"This remarkable sequel to Wigg extends the Madeline G. story over _ ... a manner that is edifying and compelling. With a new set of expert collaborators employing updated tests and advances in assessment paradigms, Hopwood and Waugh's text delivers vital applied learning, illustrating the power of a longitudinal frame of personality assessment that reveals trait consistency, age-related drifts, and new adaptations. It is ultimately person-centered and empathic. This is an essential read for personality assessors and therapists alike."

Radhika Krishnamurthy, Psy.D., ABAP, Clinical Psychology Professor, Florida Institute of Technology

"Drs. Hopwood and Waugh have assembled a remarkable revisiting of the classic 2003 work by Wiggins, viewing the contemporary status of the original case of Madeline through the lens of different paradigms of personality assessment. Providing both continuity with the original as well as insight into advances in recent years, this volume is an assessment tour de force that should be required reading for anyone wishing to understand the state of the art in the field."

Leslie C. Morey, Ph.D., George T. and Gladys H. Abell Professor of Psychology, Texas A&M University

"*Personality Assessment Paradigms and Methods: A Collaborative Reassessment of Madeline G.*, edited by luminaries Christopher Hopwood and Mark Waugh, demonstrates the power of personality assessment to reveal the inner workings of a person with a depth that is almost startling. This book presents a mosaic of carefully hewn pieces, perspectives yielded from the application of five paradigms for examining psychological assessment data, which, when melded together reveal Madeline in her uniqueness and complexity. I cannot imagine a more captivating way for students to learn about psychological assessment or for more senior assessors to expand their interpretive repertoires. With chapters written by of roster of our most distinguished, talented personality assessors Madeline G. 2.0 is a triumph."

Virginia Brabender, Ph.D., ABPP (cl), Distinguished University Professor (2017–2020), Institute for Graduate Clinical Psychology, Widener University

"Destined to become a classic in 21st century personality assessment, Hopwood and Waugh's *Personality Assessment Paradigms and Methods* should be on every clinician's bookshelf. With chapters written by luminaries in our field, this volume blends clinical wisdom with rigorous empirical evidence to illuminate the nuances of human behavior and mental life. Students and seasoned professionals alike will benefit from this incisive, engaging book."

Robert F. Bornstein, Ph.D., Professor of Psychology,
Adelphi University

"With the reassessment of Madeline G. almost two decades later, this book re-invigorates Wiggins' seminal text on personality assessment. It provides an updated, comprehensive overview of how different personality assessment paradigms answer three important questions: "What is personality?" "How do we measure it?" and "What should we measure?" The captivating Madeline G. brings each paradigm to life. This is a must-read for practitioners and trainees and belongs on the syllabus of every course for the next generation of personality assessors."

Nicole M. Cain, Ph.D., Associate Professor of Clinical
Psychology, Graduate School of Applied and
Professional Psychology, Rutgers University

Personality Assessment Paradigms and Methods

This book is an update of *Paradigms of Personality Assessment* by Jerry Wiggins (2003), a landmark volume in the personality assessment literature. The first half of Wiggins (2003) described five major paradigms: psychodynamic (as exemplified by the Rorschach and TAT), narrative (interview data), interpersonal (circumplex instruments), multivariate (five-factor instruments), and empirical (MMPI). In the second half of the book, expert representatives of each paradigm interpreted test data from the same patient, Madeline.

In this follow-up, personality experts describe innovations in each of the major paradigms articulated by Wiggins since the time of his book, including the advancement of therapeutic assessment, validation of the Rorschach Performance Assessment System, development of a multimethod battery for integrated interpersonal assessment, publication of the Restructured Form of the MMPI-2, and integration of multivariate Five-Factor Model instruments with personality disorder diagnosis. These innovations are highlighted in a reassessment of Madeline 17 years later.

This book, which provides a rich demonstration of trans-paradigmatic multimethod assessment by leading scholars in the personality assessment field in the context of one of the most interesting and thorough case studies in the history of clinical assessment, will be a useful resource for students, researchers, and practicing clinicians.

Christopher J. Hopwood, Ph.D., is Professor of Psychology at the University of California, Davis.

Mark H. Waugh, Ph.D., ABPP, is Staff Psychologist at the Oak Ridge National Laboratory; Adjunct Clinical and Teaching Faculty at the University of Tennessee, Knoxville; and in private practice in Oak Ridge, Tennessee.

Personality Assessment Paradigms and Methods

A Collaborative Reassessment
of Madeline G.

Edited by Christopher J. Hopwood
and Mark H. Waugh

Routledge
Taylor & Francis Group
NEW YORK AND LONDON

First published 2020
by Routledge
52 Vanderbilt Avenue, New York, NY 10017

and by Routledge
2 Park Square, Milton Park, Abingdon, Oxon OX14 4RN

Routledge is an imprint of the Taylor & Francis Group, an informa business

Library of Congress Cataloging-in-Publication Data
Names: Hopwood, Christopher J., 1976– editor. | Waugh, Mark
H, editor.
Title: Personality assessment paradigms and methods : a
collaborative reassessment of Madeline G / edited by
Christopher J. Hopwood and Mark H. Waugh.
Description: New York : Routledge, 2019. | Includes
bibliographical references and index.
Identifiers: LCCN 2019038982 (print) | LCCN 2019038983
(ebook) | ISBN 9781138310148 (hardback) | ISBN
9781138310162 (paperback) | ISBN 9781315143620 (ebook)
Subjects: LCSH: Personality assessment. | Wiggins, Jerry S.
Classification: LCC BF698.4 .P476 2019 (print) | LCC BF698.4
(ebook) | DDC 155.2/8—dc23
LC record available at https://lccn.loc.gov/2019038982
LC ebook record available at https://lccn.loc.gov/2019038983

ISBN: 978-1-138-31014-8 (hbk)
ISBN: 978-1-138-31016-2 (pbk)
ISBN: 978-1-315-14362-0 (ebk)

Typeset in Sabon
by Apex CoVantage, LLC

Contents

Contributors

Yossef S. Ben-Porath, Ph.D, is Professor of Psychological Sciences at Kent State University. He received his doctoral training at the University of Minnesota and has been involved extensively in MMPI research for the past 34 years. He is a co-developer of the MMPI-2-RF and co-author of test manuals, books, book chapters, and articles on the MMPI instruments. He is Editor-in-Chief of the journal *Psychological Assessment*. Dr. Ben-Porath is a board-certified clinical psychologist (American Board of Professional Psychology-Clinical) whose clinical practice involves supervision of assessments at Kent State's Psychological Clinic, consultation to agencies that screen candidates for public safety positions, and provision of consultation and expert witness services in forensic cases.

Cristina Crego, Ph.D., obtained her Ph.D. in clinical psychology and is completing a Post-Doctoral Scholar position at the University of Kentucky under the mentorship of Dr. Thomas A. Widiger. She began as an assistant professor of Psychology at Longwood University in the fall of 2019. Her research interests center around diagnosis, classification, and treatment of maladaptive trait models and personality disorders.

Sindes Dawood, M.S., is a doctoral candidate in the clinical psychology program at the Pennsylvania State University under the guidance of Dr. Aaron L. Pincus. She received her B.S. in psychology with honors from Michigan State University and her M.S. in psychology from Pennsylvania State University. Her research interests largely focus on 1) personality disorders and personality pathology (especially narcissism), 2) interpersonal personality dynamics, and 3) personality assessment.

Stephen E. Finn, Ph.D., is the founder of the Center for Therapeutic Assessment in Austin, TX, and Clinical Associate Professor of Psychology at the University of Texas at Austin. Dr. Finn received his Ph.D. in clinical psychology in 1984 from the University of Minnesota. In 2011, Dr. Finn was given the Bruno Klopfer Award from the Society of

Personality Assessment for distinguished lifetime contributions to the field of personality assessment; in August 2017, he received the award for Distinguished Scientific Contributions to Assessment Psychology from Section IX (Assessment) of the Society for Clinical Psychology (Division 12 of the American Psychological Association); and in 2018, he was given the Carl Rogers Award for outstanding contributions to the theory and practice of humanistic psychology from the Society for Humanistic Psychology (Division 32 of the American Psychological Association).

Christopher J. Hopwood, Ph.D., is Professor of Psychology at the University of California, Davis. He completed his doctorate at Texas A&M University and his clinical internship at the Massachusetts General Hospital, Harvard Medical School. Dr. Hopwood has served on the board of the North American Society for the Study of Personality Disorders, the Society for Interpersonal Theory and Research, and the Society for Personality Assessment, and as an Associate Editor for *Assessment*, the *Journal of Personality Assessment*, the *Journal of Personality Disorders*, and the *Journal of Personality and Social Psychology*.

Gregory J. Meyer, Ph.D., is Professor of Psychology at the University of Toledo. He completed his doctorate at Loyola University of Chicago and his clinical internship at the University of Chicago Medical Center, where he subsequently worked as the director of the inpatient and outpatient Psychological Assessment Service. His research focuses on psychological assessment, with an emphasis on the integration of assessment methods, and he is the co-developer of the Rorschach Performance Assessment System (www.r-pas.org). He is a former editor of the *Journal of Personality Assessment* and is a fellow of Division 5 (Evaluation, Measurement, and Statistics) of the American Psychological Association and of the Society for Personality Assessment.

Joni L. Mihura, Ph.D., ABAP, is Professor of Psychology at the University of Toledo. She completed her doctorate at Oklahoma State University and her clinical internship at Massachusetts Mental Health Center, Harvard Medical School. Her research focuses on psychological assessment with an emphasis on systematic reviews and meta-analyses of the literature. She is the co-developer of the Rorschach Performance Assessment System (www.r-pas.org). Dr. Mihura is a board-certified assessment psychologist (American Board of Assessment Psychology). She is Fellow of the Society for Personality Assessment and has served on the Board of Trustees.

Aaron L. Pincus, Ph.D., is Professor of Psychology at Pennsylvania State University. He received his B.S. in psychology from the University of California, Davis; his M.S. in psychology from the University of California, Berkeley; and his Ph.D. in clinical psychology from the University of British Columbia. His research focuses on integrating personality, psychopathology, and psychotherapy from the perspective of Contemporary Integrative Interpersonal Theory. He is Fellow of the Society for Personality Assessment and recipient of the Theodore Millon Award for contributions to personality psychology.

Krista K. Trobst, Ph.D., is Associate Professor of Psychology at York University in Toronto, Canada. She received her Ph.D. in clinical psychology from the University of British Columbia. She completed her internship in neuropsychology at Yale University, Connecticut Mental Health Center and Gaylord Rehabilitation Hospital in Wallingford, Connecticut. She was a two-year post-doctoral fellow in the Laboratory of Personality and Cognition at the National Institute on Aging, National Institutes of Health in Baltimore, Maryland. She has conducted research in personality assessment, particularly with respect to the Interpersonal Circumplex Model.

Mark H. Waugh, Ph.D., ABPP, is Staff Psychologist at the Oak Ridge National Laboratory; Adjunct Clinical and Teaching Faculty at the University of Tennessee (Knoxville); and in private practice in Oak Ridge, Tennessee. A Fellow in the Society for Personality Assessment, he graduated from the University of Florida and completed internship training at University of Texas Health Sciences Center at Dallas and a post-doctoral fellowship at Yale Psychiatric Institute. He has a long-standing clinical and scholarly interest in personality assessment, personality theory, and personality disorders as well as graduate education in these areas.

Thomas A. Widiger, Ph.D., is the T. Marshall Hahn Professor of Psychology at the University of Kentucky. He received his Ph.D. from Miami University with Len Rorer as his mentor (close colleague of Jerry Wiggins). He is Editor of *Personality Disorders: Theory, Research, and Treatment* and Co-Editor of the *Annual Review of Clinical Psychology*. He received the 2010 Distinguished Scientist Award from the Society for the Science of Clinical Psychology, the 2013 Senior Investigator Award from the North American Society for the Study of Personality Disorders, the 2013 Joseph Zubin Award from the Society for Research in Psychopathology, and the 2018 Bruno Klopfer Award from the Society for Personality Assessment.

Preface[1]

It is tremendously gratifying to write a preface for a sequel to Jerry Wiggins' (2003) *Paradigms of Personality Assessment*, which was Jerry's last academic contribution. That his last book would prompt others to write a follow-up would undoubtedly have pleased him tremendously, particularly given that the project nearly became the book that never was.

Paradigms of Personality Assessment was written in order to provide a book for graduate students and practitioners to have a simple way to familiarize themselves with the primary approaches to personality assessment so that they could make a reasoned and personal decision regarding which of the methods they would like to adopt. Jerry had come to realize that individuals typically continue to use whichever personality assessment approach was favored where they went to graduate school (or did their internships) and that they were not making a purposeful and informed choice. Jerry was rather uniquely positioned to write such a book, having been involved in nearly all of the traditions at some point in time and having a heartfelt appreciation for them all.

Jerry had been much less certain about the inclusion of the multimethod case study (Madeline G.) that served as the primary impetus for the book contained here. There were many factors that needed to be considered in selecting a subject, not the least of which was finding someone who was both interesting and willing. That process became much less difficult than Jerry had feared as his significant charm and graciousness endeared him immediately to Madeline who became eager to help. Madeline was also delighted that the reason she had been approached about being the subject for this project was that she was interesting. Flying to a few places to meet some of the most respected personality assessment scholars in the world also appealed to her a great deal (the meeting of them that is, not their would-be assessments of her). Despite having found a suitable participant, Jerry still had concerns, the greatest of which was that somehow one of the paradigms wouldn't shine as brightly as the others. Perhaps the subject wouldn't be equally cooperative and forthcoming with all assessors. What if her level of pathology (or lack thereof) would be a better "fit" for the *foci of convenience* (Wiggins, 2003) of some of the approaches over others? That the reader come away with an appreciation for *all* of the approaches was his aim.

The *Paradigms* book nearly didn't make it to print because Jerry became incapacitated (due to a catastrophic stroke) in September of 2002, prior to completion of the book. Thankfully, Part I of the book, within which each of the respective paradigms are discussed, was written. Also, thankfully Jerry had still been cognizant when each of the assessments of Madeline G. were submitted so that he'd been able to have the relief and joy that came from knowing how beautifully it had all turned out.

The book contained herein is written by Jerry's contemporary *Dream Team*. The vagaries of the passage of time has meant that some of the authors involved here have joined since the publication of first book. These new contributors represent the changing times and the wonderful advances in our field. The operations within each of the paradigms have evolved since the 2003, and these important advances are discussed within the chapters presented here. The original assessment of Madeline was groundbreaking and impressive but is outshone by the richness and sophistication of this reassessment of Madeline that would not have been possible with the state-of-the-art methods 20 years ago.

I suspect many of the contributors have wondered "What would Jerry think?" as they wrote their chapters or read the chapters of their co-authors. In some instances, Jerry had seen the advances coming within the paradigms (e.g., removal of the common factor within the MMPI, multifaceted interpersonal circumplex assessment coordinated across various interpersonal domains), and he was excited by the developments. The additional improvements that were not in his mind's eye might have pleased him even more (e.g., enhancing validity and re-establishing the Rorschach, the growth and refinement of *Therapeutic Assessment*). Jerry left the field in great hands.

Jerry was "one of the giants of personality assessment" (Ben-Porath, this volume), and he has left us with a great legacy. His methodological and theoretical sophistication improved our understanding and measurement of personality in innumerable ways. Having his last book be one that is meant to enhance appreciation for *all* the major approaches to personality assessment would surely strike him as *apropos*. That the case of Madeline G. was so well received that it is spurring continuing and ever-increasing interest would surely please him. That the results of the reassessment would have the intricacy and insight evidenced here likely would have left him a bit in awe.

> Madeline G. may go down in history as one of the best case studies ever published.
>
> (Strack, 2005, p. 106)

With a reassessment of Madeline being presented in this volume, Strack's observation appears prescient. Although sequels in the movies may often disappoint, Madeline 2.0 has benefitted from the extraordinary talents of the authors and the technological advances in the field to provide a richer and more sophisticated analysis of Madeline than could be achieved with her original assessment. Whether new to Madeline or checking in to see how she is doing 20 years later, readers are sure to find her captivating and the power of personality assessment nowhere better demonstrated.

As always, the greatest thanks go to Madeline.

Krista K. Trobst, Ph.D.

Note

1. Krista K. Trobst completed Jerry Wiggins' (2003) book when he became infirm and was unable to do so. Krista had primary responsibility for the original Madeline G. case study and contacted Madeline a few years ago to inquire if she would be willing to undergo a reassessment. She accompanied Madeline to Texas for her reassessment and follow-up appointments. She is Jerry Wiggins' widow. She is a psychology professor at York University, Toronto, Canada.

Chapter 1

Madeline G. and Five Assessment Paradigms Two Decades On

Christopher J. Hopwood and Mark H. Waugh

It can be overwhelming to learn a new clinical assessment method or psychotherapeutic technique. Competent clinical practice entails digesting a large body of validity evidence as well as the nuances of successful delivery. Even the most skilled clinicians meet help-seeking clients in the clinic with anxious anticipation, privately wondering how effective they will be. Our clients are living, breathing people whose personalities and life problems are "messy." They typically do not fit neatly into the boxes and categories of DSMs or offer perfect matches to manualized protocols and procedures. How do we integrate our client's experience, our experience of the client, the deluge of clinical data, and the many perspectives on personality and psychopathology that may pertain to determine how we can be helpful?

It is natural to want help from someone who knows what to do. We regularly seek consultation—recall in our minds the lessons we have learned—from teachers, supervisors, workshops, scientific articles, case reports, and technical manuals. But sometimes it would be better to observe a master of the craft in action. We want to ask this master to explain the what, why, and when of their technique. The goal of this book, a sequel to *Paradigms of Personality Assessment* (Wiggins, 2003), is to give the reader the opportunity to have this experience with master personality assessors.

In the first half of *Paradigms of Personality Assessment*, Wiggins described the historical roots, assumptions, and methods associated with five major paradigms of personality assessment: personological, psychodynamic, interpersonal, multivariate, and empirical. In the second half, representative experts of the five paradigms independently interpreted assessment data from the same person, Madeline G. Trobst and Wiggins (2003) concluded the book with an integrative formulation that incorporated insights from each paradigm. The goals of this book are twofold. First, experts from five major personality assessment paradigms provide updates about progress in their paradigm since Wiggins (2003). Second, these experts describe how to interpret data from their preferred instruments, collected from Madeline G. nearly two decades later, in order to describe what she is like now, how she has changed, and how we might answer questions she has about herself.

The remainder of this chapter is divided into four parts. We first discuss what Wiggins (2003) meant by the term paradigms and how we understand the five paradigms reviewed in this text. In the next section, we discuss some of the major trends in personality assessment during the two decades since Wiggins initiated the *Paradigms of Personality Assessment* project. We then describe Madeline G. in 1999/2000 and briefly introduce her in 2017. We conclude by outlining the plan for the rest of this book.

Paradigms

The term *paradigms* is borrowed from Kuhn (1962/2012) to refer to the idea that there are different ways of thinking about a field of inquiry or common issue—in this case, how to measure and conceptualize a person's personality. This kind of situation is common in the sciences (e.g., the transition from Newtonian physics to Einstein's general theory of relativity). Paradigms also occur in neighboring areas of psychology (e.g., different schools of psychotherapy or the person-situation debate). Wiggins focused on five paradigms and associated exemplar tests and methods: personological (narrative assessment), psychodynamic (Rorschach, storytelling tasks, and other performance-based measures), interpersonal (interpersonal circumplex [IPC] instruments), multivariate (factor-analytically derived trait questionnaires) and empirical (Minnesota Multiphasic Personality Inventory [MMPI]). Wiggins elaborated how the paradigms give different answers to three questions: "'What is personality?', 'How do we measure it?', and 'What should we measure?'" (Wiggins, 2003, p. 1). The personological tradition emphasizes the individual's life story, which is measured by culling the themes and patterns of personal narratives for meaning. The psychodynamic perspective is most sensitive to implicit and unconscious dynamics as assessed through relatively indirect approaches such as inkblot tasks or storytelling techniques. Interpersonal theorists understand personality in terms of how people relate to proximal and internal others, the dynamics of which are structured around agency and communion and measured using multi-informant and observer methods. The multivariate paradigm asserts that factor analyses of items that reflect the variation with which people describe one another reveals the structure of personality, generally in the form of a hierarchical Five-Factor Model (FFM). The empirical paradigm interprets personality via the MMPI, a measure of hypothetical diagnostic constructs whose meaning is inferred by a broad network of observed correlates.

Wiggins (2003) also elaborated the ways in which personality assessment paradigms differ from scientific paradigms as defined by Kuhn. For instance, unlike Kuhnian paradigms that are fundamentally incommensurable owing to their different vocabulary, concepts, and acceptable methods, personality assessment paradigms can be integrated, as Trobst and Wiggins (2003) artfully showed in their conclusion to *Paradigms of Personality Assessment*. Kuhn (1963) himself suggested the professions such as law and medicine (and assessment psychology) do not display pure paradigm dynamics since they are shaped by societal needs as well as the so-called truth-value of their disciplines. Wiggins (2003) thus concluded that the paradigms might be better understood as "communities" with important historical, theoretical, and methodological differences. The use of the term "community" highlights a critical difference between personality assessment paradigms: the social networks that drive and define each paradigm. We think about different people when we consider the personological (e.g., Henry Murray, Dan McAdams), psychodynamic (Sigmund Freud, Sidney Blatt), interpersonal (Harry Stack Sullivan, Lorna Smith Benjamin), multivariate (Raymond Cattell, Lewis Goldberg), and empirical (Paul Meehl, Grant Dahlstrom) personality assessment paradigms. Wiggins devoted much of his initial chapters to describing each paradigm in terms of associated historical figures and tracing their imprint on the paradigms. We gather that it was not difficult for him to select individuals to represent each paradigm. It was likewise not difficult to think of people to represent the paradigms for the present book. At the same time, we can also think about people, like Wiggins, who are better known for putting different paradigms together.

Isaiah Berlin (1953/2013), borrowing from the ancient Greek Archilochus and the Medieval scholar Erasmus, labeled these two kinds of people as *hedgehogs* and *foxes*. Hedgehogs develop deep expertise in one area, hoping to identify a single, coherent solution to complicated problems. Foxes, in contrast, accept that they will never get it all at once and tend to explore various tracks and hop around in different areas. Hedgehogs seek to develop expertise in one approach, whereas foxes see multiple paths to accomplish the same goals, are attuned to the advantages and disadvantages of different approaches, and are interested in how different strategies can be integrated with one another. Foxes and hedgehogs both promote progress but do so in different ways; in turn, they are susceptible to different kinds of problems. Foxes can become unmoored and may be inclined to issues that are too distal or abstract to solve focal problems, or they may experience a kind of frustration about never having solid answers to their questions. Hedgehogs, burrowing down deep, can develop blind spots and miss opportunities for insights that may be known from other perspectives or experience a deep despair upon realizing that they will never actually grasp the full picture with their singular, dedicated approach.

How do we, as individuals, encounter the multi-paradigmatic world of personality assessment? Is it better to be a fox or a hedgehog? We are with Wiggins (2003) in proposing that we can have it both ways. The field is healthier to the extent that at least some of us act like hedgehogs at least some of the time. Hedgehogs take principled ideological stances that faithfully represent a certain perspective in the clash of ideas and that serves a deeper understanding. This is more consistent with the standard Kuhnian model. But we also need enough foxes to counter a situation in which paradigms develop into "invisible colleges" that tacitly influence the field, which is based more on historical and political factors than validity or utility (Blashfield, 1984). Fortunately, this binary choice of fox or hedgehog is not the only option. The same person can be both a fox and a hedgehog, albeit generally not at the same time. Wiggins (2003) argued that Henry Murray was both a hedgehog and a fox, and both of the authors of this chapter identify ourselves that way. A book also can be both. This volume has the dual aims to promote the unique value of individual personality assessment paradigms ("hedgehog" Chapters 2–6) and demonstrate how those paradigms can be fruitfully integrated ("fox" Chapters 1, 7, and 8).

Personality Assessment

Although Meehl (1978) warned us that progress in psychology would be slow, a lot has actually happened in personality science and assessment in the nearly two decades since Wiggins initiated his project. In fact, whereas the influence of personality assessment had been waning in some ways for decades at the end of the 20th century, during the beginning of the 21st we are witnessing a re-emergence of personality in clinical psychology. Several factors are responsible for this trend, including new evidence regarding personality stability and change, the ascendance of dimensional models of psychopathology in research and diagnosis, the rising popularity of Therapeutic Assessment (TA; Finn & Tonsager, 1997), major updates to some of the most widely used personality tests, and the Open Science movement.

Personality Stability and Change

When *Paradigms of Personality Assessment* was written, there were active debates about whether clinical psychologists should even be using a term like personality in clinical assessment. Views ranged from the perspective that personality basically never changes to the opinion that any stability observed in personality depended entirely on certain patterns of environmental consistency. Shortly thereafter, Brent Roberts and colleagues published two influential meta-analyses (2000, 2007) showing that individual differences in personality remain relatively stable across the lifespan but that there are normative changes in personality as people age that are consistent with psychological maturation. In other words, if you are more neurotic than your sister today, you probably will be more neurotic than she is tomorrow, but both of you probably will become less neurotic as you age. More recent research, again by Roberts and colleagues (2017), showed that psychotherapy can intensify these changes in the direction of maturity.

This work has important implications for clinical personality assessment. First, we can predict a great deal of consistency in the personality of a person, such as Madeline G., assessed two decades on. Second, we can predict that any changes will most likely be in the direction of greater adaptation and well-being. Third, we can predict that this might particularly be so to the degree that Madeline engaged in interventions such as psychotherapy. These were our general predictions before learning more about Madeline's current life situation, which we describe in more detail below and revisit in the concluding chapter.

Dimensional Models

Personality assessors emphasize the difference between assessment and diagnosis (Meyer et al., 2001). Diagnosis involves determining what disorder an individual "has." Diagnosis is usually an important part of an assessment, but assessment also includes understanding people beyond their diagnoses, including the textures and nuances of their histories, life contexts, and close relationships. Diagnosis is sometimes conflated with assessment, such as when the clinician presumes that the disorder explains the person's functional difficulties. Formal diagnosis has typically been emphasized in biological psychiatry, as a branch of medicine, and manualized approaches to psychiatric treatment, whereas assessment has traditionally been emphasized in clinical and counseling psychology and more traditional psychotherapy approaches. Thus, an unfortunate side effect of this difference in focus is the reinforcement of ongoing schisms between science and practice.

One of the more exciting innovations of the 21st century is that psychiatric diagnosis is becoming more dimensional and thus more similar to personality assessment qua *assessment*. This innovation has taken various forms (e.g., Harkness et al., 2014). Dimensional schemes for personality disorder diagnosis have been presented as alternatives or replacements to the traditional categorical model in both the *Diagnostic and Statistical Model for Mental Disorders* (Skodol, 2012) and the *International Classification of Diseases* (Tyrer, Crawford, & Mulder, 2011).

The Hierarchical Taxonomy of Psychopathology (HiTOP; Kotov et al., 2017) consortium has come to embody a powerful movement toward dimensionalizing other forms of psychopathology as well. The National Institutes of Mental Health Research Domain Criteria compels researchers to conceptualize psychopathology as continua rather than categories in research applications. Thus, psychiatric diagnosis increasingly resembles a multidimensional profile of scores that would be familiar to personality assessors. A major focus of this book is to conceptualize one person, Madeline G., after an interval of just less than 20 years, using several such multidimensional profiles that reflect the riches of five major paradigms of personality assessment.

Therapeutic Assessment

Another area in which traditional personality assessment has exerted its influence in the beginning of the 21st century has to do with how an assessment is conducted. There has been a long and interesting history of using assessment to go beyond the task of description or diagnosis and for the clinicians to relate to, or "get in the shoes of", their clients (e.g., Fischer, 1985/1994; Handler, 2006) that received a shot of energy from Finn's (2007) formalization of Therapeutic Assessment (TA) as a semi-manualized model of this approach. TA blends assessment and psychotherapy, with the idea that therapy is more effective when based on powerful personality assessment technology, and personality assessment achieves its full potential when it helps people understand themselves. In TA, assessment tools are regarded as 'empathy magnifiers' that help clients, mental health professionals, and important others understand clients' 'dilemmas of change.' Although TA has theoretical origins in humanistic and phenomenological psychology, as a set of techniques it is congenial with all paradigms and tests (and in some ways is similar to motivational enhancement, which comes from a more behavioral/humanistic tradition). As an attitude toward mental health, TA is in keeping with current standards of collaborative care (Berry & Dunham, 2013). TA has had such an impact on personality assessment that not including it in this project would have been a major omission. We accordingly replaced the personological-narrative approach from Wiggins (2003) with a TA, conducted by Stephen E. Finn. This had several implications for other aspects of this project, as we describe in detail below.

Test Updates

Paradigms generally stay alive to the degree they can evolve and adapt. The four paradigms in this book that are generally associated with specific measures have each witnessed dramatic within-paradigm evolution during the last two decades. The most direct way to evolve in the area of personality assessment is to revise an instrument. Test revisions often involve more than new data, norms, and scores; they also can reconceptualize aspects of the instrument and its constructs. In two cases, there were major revisions to the central representative instrumentation. Within the psychodynamic paradigm,[1] the *Rorschach Performance Assessment* System (Meyer, Viglione, Mihura, Erard, & Erdberg, 2011) is an evidence-based approach to using the Rorschach Inkblot Task that solves several issues in earlier models of administration and focuses on scores with established empirical evidence. The Social Cognition and Object Relations (SCORS) approach to the *Thematic Apperception Test* (Murray, 1943; Morgan, 2002), which provides quantitative estimates of the respondent's social cognition, has gained considerable popularity in a relatively short time (Stein & Slavin-Mulford, 2018). Within the empirical paradigm, the MMPI-2 has been updated to the MMPI-2-RF in an effort to address issues related to discriminant validity and to align the measure with popular contemporary models of psychopathology (see Sellbom, 2019). It is an ascendant approach to MMPI-based personality assessment that will serve as the basis for the upcoming MMPI-3.

In two other cases, paradigms have expanded their reach. The interpersonal paradigm has been at the forefront of dynamic assessment procedures designed to capture different levels of personality within a person, as assessed by instruments that target different interpersonal surfaces, and to quantify how individuals change over time, the assessment of which has been made possible by recent technological advances. The multivariate paradigm, and its most popular representative, the Five-Factor Model (FFM), have made perhaps the greatest inroads into psychiatry. This includes the development of a range of instruments based on or structurally congenial to FFM traits designed to measure disorder constructs, as well as a large body of research showing that psychiatric phenotypes can be organized around a hierarchical five factor structure that is very similar to the FFM. The authors of Chapters 3–6 describe these innovations within their paradigm in detail, in addition to their interpretations of Madeline G.'s data.

Open Science

Meehl's (1978) paper foreshadowed what has become a critical development within the last two decades. He warned that the field was focusing too much on p-values and that this would eventuate in a pseudo-science build on "statistical power functions" rather than actual evidence. This is essentially what happened. It is now clear that a large body of psychological "evidence" was generated through questionable research practices. Hopeful antidotes such as preregistration, full reporting of all data, power analyses, large samples, changes in journal practices, and replication are becoming more the norm as a corrective. These changes have been very active in personality psychology, yet they have been somewhat slow to influence clinical psychology (Hopwood & Vazire, in press; Tackett et al., 2017).

How is the practicing personality assessor to respond to all of this? The implications for the researcher are clear, and one of the loudest messages is that samples need to be larger. But how does this apply to practicing personality assessors? One implication is that they can have perhaps even less confidence in the psychological research as a guide to practice, which is hardly encouraging. But a slightly different angle is to double down on what Stricker and Trierweiler (1995) called Local Clinical Science (LCS). LCS means treating each individual case like a scientific experiment. Generate hypotheses, collect data to test those hypotheses, incorporate checks against confirmation bias, and be open to changing formulations based on evidence. This is what good personality assessors already do when appropriate resources are available. It is also a major feature of this book: a wide range of multimethod approaches were administered to one person, Madeline, and exemplar assessors applied their knowledge base and clinical reasoning in their evaluations.

Madeline G.

Wiggins chose Madeline G. for this project in consultation with his partner, Krista Trobst, who collaborated on the project. Madeline G. consented to participate. Much of her life story is described by Dan McAdams (2003), who interviewed Madeline in person in December 1999 for a little over three hours. She is also described by Trobst and Wiggins (2003) in their summary chapter, from the perspective of people who knew her personally at that time. When the first assessment occurred, Madeline was a 35-year old woman working as a defense attorney and partnered for 6 years with her common-law husband. Madeline herself divided her life into three segments: "Childhood, Jail, and The Present." Madeline was born in a small Native American community in which her father had a degree of social status. She described exposure to extensive substance use and severe abuse throughout childhood. For example, Madeline said that at one point a teacher would not let her put on shorts and a T-shirt for gym because other children were frightened by all the bruises on her body. There was also a notable absence of warmth or affection in her family. For instance, when Madeline visited her mother in the hospital, afraid she would die, her mother refused a kiss good-bye.[2]

Madeline spent considerable time in jail during her teens. She did not say why she was jailed but noted "I did everything." She apparently had her own history with substance abuse and violent relationships during this time. While she was in prison, she began reading books and planning for her future. After prison, she got a job and began preparing for an advanced education. She was eventually admitted to a top law program and ultimately passed the Bar exam, a major achievement and source of pride for her.

Madeline met her partner around the time she graduated from college, which she noted with pleasure was a high point in her life. At the time of the assessment, she had built a strong reputation for defending people from an underprivileged community like the one she had grown up in and was about to begin a new job at a prestigious firm. Trobst and Wiggins (2003) provided a brief follow-up from three years after the assessment. Madeline was successfully running her own five-person law firm and regularly winning cases. However, her partner had left her unexpectedly about a year and a half after the assessment. This precipitated a bout of depression, sleeplessness, and passive suicidal ideation that she found confusing and foreign. She eventually realized he would not be coming back, and her depression slowly abated, which coincided with a reinvestment in her work and to her firm, accompanied by no interest in having another intimate relationship.

Madeline's story as of 2017 is described in detail in Chapters 2 and 3 of this volume. Briefly, this reassessment occurred at a strategic time for her because she had been away from work for some time and was considering if, when, and how to re-engage. She also had a personally meaningful recent experience caring for an uncle who passed away. He had been one of the few family members she said had shown tenderness and protectiveness toward her as a child.

Plan of This Book

As mentioned above, the first half of *Paradigms of Personality Assessment* is devoted to describing the theoretical and historical background of the five assessment communities. We refer the interested reader to that book for this material. The goals of the current book were to describe updates within each of the paradigms and interpret data from Madeline G.'s second assessment.

Our specific procedures changed somewhat across assessments, as can be seen in Table 1.1. First, we replaced the personological-narrative paradigm with Therapeutic Assessment for reasons described above. There were also some similarities and differences in instrumentation. We did not readminister the questionnaires that had been given by Dan McAdams, nor did we readminister an intellectual or cognitive measure. Within the psychodynamic paradigm, the Washington University Sentence Completion Test (WUSCT; Hy & Loevinger, 1996) was added, and the Rorschach

Table 1.1 Assessment of Madeline G. in 1999 and 2017

Paradigm	1999		2017	
	Instruments	Assessors	Instruments	Assessors
Narrative/ Therapeutic Assessment	Life Story Interview, Thematic Apperception Test, Loyola Generativity Scale, Big Five Inventory, Personal Strivings, Satisfaction with Life Scale	Dan McAdams		Stephen E. Finn*
Psychodynamic	Rorschach, Object Relations Inventory, Thematic Apperception Test, Wechsler Adult Intelligence-Scale-III	Rebecca Behrends and Sidney Blatt	Rorschach Performance Assessment System, Thematic Apperception Test, Object Relations Inventory, Washington University Sentence Completion Test	Greg Meyer,* Joni L. Mihura, and Mark H. Waugh
Interpersonal	Inventory of Interpersonal Problems Circumplex and Interpersonal Adjective Scales, self and informant report	Aaron L. Pincus and Michael Gurtman	Inventory of Interpersonal Problems Short Circumplex and Interpersonal Adjective Scales, self and informant report; Circumplex Scales of Interpersonal Values, Interpersonal Sensitivities Circumplex, Circumplex Scales of Interpersonal Efficacies; Continuous Assessment of Interpersonal Dynamics	Aaron L. Pincus, Sindes Dawood, and Christopher J. Hopwood
Multivariate	Revised NEO Personality Inventory, self and informant report	Paul Costa, Jr. and Ralph Piedmont	Revised NEO Personality Inventory, self and informant report	Thomas A. Widiger and Cristina Crego
Empirical	MMPI-2	Yossef S. Ben-Porath	MMPI-2-RF	Yossef S. Ben-Porath

* participated in in-person assessment.

Performance Assessment System (R-PAS) approach was used to administer, code, and interpret the Rorschach. As noted above, the SCORS-G was used to code the TAT. Several instruments were added to the interpersonal paradigm, consistent with a more contemporary approach to interpersonal assessment as described above. The MMPI-2-RF was given in lieu of the MMPI-2. We had hoped to identify the MMPI-2 raw data from Madeline's first assessment in order to provide a direct comparison of MMPI scores across time, but, unfortunately, we were unable to locate those data. The approach to multivariate assessment remained the same, albeit with a different informant.

As in Wiggins (2003), we were motivated to find the very best representatives for each paradigm. Steve Finn was a natural choice to lead the TA. Greg Meyer and Joni Mihura have led the development of the R-PAS and have a distinguished history in the areas of performance-based personality and multimethod assessment. Mark Waugh has decades of experience practicing, teaching, and supervising personality assessment from a broad psychodynamic perspective. Aaron Pincus and Sindes Dawood have recently published guidelines for the interpretation of multisurface interpersonal assessment data, and Chris Hopwood has expertise coding interpersonal behavior and conceptualizing the role of interpersonal phenomena in personality assessment and PD. Tom Widiger is the foremost authority on the clinical assessment with the FFM and has left an indelible stamp on the field of clinical and personality psychology more generally. Finally, as a co-author of both the MMPI-2 and MMPI-2-RF, Yossef Ben-Porath remains the foremost authority on the MMPI that he was two decades ago.

Our process was as follows. Krista Trobst located Madeline in 2016 and asked if she would be interested in participating in a reassessment, and Madeline tentatively agreed. We then asked a representative of each paradigm whether they would be interested in participating in this project, and again they agreed. We arranged for Madeline, Krista, and Greg to go to Steve's center in Austin, Texas, for the initial assessment in January 2017. Krista accompanied and supported Madeline during her trip, which was supported financially by the editors and lead authors in this book. After consenting to participate, Madeline spent two days with Steve and Greg, as described in detail in Chapters 2 and 3. While in Austin, Madeline asked four TA questions about herself that could help guide the interpretation of assessment data, as is standard in a TA. Madeline completed some of the assessment data while in Austin and other questionnaires upon returning home. She also found a male platonic friend who completed informant assessments. Assessment data were sent to each of the experts, who provided Steve and Greg with summary interpretations, organized around Madeline's initial questions. Brief videos, selected by Steve, were also sent to Chris for interpersonal coding. Apart from Steve and Greg, none of the experts saw data from tests that were not in their paradigm, nor were interpretations shared. Madeline, Krista, and Greg returned to Austin about a month later for an Assessment Intervention and Summary/Discussion Session, as described in Chapter 7. At that point, she changed her questions somewhat. Following this summary, Greg and Steve prepared a brief document describing the overall process and Madeline's reaction. Chapters 2–7 were then written independently. This chapter and the final, concluding chapter were written after Chapters 2–7 were completed. As in Wiggins (2003), all assessment data are included in this volume, as are a number of rich details about the assessment and Madeline's life.

Notes

1. As emphasized by Meyer, Mihura, and Waugh in Chapter 3, the Rorschach and other instruments are not, themselves, "psychodynamic", although they can be and often are interpreted using psychodynamic theory.
2. In a response she gave to the ORI in 1999, Madeline said, "The first time I ever kissed my mother was when she was lying in the hospital, having just slit her wrists on the kitchen table. I saw my cousin brushing her hair, and I was green with envy" (Wiggins, 2003, p. 342). It is unclear if these are two different moments or alternative depictions of the same experience.

Chapter 2

Therapeutic Assessment of Madeline G.

Stephen E. Finn

I long admired Wiggins' (2003) book, *Paradigms of Personality Assessment*, and viewed it as a groundbreaking work that cemented the place of multi-method personality assessment in our field. Thus, when Hopwood and Waugh approached me about taking part in a reassessment of the book's principal subject, Madeline G., and filling in for Dan McAdams, I was intrigued. After some thought, it became clear that I could not successfully represent McAdam's narrative assessment model, but I would collaborate if the reassessment were done as a Therapeutic Assessment, my area of expertise and a close "cousin" to the narrative approach. Hopwood and Waugh readily agreed, and Krista K. Trobst checked with Madeline, who was open to the idea and gave Krista permission to share her contact information with me.

I also proposed a new format to the assessment process in which Madeline would come to Austin, where she would be given all the tests. Our group of experts would then collaborate with me on interpreting the tests, and I would give oral and written feedback directly to Madeline. I had been part of a team in the past that used a similar collaborative case study approach, and it had proved to be very therapeutic for the client (Engelman, Allyn, Crisi, Finn, Fischer, & Nakamura, 2016). I also asked that Greg Meyer join me for the in-person sessions with Madeline; to my great pleasure, he agreed. I was excited and curious to see how Therapeutic Assessment might affect Madeline's experience of psychological assessment.

Overview of Therapeutic Assessment

Therapeutic Assessment (TA) is a relatively new paradigm of psychological assessment in which tests are used not only to understand individuals and assist in making important decisions but also to help people understand *themselves* in new ways and resolve problems in their lives (Finn & Tonsager, 1997; Finn, 2007; Finn, Fischer, & Handler, 2012). TA was informed by Collaborative Assessment (CA), an approach developed by

Fischer (1985/1994), Handler (2006) and others; thus, in TA, clients are treated as essential co-participants in every step of the assessment process. The core values of TA are "collaboration, respect, humility, compassion, and curiosity" (Finn, 2009). I will now describe briefly the semi-structured format of a full adult TA. More detailed accounts are available elsewhere (e.g., Finn, 2007; Finn & Martin, 2013).

Steps in Adult TA

Initial Phone Contact

Although it varies by setting, most TAs of outpatient clients begin with a phone conversation between the client and assessor. This call is viewed as an opportunity to begin enlisting clients as collaborators. The assessor provides information, responds to questions about TA, and then asks, "What questions do you want to have answered through the assessment?" These questions/goals are discussed briefly, and the client is encouraged to think of others. Assessor and client agree on an initial meeting, and the client is sent an information sheet that more fully explains the process of a TA.

Initial Session(s) and Collection of Assessment Questions

The initial session(s) of a TA are one of the most important steps as they set the stage for the therapeutic process to unfold. First, assessors continue the process of co-creating Assessment Questions (AQs) that will guide the rest of the TA. These AQs serve a number of purposes. They: 1) enlist clients as collaborators, 2) lower clients' anxiety about the assessment, 3) give information about where clients are open to input, and 4) provide windows into a client's existing narrative about self and the world. Throughout the initial session, assessors pay special attention to building a secure alliance with clients by listening closely, mirroring clients' dilemmas, and avoiding comments that might elicit anxiety and/or shame. Research has shown that after an initial session, most clients feel more curious, hopeful, and excited about the assessment (e.g., Finn & Tonsager, 1992).

Standardized Testing Sessions and Extended Inquiries

Once the AQs are developed, assessors choose standardized psychological tests (i.e., with empirical norms and formal methods of interpretation), and clients and assessors work with these tests in a series of meetings. It is recommended that assessors explain to clients how each test is relevant to their AQs and that assessors begin with tests that by their face validity appear closely connected to clients' major concerns. This kind of transparency helps clients fully engage with each test. Another common practice in TA is that after a standardized test has been administered, assessors typically involve clients in discussing their experiences and test responses and how those are relevant to their AQs and to life outside the assessment room. This process is called an Extended Inquiry (Finn, 2007), and experience has shown that it can be highly emotional and transformative for clients. Successful Extended Inquiries often rely on assessors' ability to use scaffolding to help clients understand emotions or behaviors of which they were previously unaware (Kamphuis & Finn, 2018). This process of "co-constructing a new narrative" is continued in the subsequent step.

Assessment Intervention Session(s)

Following standardized testing, TA assessors examine all test findings, construct a tentative case conceptualization, and divide insights and findings that have emerged thus far in the assessment into three categories (Finn, 2007): *Level 1 information*—findings that are consistent with a client's existing narrative about self and the world; *Level 2 information*—findings that are somewhat discrepant from a client's existing views and that might elicit anxiety, shame or defensiveness; and *Level 3 information*—understandings that are so discrepant from a client's current way of thinking about self and the world that they are likely to be rejected due to the natural human tendency toward self-verification (Swann, 1997), or they may cause a disintegration experience for clients, i.e., a terrifying sense of confusion and panic that can result when their basic views of self and the world are challenged in fundamental ways (Kohut, 1984).

In Assessment Intervention Sessions (AIS), assessors target Level 3 information that is potentially crucial to answering clients' AQs and create experiential opportunities that may help clients "discover" this information with assistance from the assessor. Assessors may use psychological tests in nonstandardized ways or invite clients to do role-plays, art therapy projects, or other relevant "experiments." The major goals of the AIS are to test the current case conceptualization and decrease the "shock" value of Level 3 findings by helping clients begin to grasp them on their own.

Summary/Discussion Sessions

Often called "feedback sessions" in traditional assessment, these meetings are where assessors verbally present test results, their case conceptualization, and recommendations to clients and then involve clients in answering the AQs developed at the beginning of the assessment. Rather than consisting of a monologue from an "expert" psychologist, Summary/Discussion Sessions are collaborative dialogues where clients are asked to confirm, modify, or reject possible interpretations of test scores and give examples of how such findings show up in their lives. Research and clinical experience have shown that in general the greatest therapeutic benefits occur when assessors first discuss Level 1 findings, then Level 2, and finally Level 3 information (e.g., Schroeder, Hahn, Finn, & Swann, 1993).

Written Feedback

Generally, written feedback in TA is in the form of a letter from the assessor directly to the client, and this document recaps the collaborative understandings that emerged in the Summary/Discussion Session. Again, the emphasis is on answering the client's AQs and writing about test results in language that is comprehensible and accessible to clients. Typically, feedback letters are mailed to the client a month or more after the Summary/Discussion Session. Research has shown that the combination of oral and written feedback has the greatest therapeutic effects on clients (Lance & Krishnamurthy, 2003).

Follow-Up Session(s)

Follow-up Sessions are typically scheduled six to eight weeks after the final Summary/Discussion Session, and almost all clients return for these meetings. They provide an opportunity for clients and assessors to continue discussing the assessment experience and results, for clients to update the assessor on how they are doing, and for reviewing and possibly revising any suggestions that came out of the assessment.

Feedback From Client

When the TA is completed, clients are asked to provide written feedback about their experiences, by both responding to open-ended questions (shared later) and completing a standardized satisfaction measure, the Assessment Questionnaire (Finn, Schroeder, & Tonsager, 1994).

Research on TA

There are several recent reviews of research on the effectiveness of TA and its "close cousin," Collaborative Assessment (CA) (Aschieri, Fantini, & Smith, 2016; Aschieri, De Saeger, & Durosini, 2015; Finn & Martin, 2013; Kamphuis & Finn, 2018). In addition, a relatively recent meta-analysis (Poston & Hanson, 2010) of psychological assessment used as an intervention showed large effect sizes for treatment process variables such as alliance and client satisfaction and moderate effects for treatment outcome variables such as symptom improvement or increases in self-esteem. Overall, the research shows that TA can benefit clients with many different problems in living, including depression, psychosis, anxiety, severe personality disorders, suicidal ideation, substance abuse, chronic pain, and complex PTSD, among others (see Kamphuis & Finn, 2018 for individual references). In some instances, clients' problems in living decrease during or immediately after a TA, and these improvements persist and grow for two to eight weeks afterward. Also, in numerous studies, clients who participate in TA are more open to subsequent treatment, more motivated, and have better alliance with treatment professionals than are other clients.

Two studies seem particularly relevant to the current project. Recently, my colleagues and I conducted a Randomized Control Trial (RCT) with 74 clients with severe personality pathology awaiting residential treatment at a tertiary care hospital in Holland (De Saeger et al., 2014). The five-session TA showed no impact, relative to a credible control treatment, on self-reported symptomatology. However, clients in the TA condition were more motivated and hopeful about their upcoming treatment, showed better alliance to the clinician working with them, and felt they had progressed in being able to make use of treatment. A subsequent qualitative follow-up study (De Saeger, Bartak, Eder, & Kamphuis, 2016) shed light on clients' positive experiences of the TA, revealing that they felt empowered and validated by the TA and were impacted by being treated as valuable and equal partners in a process whose goal was to understand them as individuals.

How and Why TA Works

Although the specific therapeutic mechanisms of TA are still being investigated, several dominant theories exist to date.

Changing Core Narratives

My colleagues and I have written extensively (e.g., Finn, 2007; Finn & Martin, 2013; Smith & Finn, 2014) about our belief that TA leads to lasting change when it helps clients revise central aspects of their "stories" about themselves and the world. As any clinician appreciates, many people seeking psychological services have deeply embedded, and often unconscious, views of themselves that are inaccurate (e.g., "I am deeply flawed"). Often, these implicit narratives were developed on the basis of messages from important attachment figures early in life and presumably were adaptive or functional in those contexts. Often, however, such narratives become self-fulfilling prophesies that are related to a host of problems in adulthood. A vast psychological literature exists about the human tendency to "screen in" information that confirms our existing narratives and "screen out" information that contradicts them—what Swann (1997) termed "self-verification." The relational stance and techniques of TA are specifically designed to address self-verification and help clients change core narratives by: 1) enlisting clients' curiosity about their problems in living at the beginning of an assessment, for example, by co-constructing AQs; 2) creating an atmosphere of safety and emotional support that allows clients to tolerate the difficult emotions that come from new ways of thinking; 3) using psychological tests as "empathy magnifiers" (Finn, 2007) to identify those aspects of clients' narratives that are open to change and what alternatives will be accepted; 4) lowering clients' anxiety and guarding against disintegration by verifying certain aspects of clients' narratives; 5) involving clients in "co-editing" old narratives and "co-authoring" new ones that are more coherent, accurate, compassionate, and useful than those they held previously; and 6) encouraging clients to reject assessment findings that are too threatening or that do not seem accurate or useful.

Reintegrating Split-Off Affect States

The avoidance or suppression of core emotions, called "affect phobia," is a frequent result of early trauma and has been implicated in a host of psychopathological conditions, including personality disorders (McCullough et al., 2003). Sometimes, during TA, clinicians are able to support clients in accessing emotional states that have been previously dissociated so they can begin to "re-integrate" them, and this leads to significant behavioral changes (Finn, 2012). TA assessors may intentionally elicit such disavowed emotions by using performance-based personality tests such as the Rorschach or the Adult Attachment Projective Picture System (AAP; George & West, 2012). Research has shown that such tests are highly activating of areas of the brain associated with emotional experience and expression (Asari et al., 2010a; Bucheim et al., 2005) and hence often provide information that cannot be gleaned from interviews or self-report tests. Assessment Intervention Sessions—the third step of TA—often directly target split-off emotions with the aim of helping clients see how avoiding them is connected to their major problems in living (see Aschieri et al., 2016; Finn, 2012).

Shame Reduction

Many clients who seek psychological services suffer not only from painful emotional difficulties (e.g., depression, anxiety, eating disorders, intimacy problems) but also from feelings of shame about those very conditions, which then intensifies their distress (Aschieri, 2016; Finn, 2007). TA addresses clients' shame in a number of ways—for example, by inviting them to be curious about their struggles and to explore them and learn about them with the help of an empathic, nonjudgmental assessor (Aschieri et al., 2016). Perhaps the most effective TA intervention for shame is its deliberate, careful involvement of the clients in co-constructing new narratives that explain their problems in living in compassionate ways. Our experience is that when shame about a certain difficulty decreases, often clients find ways to address that difficulty that previously were blocked.

Restoring Epistemic Trust

Recently, Kamphuis and Finn (2018) re-examined the empirical evidence of TA's efficacy in light of a concept from evolutionary psychology, *epistemic trust*. Healthy epistemic trust is derived from early secure attachment experiences, and it results in the ability to appropriately discriminate in adult relationships whom one should trust and learn from and whom one should distrust and treat with skepticism. Recent research has documented that many clients, especially those with personality disorders, are unable to exercise appropriate epistemic trust and instead live in a condition of *epistemic hypervigilance*, in which they maintain rigid internal "working models" (i.e., narratives) that are never updated interpersonally (Fonagy & Allison, 2014; Fonagy, Luyten, & Allison, 2015). As most clinicians know, such individuals are extremely difficult to treat in psychotherapy. Kamphuis and I contend that TA is particularly successful within a relatively short period of time with clients with epistemic hypervigilance because so many of its principles and techniques address epistemic trust (Kamphuis & Finn, 2018). Comments related to renewed epistemic trust were frequent in the comments of personality disordered clients interviewed post-TA in the qualitative study mentioned earlier (De Saeger et al., 2016).

Madeline's First Visit to Austin; January 6–7, 2017

Before going into detail about the Therapeutic Assessment of Madeline, let me say that it was one of the most interesting, exciting, challenging, and moving clinical experiences I have had in over 35 years of practice, and I was left with an enormous appreciation for Madeline and what she has achieved in her life.

Preliminary Phone Contact

Once Krista K. Trobst gave me Madeline's real name and contact information, I called her on December 6, 2016, to discuss her willingness to do the reassessment. Madeline told me that she thought it was "really cool" to be asked to be retested and that she was "totally willing" to be "a subject for science." When I explained the Therapeutic Assessment paradigm, she grasped it immediately and said, "Your timing is great!"

She then explained that she was in the middle of a "huge professional transition" and a "huge period of turmoil" where she wanted to "redefine moving forward in life." She said she was exhausted by the work she had been doing for years as a defense attorney for underprivileged clients and had decided to close her practice. When I said that choice must be disorienting, Madeline seemed to feel understood and became even more open, saying, "I have always been so goal oriented and task driven. Now I feel really ungrounded. Not having a goal makes me question everything." I asked Madeline if she could think of any particular questions she wanted to address through the assessment; she laughed and said, "Now who am I?" I laughed also and told her that was an excellent question that I was sure we could address. Madeline responded, "What a bonus—an added bonus this time! So, you'll give me feedback?" I assured her Greg Meyer and I would go over the test results with her at the second meeting, and she then said that she never got feedback from the previous assessment. When I asked if she had read the Wiggins (2003) book, she seemed surprised and said, "I never knew there was a book." This startled me, but I just assured her that this time we would give feedback and answer her questions. When we hung up, I was struck by how pleasant the conversation was and how open Madeline had seemed on the phone. I had several more interactions with her by email regarding travel arrangements before she came, and these were equally pleasant.

Plan for Initial TA Sessions

Greg Meyer and I met with Madeline on January 6 and 7, 2017, for the initial part of the TA. On the first day, we collected Assessment Questions from Madeline and then gave her the MMPI-2-RF, NEO-PI-R, Washington University Sentence Completion Test (WUSCT), and the interpersonal rating forms. Madeline had already agreed to give the informant versions of the NEO and of the interpersonal rating forms to a good friend to complete. On the second day, we checked in with Madeline, and Greg administered the Rorschach (which took almost three hours) and the TAT. After lunch, we did an Extended Inquiry of certain Rorschach responses. Krista K. Trobst traveled separately to Austin and spent time with Madeline each day after our sessions and part of the day following, before they returned to their respective homes.[1]

Initial Impressions

Greg and I met at my office before we were to see Madeline, and at the appointed hour (10 AM), I opened my door and was heading down the hall to see if she had arrived. I said to Greg, "I don't think she's here yet, but I'll check." As I rounded the corner to the waiting room, I saw a dark-haired woman who clearly had heard me and protested loudly, "Why didn't you think I was here?! I can navigate and drive a car!" I was taken aback and explained that I had been listening for the door to the waiting room to open and hadn't heard it, to which she exclaimed, "I have stealth powers." I thanked her for coming, shook her hand briefly, and watched as she gathered up her hot tea (available in my waiting room) and backpack. Madeline then complained about the unseasonably cold weather in Austin and also about how hard it was to be someplace (Texas) where "everyone had voted for Trump." I said, "I know exactly what you mean!" and she smiled and seemed to relax a bit. I led her to my office where she shook Greg's hand and settled on the sofa facing us, and I took the time to notice her appearance: an attractive middle-aged woman with curly dark hair, dressed in a white linen shirt, form-fitting pants, and lace-up boots. I remember thinking, "She's younger and more attractive than I imagined," and making a quick assessment of how to be with her, I summoned the most attentive and extraverted part of me to our interaction. I asked Madeline if she had had any trouble getting to the hotel the night before, and she recounted animatedly that she had gotten lost multiple times, never used the GPS on her cell phone, and had pulled over a public transit bus to ask the driver for directions. At one point, she seemed to admit that finding her way was challenging, but she also said that she liked getting lost and finding her way and found it an adventure. I was left confused if she had been scared, excited, or both. Madeline said that she had gotten a map from the hotel staff to get to my office and that it had been very direct and easy (which I knew when I chose the hotel). We then asked Madeline to read a series of release forms (regarding HIPAA, the current project, and a consent to videotape) and proceeded with the meeting.

Madeline's View of the Previous Assessment

Early in the first session, Madeline began to talk about the previous assessment, and this topic came up at various points over the two days. Strikingly, Madeline claimed that she had almost no memory of the earlier assessment and said, "When Krista approached me this time, I had completely forgotten I had done it." As Greg and I asked questions and answered hers, Madeline was not aware that she had traveled to Chicago to be interviewed. She had a clearer recollection of going to Yale and told of traveling to New Haven for the testing with Rebecca Behrends. Apparently, she had struck up a conversation with people on the train and had gone out drinking with them the night before meeting with Dr. Behrends. She laughed as she told about being really hungover when she met with Dr. Behrends and how she had been sound asleep when Dr. Behrends had called her at the hotel after she failed to show at the time of her appointment. At various points over the two days, she complained about

Behrends: "I had never met a psychologist so tight. She was so distrustful." This was surprising to Greg and me as we had heard that Dr. Behrends was a very kind and empathic person.

At one point, I attempted to get Madeline curious about her lack of recall of the previous assessment, and I even invited her to pose a question about this for the assessment, but she declined to do so. When we were discussing possible explanations, I wondered aloud if there had been anything anxiety-provoking or difficult about the experience, and Madeline rejected this immediately, saying instead that most likely the assessment "hadn't been that important" to her and that she had been occupied with her life at the time. Madeline did say that Krista had told her that Madeline knew at one point that there was a book. (These discussions are recounted in the closing chapter of the 2003 book.) Madeline tentatively wondered aloud several times if she might want to read it. Greg and I reassured her that even if she didn't, we would still certainly tell her about how her test responses had changed over the 20 years, and this offer seemed to relieve her and pique her curiosity.

Development of Assessment Questions (AQs)

The following AQs were developed during the morning of the first assessment day. I write more about the process of gathering the questions below; at this point, I share the AQs with relevant background information.

Assessment Question 1: "Who the Hell Am I Now?"

This is a version of the question Madeline gave me during our initial phone conversation. As mentioned earlier, Madeline reported she had essentially closed her practice as a criminal defense attorney, saying that she finished her last case over one year ago and had been living on savings. She had done a bit of work for former clients recently and also had pursued collections from government sources for previous cases. She agreed that the defense work itself was demanding but said that this was not what led to her decision to change her work; mainly, she was exhausted by the constant struggle to collect payments for work she did for indigent clients and to get funding approved for expert witnesses she needed to successfully defend her clients. She summed up her feelings with, "I am so fucking fed up with having to keep asking for money. I don't like begging!" When I asked what she would do if money were not an issue, Madeline claimed, "If I had 10 million dollars, I would do what I did before."

Although she seemed to pin much of her current disorientation on her work plans, Madeline also disclosed that she had recently been through a life-changing experience: she originally left her practice a year earlier to care for an uncle, her father's younger brother, who had leukemia. This was a man she felt very attached to, saw as her only family, and described as being the only source of positive parenting during her childhood and adolescence. Beginning in January 2016, she had devoted all her time to taking care of him as he got increasingly ill and eventually died 9 months later (at age 67). In an effort to help her uncle, Madeline had also reconnected with family members she had not spoken to in years in order to have them visit. These included her older brother, who flew in two times to see the uncle. Madeline discovered that she liked and felt connected to this brother, and they had been having regular contact since. She said she didn't expect to have this connection, explaining, "I don't trust very easily." The day after her uncle died in September, Madeline reported she had asked herself, "Now what?" and was disturbed that she didn't have an answer. After telling about the time with her uncle, she expressed other misgivings about her previous work beyond the difficulties of asking for money: "My work became who I was. I still want to help, but I'm not sure what I want to do. I used to say my work was 'what I do, not who I am,' but I now see I was kidding myself."

Assessment Question 2: "After All This Time, How Is It That I Have Yet to Find My New Direction?"

Madeline expressed frustration that she hadn't yet been able to think of work she would find interesting and that would give her purpose, explaining, "I know myself, and I'm smart. How can I still be confused about this?" She went on to say that she was not an indecisive person and normally made decisions quickly. She felt she doesn't recognize herself lately and that she was "bitchier" to people, "shorter"—instead of fun and engaging as she liked—and found herself not looking at people and disengaging. When I asked if she had any guesses about why it had been so hard for her to find direction, she said, "I'm not that driven right now." This led to her next assessment question.

Assessment Question 3: "Why Am I Not so Driven Right Now? Where Has That Gone?"

Madeline explained that she felt less "driven" than she was accustomed to and was sleeping more than usual. [Incidentally, she reported long-term problems sleeping, often getting only four to five hours of sleep a night total in periods of one-and-a-half to two hours.] We asked when the feeling of being less driven had started, and Madeline said she first noted it during the period after her uncle died. She said, "The wind got sucked out of me" and that it had never come back. When I wondered if the grief about her uncle was taking energy, she said she wasn't sure and that mainly the lower energy "pisses me off." She said that she was drinking more than she used to; when I asked if she was concerned, she said, "A bit." In this context, she noted that both her parents were "raging alcoholics."

Assessment Question 4: "How Do I Redirect My Sense of Self?"

This question was clearly related to the first question Madeline posed ("Who the hell am I now?"), but I experienced it as more vulnerable in that she was clearly asking for Greg's and my help. At first, she kept fairly close to aspects of self that were related to her job, describing her dilemma as no longer wanting to do the work she had done but also not wanting to "ascribe to mediocrity." She said she longed for something she could be "just as passionate about" as her previous work, but she didn't know what that was. We discussed various options that seemed open to her with her law degree, including teaching, which she rejected immediately, telling us, "Those who can, do; those who can't, teach." We let this aphorism go by at first, but I later returned to it and asked if this is always true. It became clear that part of Madeline's dilemma was that she had seen herself as a "warrior for justice" of native peoples, and, in her mind, "teacher" was nowhere near "warrior." However, she began to tell us about a volunteer job she had done, mentoring native attorneys and court workers in "mock trials" she set up with actual judges and court personnel. This had been fulfilling, and coincidentally she had received a call just before she left for Austin that she believed was an offer to do this work for pay. I wondered if she could see herself as a "magician" or "wizard" instead of a teacher, and she seemed bemused but not very open to the idea.

Another theme regarding self-definition emerged when Madeline confessed that for some years, she had never envisioned herself being alone at her current age. We learned about the end of the relationship with her former partner, related in the closing chapter of the 2003 book. Madeline explained that she had "settled into" the relationship with this man, which lasted from 1993 to "one month before 9/11." She confessed that she was caught off guard when her partner announced that he was ending the relationship and moving out and had already rented another place to live. It was painful over the next four to six weeks to have him return to their house and slowly move his belongings out. Madeline said he didn't explain why he was ending the relationship, except that he was "doing the right thing for him." She appeared completely accepting of the legitimacy of his sudden, unexplained leaving but confessed, "I almost didn't get through it. I damn near imploded. He was the first person I really let in. . . . I got so depressed I almost killed myself." (This event is described by Krista K. Trobst in the 2003 book on p. 321.) Madeline described retreating into an inner room in her house and not answering phone calls or the door when friends reached out. They would come by and leave food on her doorstep. Gradually, over several years, she recovered and threw herself even more into work. In 2007, she did have a ten-month relationship with another man who was in the legal profession, but it was uncomfortable, Madeline said, because colleagues knew of their relationship and she is "a private person." The relationship ended because this man was diagnosed with prostate cancer, their sexual relationship understandably suffered, and Madeline "didn't want to stick around for all that."

Madeline related she had not had a serious dating relationship since 2007, saying "I haven't kissed a person since then." When we asked why, she said, "I have high standards" and explained that she needed a man, like her former partner, who was "not threatened by me." She then described her ex- in glowing terms, saying he didn't have problems with her being independent and had taught her a valuable lesson that changed her, "Don't mistake kindness for weakness." She also said the relationship had changed her for the better and had "smoothed out" her "rough corners." She said still had some contact with him and thought of him as positively as ever. I pushed on this story a bit, asking if one of the reasons Madeline was still alone was because she had "put a wall" up because of being hurt by the ex-partner's nonrelational way of ending the relationship. She strongly rejected this possibility. When I asked if she had ever learned why he had left, she said, "No, I don't need to know." When I asked if she had any guesses, she told of the partner's deep loyalty to his parents, who had never liked Madeline. She explained that his father had become ill, he needed to devote more energy to them, and the relationship with her was an impediment. Again, there was no rancor or bitterness about the idea that he had chosen his parents over her.

Process Observation

One dynamic I was aware of throughout the entire morning was the importance of mirroring Madeline's obvious strengths versus her vulnerability. When I invite clients to pose AQs at the beginning of a TA, I am aware that I am inviting them to reveal where they are confused or unhappy and where they want help. Madeline was both open and excited about getting information from the TA, but I also quickly learned when she spoke about struggles not to make empathic comments of the type, "That sounds hard." Such comments seemed to invoke shame about "weakness," and generally, Madeline would swat such statements away, saying something like, "Well, of course! But I got through it." Fortunately, the collaborative stance underlying TA aptly addresses this type of dynamic by reducing clients' sense of vulnerability, and Greg and I underlined it: we were experts on tests, not on Madeline, and it was by jointly discussing test results and our impressions that Madeline might achieve new insights. My sense was that this approach successfully began to lower Madeline's epistemic hypervigilance.

Self-Report Test Administration

After lunch on the first day, Greg and I checked in with Madeline. She regaled with the story of a conversation she had initiated over lunch with two men about why they had voted for Trump for President, and I was struck again by her extraversion but also by her apparent diplomacy. It was clear that she had continued to think about how the major events she had told us about had affected her (her partner's leaving, her uncle's death, and her closing her practice). She said, "I guess these things softened a lot of edges, and that is a mixed thing." With this tone in the air, we then led Madeline to a testing room in my office suite where she completed the assessment measures.[2] She worked diligently and almost without interruption for over two hours, only taking a short break for a cigarette after all the forms had been completed.

Extended Inquiry of Self-Report Measures

After the break, the three of us met to discuss Madeline's impressions. She remembered some of the self-report instruments and was excited to see how her current scores would compare to those from 20 years previously. During the break, Greg and I had selected certain of Madeline's responses to the WUSCT (see Table 3.4), and we asked her about those in an Extended Inquiry; this proved useful in giving us information on topics that were not ostensibly related to her assessment questions.[3]

Two responses we asked about were items 7 ["My mother and I . . . *are not compatable*" (sic—Madeline's response in italics)] and 12 ("A good father . . . *is an anomaly*"), and Madeline revealed more information about her early life than we knew from the 2003 book. She described her father as an abusive, psychopathic man and her mother as a "vicious, violent, self-destructive liar" who only contacted Madeline over the years when she wanted money. Her mother is the oldest of 14 children, and one of the mother's younger sisters was given her same name because the parents forgot they had already used it. Madeline's father was one of ten children, and, as previously mentioned, both parents were "raging alcoholics." Madeline was off and on again in foster care from ages 6–12, which she said she "hated." She ran away and began living on her own starting at age 12. At age 14, she went to prison for the first of two times because a "cop with a beef against the family" had lied and "framed" her. She believes this experience was influential in her decision to become an attorney and work for justice for underprivileged native people. As mentioned earlier, these topics were delicate to discuss in that Madeline made it clear that she didn't want to be seen as a "trauma survivor," which she associated with being pitied—a stance she despised. At this point, both Greg and I honored this point of view by mirroring Madeline's prized sense of strength and letting her decide what to reveal. I was aware of many questions I chose not to ask.

WUSCT item 8 ("What gets me into trouble is . . . *my imagination*") provided more information about the excitement-seeking aspect of Madeline's personality. In discussing her response, Madeline said, "I can be ridiculously spontaneous;" when I asked for an example, she told of one day going to the airport not knowing where she would go, choosing to fly to Istanbul, then making her way to Cyprus. There, one night in a bar, she met a Russian man who offered to take her on a boating trip the next morning to see a statue of Aphrodite. According to Madeline, the boat strayed into forbidden waters, was stopped by the Turkish police, and turned out to be loaded with boxes of smuggled guns. She said she got out of the situation eventually and summed it up with a favorite phrase she said she uses to reassure herself, "I've been further from home and more scared." She also expressed her belief that experiences matter most in the end: "He who's got the best stories wins!" A frequent theme during our conversations was Madeline's love of adventure, susceptibility to boredom, desire to keep active, and tendency to act on the spur of the moment.

The Extended Inquiry of WUSCT item 22 ("At times she worried about . . . *the unknown*") led me to think the Madeline's forward motion was one way she dealt with existential anxiety. When I asked what was scary about the unknown, she used the metaphor that "life is like a roll of toilet paper that turns faster and faster as it reaches the end." She said she felt less invincible as she ages and that she was anxious about getting older. When I asked Madeline what her biggest fears were, she said, "Running out of money" and "Not being independent." Returning to the work theme, she then said she "wants to keep her fiefdom" and "never expected to be here at this age." I felt more and more empathy for the disorientation Madeline was experiencing given that her previous work no longer felt right.

This discussion also allowed Greg and me to appreciate Madeline's allowing herself to "sit with" the discomfort she was experiencing, rather than doing any of a myriad of things that would get her out of the feeling (e.g., drinking, traveling, or taking the first job that came along.) She accepted this feedback and said she had come too far to set off on a path that would make her unhappy. We all agreed that it was fortunate that the opportunity for the TA had come along at that particular point in time, and we checked in about how the day had gone for her. Madeline confessed that it was new and uncomfortable to be in the position of the "helpee" rather than the "helper." We again told Madeline that we saw her as a highly capable person who happened to be in an uncharacteristic position of not knowing her next "place just right," and this seemed to sit well with her.

After Madeline left, Greg and I reflected on the day and agreed that we had established a good initial alliance. We began to anticipate what it would be like for Madeline to take the Rorschach.

Check-In on Second Day

Madeline arrived a few minutes early on the second day, and we began by asking about her evening and her thoughts about the previous day. She told about lively conversations she had had with people in the hotel bar while listening to live music and that she had told Krista K. Trobst over dinner that her time with us was fun and had gone by quickly. She said she was curious (not "disturbed," when I inquired) that she had no memory of being interviewed by Dan McAdams in Chicago. Once again, she rejected my suggestion that it might have been overwhelming to recount her life narrative, bluntly saying, "It probably wasn't." This gave us another opportunity to mirror her resilience; at first, she had a hard time accepting this, saying that she "couldn't imagine" allowing herself to be "haunted" by her traumatic childhood. Gradually, she accepted that this was a unique quality of hers, and in retrospect, I believe this discussion set the stage for the Rorschach Extended Inquiry.

Rorschach Administration

In Chapter 3, Greg Meyer describes the administration of the Rorschach Performance Assessment System (R-PAS), which as previously mentioned took almost three hours. Let me share what was in my mind as we approached the Rorschach with Madeline.

I believe that the Rorschach is an incredibly valuable tool when assessing clients like Madeline, whose problems in living typically reflect the costs of psychological coping mechanisms they have used to manage traumatic experiences, memories, and emotions. My experience is that when a good therapeutic alliance is established before the Rorschach administration (in part by co-constructing Assessment Questions), clients often produce protocols that have great added value in answering their Assessment Questions. This is partly because the Rorschach excels at revealing aspects of clients' situations that do not emerge in interviews or on self-report tests (Finn, 1996b) and also because of the sensitivity of the Rorschach to unresolved trauma (Finn, 2011, 2012). I was convinced that both the Rorschach scores and the Extended Inquiry would be very valuable for Madeline's TA.

I was also acutely aware that the Rorschach might be an extremely challenging experience for Madeline, in part because of her comments that Rebecca Behrends (who administered the test in the previous assessment) had been "very skeptical and challenging" of Madeline's responses and had "not liked them." I imagined this was how Madeline interpreted Dr. Behrend's inquiry of her free responses. I also knew from work with similar clients that Madeline might feel out of control in the ambiguous situation of the Rorschach or even one-down and that this could lead to her going one-up. I realized that if such a response occurred it would be illuminating of Madeline's personality structure; however, for therapeutic reasons, I wanted to ensure that the administration was not so stressful as to mobilize all her character defenses. Thus, I suggested to Greg that we preface the Rorschach administration explaining to Madeline that our averted gaze and lessened responsiveness was because of the "rules" of the test administration and not a reaction to her responses. I also suggested that 1) we introduce the clarification phase by emphasizing that we were trying to see things as Madeline saw them, and 2) if at all possible we avoid clarification prompts such as, "I'm not sure I see it as you do" as she might feel criticized. Greg agreed with my suggestions.

As Greg writes in Chapter 3, in fact the Rorschach administration was a highly significant assessment event. Greg took the lead, typing responses on his laptop, while I sat off to the side and attempted to be unobtrusive. Madeline "threw herself into" the initial response phase, giving rich, detailed responses; speaking animatedly and dramatically; and—in spite of (or challenging?) our warning that we would be less engaged—frequently trying to engage both of us by pointing to the cards, asking direct questions, and making gestures with her hands and body to demonstrate her percepts. When Greg was typing, often she would turn to me to make visual or verbal contact. It was fascinating to see how she related to the structure Greg imposed during the administration: at several points asking permission to give an additional response beyond the four allowed by the R-PAS administration, "poking" Greg repeatedly about his "slow" typing while also patiently waiting for him to catch up, and challenging Greg forcefully on Card X when he requested a second response in keeping with the administration guidelines. In the latter instance, it's possible Madeline was balking at being "controlled," but my impression was that a deeper dynamic was involved. Throughout the test, she had vacillated in giving responses with a positive affective tone and others with negative, disturbing images. Her first response to Card X was very high energy and exuberant. She tried to hand the card back to Greg at the end of the response and appeared incredulous when he asked for a second response. She protested, "Don't be greedy! This is the party picture!" Then at Greg's urging, she looked at the card again and accused him, "Shit, you blew it for me!" and proceeded to give a very disturbing image as her closing response. In my mind, Madeline had wanted to end with the positive image.

Also, in spite of our framing of the Clarification Phase as trying to "get in her shoes," Madeline initially seemed both confused and offended by the clarification questions, asking at first, "Isn't it evident?" and then appearing to take umbrage when Greg made detailed queries to help with the scoring. At one point, when Greg queried a "boat" Madeline saw on Card I, she said, "Patently obvious. . . . You didn't see it before?" I explained, "some people might see boats but not see it the way you saw it. So, that's why we're asking. I don't want to assume your boat is the one I see." After repeated versions of this statement, Madeline eventually seemed to take the clarification questions less personally, to enjoy helping us see "through her eyes," and to become excited by the idea that people see the cards differently ("Oh, okay. I bet everyone sees something different, don't they? . . . Isn't that fascinating?").

Rorschach Extended Inquiry

I saw the Extended Inquiry as an opportunity to explore Madeline's underlying vulnerability to painful affect states and the ways she coped with those, which I believed was essential to addressing her AQs. Both Greg and I suspected that Madeline's sense of disorientation and lack of energy at that time in her life were related to courageous choices she had made to be present for her uncle's illness and death, reconnect with her brother, and put aside work that had very effectively given her a sense of value and purpose and managed a number of emotional states (aggression, shame, depression, etc.) that were related to 1) her early trauma, 2) existential issues related to aging and her recent encounter with death, and 3) the loss of the attachment relationship with her partner. I believed that by discussing Madeline's Rorschach responses with her, we would get a sense of how close she was to acknowledging these difficult emotions, i.e., what was Level 1, 2, and 3 information (see p. 5), and also possibly increase her awareness through careful scaffolding of the costs and benefits of her current ways of coping. Over lunch, Greg and I discussed aspects of Madeline's responses that might be useful to bring up with her.

When we returned, we began by asking Madeline for her thoughts and impressions of the Rorschach. She immediately reflected on how different the current experience was compared to the previous Rorschach administration. Although her memory was fuzzy, Madeline thought that this administration had taken longer (we agreed), that Rebecca Behrends had not done a separate Clarification Phase but had queried responses at the end of each card (we said we knew this to be true), and that she was much more engaged in the test, although she knew she had tried hard and taken the test seriously the first time. We brainstormed about why

Madeline felt more involved in the current administration. She quipped, "Well, I wasn't hung over this time!" and we all laughed and agreed that was a possibility. But then she focused on the relational environment, saying, "there was whole different feel. I didn't feel challenged this time. I was asked to explain and expand and describe what I saw, rather than being asked, 'What the fuck are you talking about?'" This observation set the stage for us to inquire further about Madeline's responses.

I continued by explaining to Madeline that we would be scoring her responses and discussing inferences based on research and nomothetic norms when she returned one month later. She was clearly intrigued. I said that there was another interesting way to look at Rorschach responses, as possible "symbols" or "metaphors" for aspects of her life she was "working on internally" but of which she might not be fully conscious. Madeline immediately associated to two images she had seen on Card IX, where two "strong caribou" looking out over nature were followed by "two fat fucks . . . with Klu Klux Klan hats on . . . shooting at each other." She thought the second image was related to a sign she had seen on my office building prohibiting people from bringing firearms inside. I agreed that might be true but asked Madeline if she had noticed how frequently she saw very positive and negative images to each card turned in different orientations. She initially seemed to dismiss this, saying that, "Everyone has good and bad in them" and giving several examples from life. I asked, "But might you be *more* aware of the positive and brutal aspects of life than other people because you've had both types of experiences in spades?" and Madeline said, "That makes sense." She talked about how her work had exposed her to the beautiful and horrible sides of human nature but also agreed she was particularly aware of this duality from a young age. Madeline shared how her father had been "idolized" in the community they had lived in, while being an unpredictable "violent, vicious, monster" when he was drinking at home; she then associated this with how she still feels "on alert" when someone walks behind her in a courtroom. I brought up her first response to Card I: "Wily coyote sentinels . . . keeping watch . . . very observant." Madeline laughed and slapped her knee, saying, "I love that. I would never have personalized that! That's me." At that point, I felt confident Madeline grasped how Rorschach responses could hold personal meaning and that we could move ahead looking at other responses that were more connected to trauma.

Greg took the lead by showing Card IV and reminding Madeline of her sole response in the previous assessment: a scary monster spewing fire down on a little person to purposely burn him. As Greg described this, Madeline got an odd look on her face and reported that she felt a tremble/quiver run through her body from bottom to top and was close to breaking out in a sweat. She was speechless for a moment, and we

all agreed that the image was a metaphor for her experiences with her father. Madeline interjected, "See how far I've come!" and "I will never be that little bugger again!" We wholeheartedly agreed, and I brought up her response to Card IV in the current assessment: a picture of a potentially harmful Sasquatch-like figure taken by a photographer who was protected by a thick sheet of ice on which the monster was standing. Madeline said, "Isn't that funny, fire and ice!" and then, laughing with absolute delight, "Wow . . . I'm so glad I'm here! This is so frigging cool!"
I then took a risk:

SF: *See if this fits for you. . . . What that transformation from the old image to this would tell me is you were traumatized as a kid.*
M: *Yeah, fucking yes, horribly.*
SF: *When you went and did this* [test] *before, the trauma was still close.*
M: *Yes.*
SF: *Now, you're farther away. You're protected.*
M: *Safer.*
SF: *Safer. And you can look at it.*
M: *He was alive then. He's dead now.*

Madeline then told us of her father's death and of her decision at that time to let go of her hate for him. She said this choice was possible because of the unconditional love she had experienced from her partner. She also talked about her current fear and vulnerability to falling back into traumatized states and how she protected herself by keeping her focus on positive, new memories. I said, "One of the ways you've found to heal from past trauma is to create new memories. But it can never be like the trauma never happened to you." Madeline responded, "The trauma is still powerful shit. I just can't give it power."
This led to a very moving discussion of her responses to Card V, where Madeline at first saw a "blossoming cocoon" with a creature with new wings emerging. During the administration, this image had morphed into a creature whose wings were being weighed down by "trapped bodies" that were struggling to be free. Madeline had seen a "zipper" that needed to be opened so the trapped creatures could come out. She had said of the trapped bodies, there was "a possible transformation, but it will require a totally new identification." When I read this phrase back to her in the Extended Inquiry, Madeline made the connection to her fourth Assessment Question about finding a new sense of self and burst out laughing in pleasure. When we mused about the image, at first Madeline identified the trapped creatures as representing clients she had worked with who needed help and that she had to let go of when she closed her practice. We were able to extend the metaphor and suggest that they also represented traumatized parts of herself she had "repressed" (her word) to survive but

who now needed to be "unzipped" in order for Madeline to "be able to fly" better. She asked how she could do this, and I shared two important suggestions: 1) it's important not to open the "zipper" all at once, but to "unzip" a little, let a bit out, and "zip up" again, and 2) it helps to have a trusted person there who can help with the "zipping and unzipping." Madeline accepted these suggestions without challenge and then shared a new piece of information: she was regularly seeing a counselor through Legal Aid because she wanted help keeping an eye on her drinking. She said the counselor had been helpful and offered for us to talk to him. I was pleased that she felt safe to disclose this fact and saw this as more evidence of the comfort and openness we had achieved at that point.

Interestingly, as we closed our work that day, Madeline also felt clear that she was going to explore the job she had mentioned to us the first day but initially rejected: of mentoring native attorneys and court workers. Her disdain about teaching was gone, and she said this position would be a way to continue to help others but without burning out. Greg and I cheered her on and said we would be very interested in what she learned when she called. We closed by confirming the dates for her second visit to Austin one month later to discuss the results of the testing and address her Assessment Questions and saying a warm good-bye. As a parting gesture, I gave Madeline a postcard I had on my bookshelf of a watercolor impressionistic butterfly. Of course, she recognized the connection to her Card V response immediately and seemed delighted, saying the small gift would help her remember our discussions of that card.

Integrating Assessment Data, Initial Case Conceptualization, and Planning for Subsequent Assessment Sessions

Interlude Between Assessment Meetings

Following Madeline's first visit, Greg and I distributed the assessment materials to the group of experts along with Madeline's AQs, background information, and an account of our observations and experiences. Also, Greg and I kept in contact after he returned home, and we noted similarities in our experiences after we separated: both of us were exhausted, pleased with how the sessions had gone, and also struggling some with (more than typical) feelings of self-doubt and self-criticism. When we realized the latter, we were able to reassure each other and also to hypothesize that we were having a countertransference reaction that was important: we believed we were "holding" shame and insecurity that Madeline had disavowed in herself and that our interactions had awoken in us. If so, we saw this as an important clue as to what might be Level 3 information for Madeline.

I communicated briefly with Madeline about arranging the informant ratings on the NEO and the interpersonal measures. (She had already told Greg and me of the friend she had chosen to do these.) As prior to the initial meetings, our interactions were cordial and pleasant, and Madeline was conscientious in doing her part.

Notes

1. When agreeing to do Madeline's TA, I had asked that a familiar person accompany her to Austin to offer support during the assessment process. I knew from previous experience that TA can be an extremely intense and overwhelming process when it is compressed into several days. Dr. Krista K. Trobst, who knew Madeline from the previous assessment, volunteered to come to Austin during the current TA.
2. Typically in TA, the first tests administered are those that at their face value seem closely related to the client's main Assessment Questions. We deviated from this procedure in Madeline's TA, but she understood from the beginning that she would be repeating many of the self-report tests she had completed in the first assessment. Also, because Madeline was interested in seeing how she had changed over the 20 years, I was not worried about disrupting the alliance established early in the assessment by appearing to disregard her own agenda.
3. In collecting background information in TA, assessors stick closely to clients' AQs and generally do not inquire about topics that are not clearly relevant to clients' agendas. This tactic keeps clients from going "one-down" in the assessment, and is believed to lower clients' anxiety and engender epistemic trust (Finn, 2007; Kamphuis & Finn, 2018).

Chapter 3

A Psychodynamic Perspective on Madeline G.

Gregory J. Meyer, Joni L. Mihura, and Mark H. Waugh

Introduction and Rationale for This Chapter

This chapter is about seeing Madeline from a psychodynamic perspective. Several sources inform our perspective: her previous assessment, completed in December 1999 (Wiggins, 2003); talking and being with her; hearing her reported history and learning about some of the key experiences in her life, both in childhood and since her previous assessment; and observing her behavior. Our understanding is amplified further by four structured tasks that use distinct stimuli and allow for different types of open-ended responses. In these, we classified aspects of her observed response behavior and compared them to normative or developmental standards, as well as interpreted her responses idiographically to consider aspects of her performance—and her psychology—that go beyond the formally scored variables or help to personalize the formally scored variables more fully.

The four coded measures include her imagery, communications, and behavior while completing Hermann Rorschach's Inkblot Task (Rorschach, 1942); the stories she generated to people visually depicted on the Thematic Apperception Test (TAT; Murray, 1943); her open-ended descriptions of *mother*, *father*, *a significant other*, *a pet*, and *self* on the Object Relations Inventory (ORI; Blatt, Wein, Chevron, & Quinlan, 1979); and her responses to stems on the Washington University Sentence Completion Test (WUSCT; Hy & Loevinger, 1996). Despite potential misconceptions to the contrary, none of these structured testing measures are inherently psychodynamic. However, one may interpret them from a broadly psychodynamic perspective, as we illustrate.

Another important element informing our assessment concerns its context. There are several facets to this context. First, we were assessing Madeline so that authors of a book could for the second time draw on her life and test responses to illustrate particular approaches or paradigms to understanding people and their personalities. Almost none of us will ever find ourselves to be the central character of a book once in our lifetime, much less twice. Many of us also would not want to have our life and our psychological strengths and difficulties exposed and featured as the central elements of a book, much less two of them. That Madeline volunteered for this speaks both of her desire to contribute and her comfort, if not fondness, with an audience.

Second, we recorded the entire assessment on video, and being recorded affects people's behavior. Third, Madeline's assessment took place over two two-day weekends one month apart by two men who were roughly her age (Steve Finn and Greg Meyer). These later two facets also likely fostered a sense of being on display—or at least of having an interested audience. For sure, the three people present in the room felt a sense of the uniqueness, importance, and opportunities afforded by being able to engage in this reassessment. Moreover, both assessors felt some initial anxiety about it going well. Fourth, Madeline was assessed as part of a Therapeutic Assessment (Finn, 2007; Finn et al., 2012), with the explicit goal of being personally useful to her and, we hoped, psychologically transformative by helping Madeline think through and emotionally process her assessment data with us in a way that would aid in meaningfully answering the most important personal questions on her mind.

Our goal in this chapter is to draw on the various sources of information noted above, while being mindful of the particulars of this assessment context, to think about Madeline psychodynamically. A good place to start, then, is by explaining what we mean by psychodynamic.

The Basics of Psychodynamic Approaches to Understanding People

Five psychodynamic principles will organize our thinking and approach to test interpretation. The past, particularly early childhood experience, is important for understanding who we are in the present. Conscious awareness is limited, and thus we carry more with us than we recognize. Conflicts, coping styles, and self-protective psychological defenses influence our perceptions and behaviors. Affects and motives ("hot" processes) are as important to mental life as cognitions and logic ("cold" processes). Finally, we reenact core internal conflicts or complexes in our important relationships, including within ourselves (i.e., how we relate to our self).

Psychodynamic conceptualizations of personality and psychological problems, accompanied by treatable solutions that flow from them, have existed for more than 100 years, beginning with early work by Freud, Jung, and Adler. Wiggins (2003) provides a succinct overview of psychodynamic theory from the Freudian tradition. Contemporary psychodynamic thinking in this tradition incorporates ongoing advances in cognitive, developmental, personality, and social psychology, as well as advances in the neuroscience of mental processing (Bornstein, Maracic, &

Natoli, 2018; Luyten, Mayes, Blatt, Target, & Fonagy, 2015; Westen, 1998). There is general agreement that contemporary theory in the psychodynamic tradition encompasses four main schools of thought.

Drive theory is one school of thought. It continues the classical tradition started by Freud that focuses on the interplay of id, ego, and superego. In this model, the largely conscious ego navigates between the procreative (sex) and protective (aggression) drives that propel evolution (the id) and the internalized, culturally communicated moral codes that set standards for acceptable social behaviors and internal thoughts (the superego). In contrast, ego psychology emphasizes the resources available for adaptation and effective functioning that emerge innately, such as perception, language, attention, and reasoning, and that develop over time through interactions with the environment. Ego psychology emphasizes peoples' quest to cope, adapt, and attempt to succeed in functioning across life roles and to be satisfied with their wishes, ambitions, and relationships. A third school spans interpersonal (i.e., object) relations and attachment theory, viewing interpersonal relations as primary motivators in life, with personality development embedded in critical caregiver relationships that form durable mental templates of one's self and of others. Inconsistent, detached, or abusive parenting leaves people primed to develop negative and painful or shameful self-representations and to bring core mental templates of self-with-other-interactions into new relationships, creating conflict, symptoms, affective turmoil, or lonely isolation.

Self-psychology, the fourth school, was not mentioned by Wiggins (2003). More so than others, it views obtaining a cohesive, agentic, and positive sense of self as the critical challenge for development. From this perspective, healthy development is only obtained when a caregiver (or an important other later in life, including a therapist) is able to empathically see and mirror the needs of the child, including her or his wishes, ambitions, and ideals, and genuinely prize his or her steps toward obtaining them. Of equal importance, the caregiver needs to respond empathically and provide reassuring comfort to the pain or shame of instances when those efforts falter or when a lapse in empathic attunement to the child has occurred. These processes allow a child to obtain a stable sense of worth and purpose and provide the emotional resources for the child to internalize ways of managing distress without engaging in problematic symptom behavior. Ultimately, this allows the individual to navigate the challenges of intimacy and achievement, or love and work.

A Psychodynamic Approach to Assessment Methods and Their Data

Assessment methods or individual tests are not psychodynamic. They are tools. Psychologists from any assessment paradigm can use them. Thus, a psychodynamic approach to using assessment methods and their data is one informed by psychodynamic principles and one or more of the psychodynamic approaches outlined earlier (e.g., Allison, Blatt, & Zimet, 1968; Bram & Peebles, 2014; Rapaport, Gill, & Schafer, 1968; Shapiro, 1965; Silverstein, 2013). In this approach to assessment, relational representations of self and other are important, including the in vivo interaction between the respondent and the test materials or the examiner and the examiner's personal reactions to the respondent (Schafer, 1954; see also Behrends & Blatt, 2003). This approach also explicitly posits that some assessment results will reside in conscious awareness, while other results will be in partial awareness, or completely out of awareness. This approach also posits that conflicts, characterological ways of behaving, and developmentally determined psychological vulnerabilities, as well as adaptive self-protective factors (i.e., coping styles and defenses), will be evident in test responses and behavior. Finally, this approach posits that understanding a person and the factors that prompted their seeking the evaluation requires attending to their affects and motives as much as their cognitions and beliefs.

Thus, we will be considering Madeline's reported experiences, interactive behaviors, and responses to the Rorschach, TAT, ORI, and WUSCT with these ideas in mind. We will attend to what she says and doesn't say, how she says things, and whether and how that style might change as different topics or issues are considered. We will attend to how she organizes information and how she interacts with the assessors, the setting, and the tasks themselves. For two of the tasks, we will attend to what she perceives, how she perceives, and what she doesn't perceive or notice. Across interactions and tasks, we will attend to the clarity of her communication and the factors that might contribute to lapses in clarity or organization. We will look for the assets and strengths she has for coping with the demands of her life, as well as the conflicts or complexes that might limit or inhibit them.

Throughout this process, our inferences as assessors can go astray, so we follow principles to help ensure they do not. One of the best ways to ensure inferences are as accurate as possible, as well as appropriately tailored to the life of a respondent, is to conduct an assessment using a collaborative model of Therapeutic Assessment, as Steve Finn describes in Chapters 2 and 7. In addition, drawing on standard multimethod assessment sources (e.g., Weiner & Greene, 2017), as well as texts written from an explicitly psychodynamic perspective (e.g., Bram & Peebles, 2014), we briefly outline principles to guide interpretation across multiple sources of information.

First, when drawing inferences, it is essential to keep in mind the source of information under consideration, as well as the specific psychological operations engaged when obtaining information from that source.

For instance, this principle makes the processes of linguistically driven introspective recall that are used to inform self-reported information very distinct from the processes of visual-mnemonic perception that are used to formulate Rorschach responses. Second, we look for redundancy of evidence for an inference, both within and across sources of data. The more times we see evidence for a particular inference, the stronger our confidence in the inference.

Third, we look for conservative transparency in the steps that link some observed testing behavior to an inferred quality of the individual. This *response process foundation* for interpretation posits that the most trustworthy inferences are those where we can point to specific psychological operations occurring in the microcosm of the assessment task as the basis for inferring the respondent is likely to display parallel psychological operations when engaging in parallel contexts or activities in daily life. Finally, when confronting seemingly contradictory data, we do not discard or dismiss one source or another. Instead, we seek to understand how both could be true (e.g., depression not seen on self-report, but with many markers on the Rorschach task, or vice versa). That is, we seek to understand what it would mean to be a person for whom all sources of information are correct. This principle highlights how understanding a person often involves empathically conceptualizing a unique patterning of multimethod information contextualized to the life of this one person.

The Assessment Measures Used With Madeline

The Rorschach Task

Hermann Rorschach's Inkblot Task includes a standard series of ten ink-blots that he carefully created, pilot tested, and refined over time. Five are variegated black and gray, two are variegated black and gray with prominent sections of bold red, and three are fully chromatic with elements ranging from pastel to brightly saturated color. Rorschach (1942) created each inkblot on a white background that he deliberately used as part of the pattern on many cards. During administration, respondents look sequentially at each card and answer the question "What might this be?" The assessor records responses verbatim across all ten cards and then goes back through the cards to clarify each response, gaining information about where in the card response objects reside and the inkblot features that contributed to the perception.

Rorschach trained as an artist, and he used those skills to iteratively refine and embellish the inkblots over time (see Searls, 2017). His goal appeared to be to embed both a reasonably recognizable structure into each of the inkblots and a textured array of suggestive 'critical bits' (Exner, 1996) that lend themselves to incomplete or imperfect perceptual likenesses that form competing visual images available as potential responses to the task. These critical bits rely on the form, color, shading, or symmetrical features of the inkblots. They provide wide latitude for people to generate an almost unlimited number of unique and idiographic responses.

After administering the task, the assessor codes or classifies the obtained responses along multiple dimensions, summarizes the codes across all responses to generate summary scores, compares the summary scores to normative expectations, and interprets the results based on formal interpretive guidelines. The main types of variables that are coded include test-taking behaviors, locations selected for use, types of content seen, how objects are perceived, conventionality and fit of the objects seen to the location used, inkblot features that contribute to perception, logical coherence of communication, and types of themes, including the ways in which people and relationships were construed. In addition, the assessor attends to idiographic response content, the interplay of scores with card and response features, and respondent-assessor interactions.

Within the Rorschach Performance Assessment System (R-PAS; Meyer et al., 2011; Mihura & Meyer, 2018), the primary interpretive variables are displayed on two norm-based profiles. R-PAS is a replacement for and corrective to Exner's (2003) Comprehensive System, which previously was in common use across many countries. It also became a flashpoint for controversy and the subject of heated criticism (e.g., Lilienfeld, Wood, & Garb, 2000; Wood, Lilienfeld, Garb, & Nezworski, 2000; Wood, Nezworski, Lilienfeld, & Garb, 2003). The corrections introduced by R-PAS attempted to address these criticisms thoroughly. It did so by emphasizing variables with systematically gathered validity evidence (e.g., Mihura, Meyer, Dumitrascu, & Bombel, 2013), dropping variables that lacked validity or uniqueness (Meyer et al.), and adding new variables based on meta-analytic reviews (Bornstein, 1996, 1999; Diener, Hilsenroth, Shaffer, & Sexton, 2011; Graceffo, Mihura, & Meyer, 2014; Mihura, Dumitrascu, Roy, & Meyer, 2018; Monroe, Diener, Fowler, Sexton, & Hilsenroth, 2013). R-PAS also corrected problems with the Comprehensive System norms (e.g., Meyer, Erdberg, & Shaffer, 2007; Meyer, Shaffer, Erdberg, & Horn, 2015), notably reduced problems related to variability in the number of responses given to the task (e.g., Hosseininasab et al., 2019), and updated tables to classify the conventionality of perceptions (e.g., Su et al. 2015). It also provided more fully specified administration and coding guidelines to increase their reliability and uniformity (e.g., Viglione, Blume-Marcovici, Miller, Giromini, & Meyer, 2012; Viglione et al., 2015) and refined interpretation to emphasize transparent links between observed testing behaviors and inferred behavior in everyday life (Meyer et al.).

The Rorschach, possibly more than any other currently used assessment measure, is dismissed or denigrated by many psychologists, despite its supportive research base of reliability and validity, including by text-book authors, who have a responsibility to their readers to know better. Furthermore, the Rorschach research base applies to the variables that clinicians actually use in practice. This makes the Rorschach unlike the TAT, ORI, or WUSCT. These measures also have a strong research base, as we discuss shortly. However, most clinicians in practice do not score or interpret those variables, instead interpreting responses to the standardized material qualitatively, as we will illustrate.

Based on a comprehensive review of meta-analytic evidence, since 2001 researchers have known that the global validity of Rorschach variables was sound (Meyer & Archer, 2001) and equivalent to that for the Minnesota Multiphasic Personality Inventory (MMPI; see Chapter 6; e.g., both had an average $r = .32$ over all hypothesized effects). However, the data indicated the Rorschach was *generally* valid, and generally *as valid as the MMPI*, but they did not indicate which *specific scores* were valid and which were not. Notably, Garb (1999) called for a moratorium on the use of the Rorschach in clinical and forensic settings until that kind of data was available, even though no other assessment measure in use has meta-analytic support for every variable. Nonetheless, Mihura et al. (2013) systematically reviewed the published literature for the 65 variables central to interpretation in the Comprehensive System (Exner, 2003). The authors replicated the findings concerning general validity, although they also documented clear differences in validity across variables, with 13 having excellent support, 17 good support, 10 modest support, 13 no support, and 12 with no construct relevant studies in the literature.

Meyer, Hsiao, Viglione, Mihura, and Abraham (2013) surveyed 246 experienced clinicians who regularly used the Rorschach, asking them to ignore what they learned and instead rate variables on their perceived validity in practice. Across the 65 variables studied by Mihura et al. (2013), the correlation was strong (.51) between the average ratings of validity from the clinicians and the classification of the variable as having no, modest, good, or excellent validity based on the meta-analytic results. Importantly, the clinicians and the meta-analytic research diverged from Exner's (2003) authoritative review of the Comprehensive System while converging on the conclusions that some variables lack validity and probably should not be used in clinical practice and that other variables are valid and should be emphasized in clinical practice.

In response to Mihura et al.'s (2013) meta-analyses, the most vocal critics published a follow-up Comment (Wood, Garb, Nezworski, Lilienfeld, & Duke, 2015). Although fraught with problems (see Mihura, Meyer, Bombel, & Dumitrascu, 2015), Wood et al. made two noteworthy statements given the years of debate associated with the Rorschach. First, they said that Mihura et al.'s results "provided an unbiased and trustworthy summary of the published literature." Second, they rescinded Garb's

(1999) global call for a moratorium on use of the Rorschach in clinical and forensic settings.

Recent research has explored a set of 11 potential grandiosity and narcissism variables (GNVs; Gritti, Marino, Lang, & Meyer, 2018; Meyer, Gritti, Marino, & Sholander, 2019). Initial results in the R-PAS norms and a clinical sample indicated there was a primary dimension largely defined by the four variables of omnipotent attitudes and behavior, idealized imagery, justifying a response based on personal knowledge impervious to challenge by an examiner, and personalizing a response by linking oneself to it in some fashion. This dimension was strongly correlated (M r = .41) with ratings of narcissism by clinicians who were treating the patients in therapy.

One of the other GNVs also is relevant for Madeline. This code quantifies instances of positive affective states, including euphoric or energetic exuberance. Two other variables in the Rorschach literature are worth mentioning, as they emerge in Madeline's protocol. The first concerns affectively driven embellishment, where highly specific or elaborate inferences about objects go well beyond the stimulus features of the inkblot (Kleiger, 2017; Kleiger & Peebles-Kleiger, 1993). The second concerns split representations, where affectively polar opposites occur within a single object, between two objects in the same response, or across sequential responses (Cooper & Arnow, 1986). The *embellishment* and *splitting* variables have been associated with identity struggles, emotional instability, and confusion or conflict in intimate relationships, while the energetic affect and embellishment variables relate to hypomanic expansiveness (Cooper & Arnow, 1986; Kleiger, 2017; Mihura, 2006).

The Thematic Apperception Test (TAT)

The TAT (Murray, 1943) consists of 30 somewhat ambiguous pictures, with all but two depicting people and one being an all-white blank card with no stimuli. The cards are achromatic and generally have a gloomy tone. Respondents create a story with a beginning, middle, and end and describe what each character is thinking and feeling. The task elicits stories that exemplify motivations, needs, drives, and personal or interpersonal conflicts. Most clinicians administer eight to ten cards, selecting some they use with most clients and others to address referral questions based on the types of stories typically given (i.e., the thematic pull of the card). Clinicians typically interpret the TAT by identifying recurring themes or salient departures from what is typical (see Bram & Peebles, 2014; Teglasi, 2010; Weiner & Greene, 2017). This encompasses attending to the form and structure of the stories (e.g., length, vocabulary, organization, attention to details, injection of content not depicted, typicality), content themes (e.g., endings, emotional tone, omissions of typical content, recurrent adjectives, nature of interactions, characteristics of central characters), and interactive behaviors around the task (e.g., reactions to the task demands, the examiner, the narratives produced, the stimuli themselves).

Many scoring systems exist for the TAT (e.g., Jenkins, 2008). One long tradition of research examines implicit motives, including achievement, power, and affiliation or intimacy (e.g., Köllner & Schultheiss, 2014; McAdams, 1988; McClelland, Koestner, & Weinberger, 1989; Spangler, 1992; Winter, John, Stewart, Klohnen, & Duncan, 1998). Cramer (e.g., 2015) created and validated scores for three developmentally ordered defense mechanisms, denial, projection, and identification. Researchers have used her system in multiple studies examining development, personality, and psychopathology, including both experimental designs and longitudinal outcomes.

Another actively researched system is the Social Cognition and Object Relations Scale: Global Rating Method (SCORS-G; Stein & Slavin-Mulford, 2018). Judges can apply the SCORS-G to various types of narratives, although most research uses the TAT. Judges rate eight dimensions on a 1 to 7 descriptively anchored scale. Ratings from 1 to 3 are considered problematic or unhealthy, and those from 5 to 7 as adaptive or healthy. The dimensions are Complexity of Representation of People (COM), Affective Quality of Representations (AFF), Emotional Investment in Relationships (EIR), Emotional Investment in Values and Moral Standards (EIM), Understanding of Social Causality (SC), Experience and Management of Aggressive Impulses (AGG), Self-Esteem (SE), and Identity and Coherence of Self (ICS). As with all scoring systems, the cards selected for an assessment provide the stimulus context and thus influence the level of scores observed (Siefert et al., 2016; Stein et al., 2014). Reliability is generally strong, and validity is evident in multiple studies (e.g., Stein et al., 2018; Stein & Slavin-Mulford, 2018).

The Object Relations Inventory (ORI)

Clinicians can informally interpret or formally score written or oral responses to the five ORI prompts. Two common scores are Conceptual Level and Differentiation-Relatedness (e.g., Bender, Morey, & Skodol, 2011; Blatt et al., 1979; Blatt, 1981; Diamond, Kaslow, Coonerty, & Blatt, 1990; Huprich, Auerbach, Porcerelli, & Bupp, 2016), with both showing good interrater reliability. Conceptual Level reflects the degree of increasingly complex articulation and integration of personal characteristics in the description of the target using a nine-point scale.[1] Differentiation-Relatedness refers to the level of psychosocial maturation embodied in relationship descriptions using a ten-point scale, incorporating boundary problems, polarized versus differentiated relationship schemas, perspective taking, empathy, and mutuality.[2]

The ORI has been used to study personality, including attachment and reflective functioning; psychopathology, including depression and borderline personality disorder; and psychotherapeutic process and outcome (see Huprich et al., 2016, for a review). It is a conceptual forerunner (Bender et al., 2011) to the Level of Personality Functioning dimension (Criterion A) of the Alternative Model of Personality Disorders (AMPD) in Section III of DSM-5 (APA, 2013).

The Washington University Sentence Completion Test (WUSCT)

Loevinger developed the WUSCT solely to assess ego development, which is a key dimension of psychoemotional maturity, distinct from age or intelligence (Hy & Loevinger, 1996). Examiners classify each of its 36 items into one of eight levels[3] and convert them to a protocol level score. Scoring is rigorously defined and reliable (Westenberg, Hauser, & Cohn, 2004), and extensive research supports the WUSCT as a valid index of ego development (e.g., Westenberg et al. 2004). In general, the literature supports the key tenets of the ego development construct, including its unidimensionality, sequential development, and variability across individuals and within age groups. Researchers have used the WUSCT in multiple longitudinal studies, showing continuity and predictive validity for indices of adaptability, effective functioning, and theoretically consistent psychopathology variables. A meta-analysis showed just modest associations with intelligence and incremental validity predicting relevant criteria over and above intelligence (Cohn & Westenberg, 2004). As with the TAT and ORI, clinicians also interpret individual responses informally as narrative data.

Synopsis of Madeline's History and Observations

In Wiggins (2003), Dan McAdams (2003) provided a summary of Madeline's developmental history, and Krista Trobst and Jerry Wiggins (2003) provided input from her contemporary peers, as well as an update on her life from three years after the assessment. In the current book, Chris Hopwood and Mark Waugh review some of Madeline's history in Chapter 1, and Steve Finn provides additional updated information in Chapters 2 and 7. Given this, we confine ourselves to just brief notes about her background to set the stage for our chapter.

At the initial assessment in December 1999, Madeline was 35 years old; living in Albuquerque with her partner of 6 years; and employed as a defense attorney, specializing in work for Native American defendants.

She grew up with a brother and sister in a small town with many other Native American families, although hers stood out for its dysfunction. Both parents had serious drinking problems, with her father often becoming violent when drunk, beating his wife and each of the children. Madeline reported three early recollections. One was her father shooting her mother (McAdams gave no further details). A second was of her and her siblings watching through a hole in the floor at their parents fighting by the Christmas tree below as her mother stabs her father in the neck with scissors and blood spurts across the room. The third was returning home to find mother absent and father unwilling to explain why, although she eventually discovers her mother was hospitalized after trying to kill herself by slitting her wrists.

Madeline described herself as a wild and incorrigible child who began drinking early, even taking whiskey to school by the third grade. By age 12, she had moved out of the house, spending time in foster care and jail. In jail, she became a voracious reader and ultimately vowed to straighten up her life. At age 21, she moved, got a job, and eventually obtained advanced degrees in social work and law.

Madeline's peers saw her as extraverted, exhibitionistic, brash, spirited, opinionated, audacious, domineering, self-aggrandizing, manipulative to her ends, and hypomanic but also interesting, fun loving, and engaging. They also saw her as someone who works as hard as she plays, lives life fully, strives for excellence, and takes great pride in defending her disadvantaged clients from a system she sees as stacked against them.

The second assessment in January and February 2017 had fortuitous timing. Madeline was in a transition period. In January 2016, she had left her law practice to care for her uncle who had leukemia and ultimately died. She now was frustrated at her inability to decide what to do next, feeling that she was spinning or drifting without any wind in her sails. In a surprise to us, Madeline did not recall that Jerry Wiggins had published a book about her previous assessment, despite signing consents at the time, and initially she could not recall meeting with Dan McAdams in Chicago or him interviewing her for it. Madeline was pleased about the Therapeutic Assessment structure for the current assessment, as now she would be able to seek answers to her personal questions. Over the course of the first day, she developed four, as described in Chapter 2.

Fleshing out the context for these questions, Madeline added detail to her history, including the physical and psychological punishment she experienced growing up, her time in jail, the physical fights she engaged in both in and out of jail, and her college and post-graduate years. She described her mother contacting her once in the early 1990s when she needed money. Madeline loaned her a credit card, which she maxed out before disappearing again. Madeline also elaborated on her relationship with her former partner and its surprising and depressing end, which left her with suicidal thoughts and an unwillingness to have friends over for the next two years. She said he was her only true love and the only person she ever really "let in." Madeline also proudly described her successful law practice as a warrior for the underrepresented but noted her detest of the constant need to be "begging" for resources to do her job well.

For recent history, Madeline described her uncle, his role as the only source of emotional support in her youth, and the pride she felt at being able to fly in family to see him before he died. In particular, she reconnected positively with her brother, although she was shocked to learn he talked openly with others about their childhood experiences. Her brother went to live with their father for a month shortly before their father died. During that time, he called and asked Madeline if she would talk to their father. She agreed. Her father apologized for the way he was when she was young, praised her for all she had accomplished, and said he loved her. Madeline did not know what to say but politely responded in kind by telling him that it was okay because she was doing well now. She also said she loved him, too, although she was not sure that was sincere. When asked about sources of support, Madeline quickly named eight people, five women and three men, including one who has been a friend since her adolescence. She also noted that although she has no children, she has helped raise eight children of friends, with some staying with her up to two years. At the same time, she has been averse to romantic relationships, noting that she only had one relationship about ten years ago and had not kissed a person since then.

After the first meeting with Madeline, Steve and Greg individually wrote out their reactions and experiences to share with the rest of the collaborators. In part, Greg said, "Madeline is a very engaged, forthright, intelligent, articulate, colorful, provocative, and demanding person. Her 'I don't suffer fools or put up with bullshit' attitude is offset by a consistent desire to be affirmed and admired." He also noted how her stories and descriptions of events surrounding her assessment questions were generally engrossing, although they also left him feeling alternately empathizing and touched, admiring, or on occasion curiously annoyed. He described how difficult it was to administer the Rorschach with her and how, after returning home, he felt more than passing pangs of self-doubt and inadequacy over how it went. He speculated these feelings in part might have been experiential counterweights to her ascendance and dominance during the assessment. At the same time, when discussing the Rorschach with her, Greg felt an empathic connection with Madeline, as she genuinely reflected on and engaged with the potential meaning of the imagery she had produced in relation to her history and current circumstances.

When Madeline returned for the second weekend, she clearly had been reflecting on the work completed the month before and seemed to be feeling quite positive about how it had gone so far. The biggest change in her life was accepting a high-paying job for a position she helped design training legal advocates for work with Native Americans. Given this change, she felt most of her prior questions were no longer relevant. The four questions she now wanted to address were: 1) Why am I not so driven right now? Where has that gone? 2) How do I get judges I've alienated before to see the new person I'm becoming and believe it's authentic? 3) What tools do I need to effectively remain inspired? and 4) How do I deal with the [inner] chatter and the typical rumor mill? How do I address all that?

Interpreting the Measures

Rorschach Data and Results

We start by considering Madeline's R-PAS results, which provide a range of normatively referenced scores for interpretation, unlike the three other measures. Although we start with R-PAS data in this chapter, for general clinical practice, we would begin interpretation with self-report inventories, like those discussed in other chapters, to set the stage with consciously recognized and deliberately reported characteristics. In addition, we largely consider Madeline's current assessment rather than make a detailed comparison to her previous Rorschach. In part, this is because of space constraints. However, in part it is because the 1999 administration followed the Rapaport et al. (1968) method, which does not have a separate clarification phase and does not require the examiner to clarify every response. Consequently, her 1999 protocol is notably under clarified from an R-PAS perspective, with 40% of her responses receiving no clarification at all.

Madeline's current Rorschach is unusual in many ways. For starters, it took 2 hours and 45 minutes to complete, as Madeline gave 25 highly detailed responses, many of which she physically animated while seated, although she twice also stood up to demonstrate them. Her final protocol contained about 13,000 words, which is about 10 times more than most protocols (see Appendix A). Prior to her first response, Madeline asked if she could talk while doing this. Although it may not have made much difference, rather than saying she could, even though we could not say much back, her record may have been more concise if Greg and Steve instead said, "Say what it might be; what it looks like to you." It is also possible her record would have been more typical if, like her 1999 assessment, the context were one woman assessing her in a room without recording it rather than two men recording on video.

Thus, the administration context, including her ongoing interactions with two male examiners during the administration, may have contributed to the highly complex record. The administration context also challenges our use of the R-PAS norms, given that others in the norms were not assessed under parallel circumstances. At the same time, when Madeline's 1999 protocol was coded according to R-PAS guidelines, is also was above average in complexity, particularly with respect to the determinants of her perceptions, which, as we will see, is the case with her current protocol. This high level of complexity in 1999 was evident despite the fact that her protocol was notably under clarified. We return to this issue after considering her protocol in greater depth.

Overall, Madeline found the card images captivating and evocative and relished generating her complex, multifaceted responses. At the same time, she found aspects of the administration intolerable. As the protocol indicates, she hated when Greg regularly asked her to stop or slow down so he could get a verbatim record. She also hated the standard clarification phase questions, which consistently felt to her like Greg doubted her seemingly obvious perceptions. Finally, on Card X, she hated how Greg prompted for another response. Madeline clearly had understood the guidelines to "give two, maybe three responses to each card" (see the response phase for Cards I, II, IV, VIII, and IX). However, when she got to the very last card, she attempted to hand the card back after just one. Greg encouraged her to take a bit more time and try to see something else. She then became quite upset and angry with Greg because the buoyant, effusive party seen in her first response transitioned into a gruesome scene of "murder and mayhem." She experienced Greg as causing her positive response to be spoiled, and her anger about this prompted her to leave for a bathroom break (see Appendix A).

Table 3.1 provides Madeline's results,[4] encompassing the Page 1 and Page 2 Profiles, and the summary scores for all variables. Her responses and response-level R-PAS codes are in Appendix A. One R-PAS interpretive principle is to attend to what stands out on the Profile Pages as atypically high or low scores with red or black icons, while not ignoring strengths indicated by average scores with green icons. The red and black icons show what is most distinctively characteristic of her relative to what most people see, say, and do when completing the task; the green icons show how she is like others in the same respect. Before turning to the results, however, readers should first review the response phase communications in Madeline's record (Appendix A), optimally with the inkblots in hand to understand her responses in context. Although it is a long record to read in its entirety, doing so will provide an even better foundation for understanding her profiled scores and our interpretation.[5]

What is most distinctive about Madeline's protocol is its complexity (Complexity = 179, SS > 145). She exceeds the highest score in the norms by a comfortable margin, which is even more remarkable because she did so with just an average number of responses (R = 25, SS = 105)

Table 3.1 RPAS Scores

R-PAS Summary Scores and Profiles — Page 1

C-ID: Madeline P-ID: 1460 Age: 51 Gender: Female Education: 19

Domain/Variables	Raw Scores	Raw %ile	SS	Cplx. Adj. %ile	SS	Standard Score Profile R-Optimized	Abbr.
Admin. Behaviors and Obs.							
Pr	1	62	104				Pr
Pu	1	86	116				Pu
CT (Card Turning)	9	84	115				CT
Engagement and Cog. Processing							
Complexity	179	>99	148				Cmplx
R (Resources)	25	62	105				R
F% [Lambda = 0.00] (Simplicity)	0%	<1	56	<1	60		F%
Blend	21	>99	146	95	125		Bln
Sy	18	99	134	15	84		Sy
MC	29.0	>99	148	96	127		MC
MC - PPD	−1.0	59	104	78	112		MC-PPD
M	17	>99	143	94	124		M
M/MC [17/29.0]	59%	60	104	44	98		M Prp
(CF+C)/SumC [11/13]	85%	89	119	89	119		CFC Prp

(Continued)

Table 3.1 (Continued)

Perception and Thinking Problems		Raw	%ile	SS	%ile	SS		
EII-3		2.7	>99	143	97	129		EII
TP-Comp (Thought & Percept. Com...)		2.3	95	125	74	109		TP-C
WsumCog		81	>99	148	>99	148		WCog
SevCog		3	98	131	98	131		Sev
FQ-%		8%	46	98	8	79		FQ-%
WD-%		4%	24	89	11	82		WD-%
FQo%		40%	7	78	34	94		FQo%
P		6	59	103	35	94		P
Stress and Distress								
YTVC'		18	99	138	93	123		YTVC'
m		8	>99	143	85	116		m
Y		7	99	133	93	122		Y
MOR		9	>99	146	99	139		MOR
SC-Comp (Suicide Concern Comp.)		9.8	>99	143	93	122		SC-C
Self and Other Representation								
ODL%		40%	98	133	98	124		ODL%
SR (Space Reversal)		0	19	87	19	87		SR
MAP/MAHP	[5/8]	62%	59	104	90	120		MAP Prp
PHR/GPHR	[9/17]	53%	80	113	80	113		PHR Prp

					Abbr.
M-	1	81	113	81	113	M-
AGC	6	91	120	75	111	AGC
H	9	99	135	83	114	H
COP	7	>99	145	98	130	COP
MAH	3	97	127	53	100	MAH

© 2010–2017 R-PAS

R-PAS Summary Scores and Profiles — Page 2

C-ID: Madeline P-ID: 1460 Age: 51 Gender: Female Education: 19

Domain/Variables	Raw Scores	Raw %ile	Raw SS	Cplx. Adj. %ile	Cplx. Adj. SS	Standard Score Profile R-Optimized	Abbr.
Engagement and Cog. Processing							
W%	76%	94	124	55	102		W%
Dd%	8%	27	91	54	101		Dd%
SI (Space Integration)	9	98	132	95	124		SI
IntCont	2	51	100	11	81		IntC
Vg%	0%	58	86	30	92		Vg%
V	3	96	126	83	116		V
FD	10	>99	148	>99	148		FD
R8910%	40%	94	123	98	130		R8910%
WSumC	12.0	>99	144	86	116		WSC

(Continued)

Table 3.1 (Continued)

		Raw	%ile	SS	%ile	SS	Graph	
C		0	36	95	36	95		C
Mp/(Ma+Mp)	[0/17]	0%	5	75	5	75		Mp Prp
Perception and Thinking Problems							60 70 80 90 100 110 120 130 140	
FQu%		52%	96	126	75	110		FQu%
Stress and Distress							60 70 80 90 100 110 120 130 140	
PPD		30	>99	143	83	114		PPD
CBlend		9	>99	148	>99	144		CBlnd
C'		8	99	134	94	124		C'
V		3	96	126	83	116		V
CritCont% (Critical Contents)		88%	>99	148	>99	139		CrCt
Self and Other Representation							60 70 80 90 100 110 120 130 140	
SumH		16	>99	139	66	106		SumH
NPH/SumH	[7/16]	44%	23	89	48	99		NPH Prp
V-Comp (Vigilance Composite)		7.7	99	138	64	105		V-C
r (Reflections)		0	36	95	36	95		r
p/(a+p)	[4/29]	14%	8	79	11	82		p Prp
AGM		4	>99	141	>99	141		AGM
T		0	28	91	28	91		T
PER		1	72	109	72	109		PER
An		4	92	122	92	122		An

© 2010–2017 R-PAS

R-PAS Profile Appendix—Summary Scores for All Variables

C-ID: Madeline P-ID: 1460 Age: 51 Gender: Female Education: 19

R & Admin.	Raw	%ile	SS	Cplx. Adj. %ile	Cplx. Adj. SS
R	25	62	105	<1	60
R8910	10	85	116	30	92
Pr	1	62	104		
Pu	1	86	116		
CT	9	84	115		
R8910%	40%	94	123	98	130

Location	Raw	%ile	SS	Cplx. Adj. %ile	Cplx. Adj. SS
W	19	95	125	26	91
D	4	8	79	18	86
Dd	2	30	92	30	92
WD	23	74	110	1	63
W%	76%	94	124	55	102
Dd%	8%	27	91	54	101

Space	Raw	%ile	SS	Cplx. Adj. %ile	Cplx. Adj. SS
SR	0	19	87	19	87
SI	9	98	132	95	124
AnyS	9	97	129	90	120

Content	Raw	%ile	SS	Cplx. Adj. %ile	Cplx. Adj. SS
H	9	99	135	83	114
(H)	2	76	110	46	98

FQ and Popular	Raw	%ile	SS	Cplx. Adj. %ile	Cplx. Adj. SS
FQo	10	18	86	4	74
FQu	13	95	125	39	96
FQ-	2	53	101	7	78
FQn	0	41	97	41	97
WDo	10	23	89	3	71
WDu	12	98	131	58	103
WD-	1	37	95	11	82
WDn	0	41	97	41	97
M-	1	81	113	81	113
P	6	59	103	35	94
FQo%	40%	7	78	34	94
FQu%	52%	96	126	75	110
FQ-%	8%	46	98	8	79
WD-%	4%	24	89	11	82

Determinants	Raw	%ile	SS	Cplx. Adj. %ile	Cplx. Adj. SS
M	17	>99	143	94	124
FM	4	68	107	3	72
m	8	>99	143	85	116
FC	2	54	101	10	81
CF	11	>99	148	99	138
C	0	36	95	36	95
C'	8	99	134	94	124

Cognitive Codes	Raw	%ile	SS	Cplx. Adj. %ile	Cplx. Adj. SS
DV1 (1)	7	>99	148	>99	148
DV2 (1)	0	49	100	49	100
DR1 (3)	7	>99	141	>99	141
DR2 (6)	0	48	99	48	99
PEC (5)	1	92	121	92	121
INC1 (2)	1	65	106	25	90
INC2 (4)	0	45	98	45	98
FAB1 (4)	8	>99	148	>99	148
FAB2 (7)	2	>99	140	>99	140
CON (7)	0	49	100	49	100
WSumCog	81	>99	148	>99	148
SevCog	3	98	131	98	131
Lev2Cog	2	97	129	97	129

Thematic Codes	Raw	%ile	SS	Cplx. Adj. %ile	Cplx. Adj. SS
ABS	0	40	96	40	96
PER	1	72	109	72	109
COP	7	>99	145	98	130
MAH	3	97	127	53	100
GHR	8	92	122	39	96
AGM	4	>99	141	99	141
AGC	6	91	120	75	111
MOR	9	>99	146	97	139

(Continued)

Table 3.1 (Continued)

	Raw				
Hd	5	97	128	97	128
(Hd)	0	26	91	26	91
A	5	12	82	12	82
(A)	0	34	94	34	94
Ad	3	62	104	62	104
(Ad)	0	43	97	43	97
An	4	92	122	92	122
Art	1	50	100	50	100
Ay	1	76	111	76	111
Bl	1	86	116	86	116
Cg	5	93	122	26	90
Ex	0	41	97	41	97
Fi	1	73	109	30	92
Sx	3	97	128	97	128
NC	13	94	123	7	78
SumH	16	>99	139	66	106
NPH	7	92	121	35	94
NPH/SumH	44%	23	89	48	99

Object Qualities

	Raw				
Sy	18	99	134	15	84
Vg	0	18	86	18	86
2	10	80	113	33	94
Sy%	72%	99	138	44	98
Vg%	0%	18	86	30	92

	Raw				
Y	7	99	133	93	122
T	0	28	91	28	91
V	3	96	126	83	116
r	0	36	95	36	95
FD	10	>99	148	>99	148
F	0	<1	56	20	88
a	25	>99	146	99	136
P	4	62	105	4	74
Ma	17	>99	148	>99	143
Mp	0	12	82	12	82
Blend	21	>99	146	95	125
CBlend	9	>99	148	>99	144
WSumC	12.0	>99	144	86	116
SumC	13	>99	145	66	106
(CF+C)/SumC	85%	89	119	89	119
MC	29.0	>99	148	96	127
M/MC	59%	60	104	44	98
YTVC'	18	99	138	93	123
mY	15	>99	143	94	123
F%	0%	<1	56	61	104
PPD	30	>99	143	83	114
MC - PPD	-1.0	59	104	78	112
p/(a+b)	14%	8	79	11	82
Mp/(Ma+Mp)	0%	5	75	5	75
Blend%	84%	>99	148	97	129

	Raw				
MAP	5	98	132	96	127
PHR	9	98	132	89	119
ODL	10	99	142	92	122
NAHP	8	99	134	95	124
MAP/MAHP	62%	59	104	90	120
GPHR	17	99	136	68	107
PHR/GPHR	53%	80	113	80	113
ODL%	40%	98	133	95	124

Other Calculations

	Raw				
IntCont	2	51	100	11	81
CritCont%	88%	>99	148	>99	139
EII-3	2.7	>99	143	97	129
TP-Comp	2.3	95	125	74	109
V-Comp	7.7	99	138	64	105
SC-Comp	9.8	>99	143	93	122
Complexity	179	>99	148		
LSO	58	98	132		
Cont	51	>99	140		
Det	70	>99	148		

Other Composite Subcomponents

	Raw				
W-SI-SY	24	96	126	4	74
(H)(Hd)(A)(Ad)	2	43	97	6	76
H(H)A(A)/SumHA	67%	38	96	22	88
VFD	13	>99	148	>99	142
(r±3+Pair)%	40%	64	105	39	96
CFC - FC	9	>99	143	>99	143

Source: Reproduced from the Rorschach Performance Assessment System® (R—PAS®) Scoring Program (© 2010–2019) and excerpted from the Rorschach Performance Assessment System: Administration, Coding, Interpretation, and Technical Manual (©2011) with copyrights by Rorschach Performance Assessment System, LLC. All rights reserved. Used by permission of Rorschach Performance Assessment System, LLC. Further reproduction is prohibited without written permission from R-PAS.

that exactly split Greg's request for "two, maybe three" to each card. Thus, her protocol is complex from its density, not response productivity. Looking at the three other subcomponents of Complexity listed in Table 3.1, we see she formulates responses that are complex in visual structure (LSO = 58, SS = 132), in range of contents (Cont = 51, SS = 140), and in rich awareness of the inkblot features that influenced her perceptions (Det = 70, SS > 145). Reading her responses, one sees how infused they are with vivid, compelling, and personally rich imagery. Thus, Madeline was highly engaged, open, and spontaneous with the task, and this likely generalizes to the ways in which others describe her as living life fully.

Except for the number of responses, as noted above, Madeline is equally elevated on all the variables that contribute to or are associated with Complexity. These include the proportion of her responses due simply to form features (Form% [F%] = 0%, SS = 56; considered inversely) and the frequency with which she simultaneously incorporates multiple perceptual determinants into the same response (Blend = 21, SS > 145). It also encompasses the frequency with which objects in a response are meaningfully related to each other (Synthesis [Sy] = 18, SS = 134) or embellished by attributes in the white backdrop to the ink (Space Integration [SI] = 9, SS = 132). In addition, it includes her efforts to exhaustively encompass the whole inkblot stimuli (Whole% [W%] = 76%, SS = 124) and her pronounced propensity to see the flat two-dimensional cards in a three-dimensional perspective (Form Dimension [FD] = 10, SS > 145; Vista [V] = 3, SS = 126; VFD = 13, SS > 145). Further, Complexity also reflects her adaptive ability to mentally enliven percepts with human activity (Human Movement [M] = 17, SS = 143) and allow that which is bright and stimulating in her experiential environment to color her perceptions (Weighted Sum of Color [WSumC] = 12, SS = 144). To generate the former requires delayed, thoughtful, and empathic reflectiveness, which is accompanied by neurophysiological representations of the action taking place in the mirror neuron system (e.g., Ando' et al., 2018; Giromini et al., 2019). The latter reflects a spontaneous receptivity to perceptual stimulation (Shapiro, 1965). Together, they suggest a highly flexible and adaptive set of internal resources for processing and responding to experiences (MC = 29, SS > 145; M/MC = 59%, SS = 104).

High Complexity and its associated variables speak to Madeline's rich mental life and potential adaptive resources for effective life functioning. However, Complexity has less healthy connotations when a protocol also has problematic score elevations in other domains, as is true for her—most notably for some of the variables in Perception and Thinking Problems, and all the variables in Stress and Distress. Under these conditions, Complexity readily can become a psychological burden. There is no inherent reason for the Rorschach task to evoke so much complex processing. Hence, it comes naturally to Madeline to immerse herself fully in what she is considering, experiencing, thinking, and feeling. However, Madeline does this so reflexively that at times it surely will be difficult for her to step back from experiences and maintain a centered distance; this also suggests some difficulty with holding a stable and cohesive sense of self. Rather, Madeline's internal mental activity consistently flows at such high speeds and her attention veers to so much so readily that she is transported along by ideas, reactions, and impulses in a process that may leave her feeling more like a bobber in a powerful stream than an agent steering her own path.

At times, these processes all take place internally, perhaps as reflected in her reclusive bout with depression. At times, these psychological dynamics will spill over impulsively and generate acting out behavior, as suggested by a spur of the moment trip to Cyprus or by standing up to behaviorally demonstrate her 13th and 15th Rorschach responses. As she told Greg and Steve, the phrase "I've been further from home and more scared" is one of her favorites, which she repeats to calm herself when she finds she is lost or somewhere unfamiliar.

An R-PAS innovation is the ability to control psychometrically for the influence of Complexity on other scores. Complexity Adjusted scores are the square icons shown on her Profile Pages when they differ by at least eight SS points from the unadjusted score. They indicate what Madeline's score would have been, had her Complexity been average. Equivalently, they indicate what Madeline's score would be if everyone in the normative sample was as highly complex as she is. From either perspective, those scores indicate what stands out for her despite her high Complexity. Most of the scores already discussed still stand out as quite notable, with the exceptions being R, F%, Sy, and W%. Two of those scores (F% and W%) are now entirely average, indicating she scored just as would be expected on them, given her level of Complexity. However, R now is much lower than average, indicating that most people who have as much Complexity as Madeline only get there by giving many more responses, as we noted previously. Sy also is now lower than average, rather than much higher than average. Like with R, most people who are as Complex as she is would achieve that degree of complexity by more frequently linking objects together.

Turning to other domains, Madeline's protocol is notable for its marked degree of confusing communications and illogical or implausible representations (Weighted Sum of Cognitive Codes [WSumCog] = 81, SS > 145), even after adjusting for her Complexity and the spontaneous openness associated with that (C-Adj SS > 145). In addition, her record is notable for the presence of several more serious lapses in plausibility and logic (Severe Cognitive Codes [SevCog] = 3, SS = 131), which occur so rarely in most adults that they are not affected by Complexity adjustment. Thus, in response to these visually evocative stimuli that intentionally have contradictory elements built into them and that tap a part of psychological experience distinct from the linguistically mediated narrative that guides day to day life most of the time, Madeline shows a significant amount of confusing, implausible, or contradictory representations. This suggests that when Madeline is confronted in daily life with similar types of conflicting perceptions that trigger or reverberate with emotionally charged personal mental imagery, Madeline's thoughts and ideas will emerge with incongruous and implausible elements intertwined based on their co-occurrence rather than their logical coherence.

For Madeline, her problematic conceptualizations or communications include coyotes watching over a church as a dogmatically righteous and appropriately headless religious figure enters, two interpersonally close women working together while sharing a heart between them, warriors joined together but with their head and hearts being torn apart, and people who are identified as cowards because they are so small. They also include an immobilized winged "bugger" with many people tightly wrapped and trapped inside its zippered body attempting to escape, an oddly juxtaposed head of a cat below which is a skinned animal hide, and two buddies zippered together in a confusing cylindrical manner with a shared party going on in their heads that lets them communicate without speaking. They also include a confusing reference to Pocahontas when explaining a percept of pixies, a playful response of bears having fun as they do laundry for people camping, and a bullet or spear shooting through a heart and making it flame. Finally, they encompass a digression about the incomprehensibility of introverts in the context of seeing one who is *desperate* to participate but cannot and armed crabs beating to death emasculated and immobilized London cops while angry rats bite their ass and piss themselves in glee.

About 73% (11 of 15) of Madeline's responses with these Cognitive Codes share a similar quality: one or more of the Critical Content[6] codes accompany them. In addition, about 85% (11 of 13) of Madeline's many responses with Critical Content scores (CritCont% = 88%, SS > 145, C-Adj SS = 139) have Cognitive Codes accompanying them. Critical Content scores have three very distinct potential interpretations: primitive psychological processes associated with severe disturbance, malingered psychopathology, and trauma. Her history does not support severe disturbance and there was no secondary gain to prompt malingering. Rather, Madeline carries with her the kind of partly disavowed but disquieting and disrupting mental imagery frequently found in people who have experienced harm, abuse, or trauma. For Madeline, this imagery is most notable for aggressive, combative, and harming interactions (Aggressive Movement [AGM] = 4, SS or C-Adj SS = 141); dysphoria and damaged objects (Morbid [MOR] = 9, SS > 145, C-Adj SS = 139); sexualized content (Sx = 3, SS or C-Adj SS = 128); and internal anatomical representations (An = 4, SS or C-Adj SS = 122). Given the absence of personal health concerns, the latter suggest some concern about her bodily or structural integrity.

Madeline's trauma-relevant representations deeply interconnect with her confusing, nonplausible representations. Thus, these data suggest that although Madeline is highly accomplished and resourceful, when faced with relative ambiguity and stimuli that can provoke strong emotion, unresolved psychological trauma from her early life can intrude on the present in ways that are confusing, disjointed, and mentally disorganizing to her. Importantly, however, Madeline perceives the most obvious features that Rorschach embedded in the inkblots (Popular [P] = 6, SS = 103) and she is not prone to perceptual distortions (Form Quality Minus% [FQ-%] = 8%, SS = 98, C-Adj SS = 79). Her sturdiness in this regard, particularly given the complexity of her record, is a genuine asset for her and her everyday functioning. At the same time, however, Madeline does not identify conventional objects in the inkblots as often as most people (Form Quality Ordinary% [FQo%] = 40%, SS = 78). She instead generally perceives things from an unusual or unique perspective (Form Quality Unusual% [FQu%] = 52%, SS = 126), which she was pleased to learn when discussing her results. Notably, these unique perceptions accompany two-thirds of her responses with markers of disorganized thought processes, and vice versa.

Large contributors to Madeline's Complexity are the variables in the Stress and Distress domain. Given their important contribution to her Complexity, it is not desirable at this stage to interpret those scores adjusted for Complexity. All the variables in this domain are implicit markers of disquieting and discomforting states that she carries with her, and the variables based on perceptual determinants are rough and indirect indicators. The absence of Stress and Distress variables in a protocol does not indicate an absence of troubling affect for a person. In addition, when these variables are elevated, as they uniformly are for Madeline, they do not indicate how she consciously represents or experiences emotions. To know the latter, we need to ask her, either in an interview or by a standardized questionnaire, or we need to discuss these scores with her to understand how they may manifest in her daily life. When Greg and Steve did that, she readily identified these states, although she also was a rather chagrined and angry to learn that so much of her well-guarded tension, discomfort, and mental agitation had shown up in the results.

For Madeline, these indirect distress markers include having her attention drawn to the imprecise, hazy, and mottled variation in ink saturation (i.e., Shading, which comes in three types: Diffuse [Y], SS = 133; tactile, or Texture [T], SS = 91; and dimensional, or Vista [V], SS = 126), and to the dark, gloomy blackness of the cards (Achromatic Color [C'], SS = 134). Together these form a composite score of Shading and Achromatic Color

(YTVC' = 18, SS = 138). Adaptively, these variables show Madeline's awareness of and ability to articulate subtlety and nuance contributing to her perceptions. However, they also seem to evidence a metaphoric form of grounded or embodied cognition (e.g., Lee & Schwarz, 2014). That is, being in a dark, hazy, or uncertain state of mind or a dark mood directs attention to parallel features in the inkblots (e.g., Giromini et al., 2016). Indeed, three times during the response phase, Madeline asks Greg if she can have cards with some color in an effort to counter the darkness and gloom associated with her percepts. Another marker of implicit distress in Madeline's protocol is the large number of inanimate objects seen in motion and action (m = 8, SS = 143). Nonsentient objects moving of their own accord link to states of mental agitation and tension of the type that can lead to distracted attention, problems focusing, and difficulty attaining or maintaining sleep, all of which are difficulties Madeline describes. She characterized the internal experience as being akin to leaves picked up by the wind and swirling around in a circle.

For Madeline, the sets of variables just described contribute to her marked elevation on Potentially Problematic Determinants (PPD = 30, SS = 143). As the name implies, there is nothing inherently problematic with a protocol having any of the variables forming this composite, but when elevated, they suggest likely liabilities against adaptive regulation of affect and coping. Reviewing Madeline's Code Sequence page shows that these variables intertwine almost as intimately with her disorganized thought processes (Cognitive Codes) and trauma related Critical Contents as the latter do with each other. Importantly, however, despite the abundance of these markers in Madeline's protocol, they are offset by an equally marked abundance of indicators for the more adaptive and effective resources discussed earlier (i.e., MC), which produces a difference score between them (MC—PPD = -1.0, SS = 104) that is entirely average. This suggests that, in general, Madeline probably contends effectively with most daily life demands, despite the large degree of potentially destabilizing factors that impinge on her. That is, she can hold it together, but it takes a lot of effort.

As noted before, Madeline's protocol also is striking for its large number of Morbid codes (MOR = 9, SS > 145). These images include a headless religious figure; a crying, sad, tearful woman powerfully singing a painful lament; the pain and suffering of a horrific genocide accompanied by torn out hearts and bleeding death; considerable sadness from multiple bodies tightly wrapped and trapped in an equally immobilized being burdened with everything inside; and a dead and skinned animal that has been cut and split open. They also include two buddies zippered together; the skull of a dead fish with its bones falling to the side; a heart shot through by a bullet or spear causing it to flame up; and immobilized London police who are cut, emasculated, and being beaten, bit, and killed, if not already dead. Some of these images seem to resonate with the recent loss of her uncle or the still painful loss of her former partner (i.e., the painful lament, torn hearts, sadness at being trapped, and the shot and inflamed heart). Indeed, Madeline links the last image to the Bon Jovi song that gives "love a bad name." Some images also resonate with the consequences of violent conflict and aggression (death from genocidal conflict, being cut and split open, shot heart, entrapped or immobilized, getting beaten), which would encompass some of Madeline's recalled images from her youth.

We noted previously as part of her complexity Madeline's pronounced propensity to see percepts in a three-dimensional perspective (VFD = 13, SS > 145). Although a cognitive resource, these types of responses also involve a process of adopting distance, seeing from a particular vantage point, perceiving depth, and taking perspective. These processes thus embody a situated need to step back from experiences and gain perspective, to find or define one's place, or to gain one's bearing or orientation. They are perceptual parallels to and aptly embody Madeline's current state of feeling as if she has lost direction and needs to regain it. Two of her dimensional percepts view into emptiness (R3) or nothingness (R17), adding a more notable quality of carrying a void or of being lost and alone.

We also previously noted the frequency with which Madeline simultaneously incorporates multiple perceptual determinants into the same response (Blend = 21, SS > 145). Nine of those instances entailed simultaneous identification of both the bright, bold, and generally positive and enlivening chromatic colors and the darker, dampening, and gloomier shading or achromatic colors, forming the Color Blend variable (CBlend = 9, SS > 145). Most people give at most one of these responses; Madeline is well above the maximum in the norms of six. Thus, she has many instances of opposingly valenced, mixed affective representations, suggesting positive affective states can readily be accompanied by or turn into negative or discomforting states. Madeline's third response embodies this process well, with the bold, powerful, open woman operatically singing the painful lament as sadness drips off her.

These variables and the other Stress and Distress variables already discussed contribute importantly to Madeline's elevation on the Suicide Concern Composite (SC-Comp = 9.8, SS = 143). People who engage in near-lethal suicide or serious self-destructive behavior generally tend to elevate this index. However, it is just one indicator of risk among many. Further, it operates implicitly, showing some of the taxing liabilities carried by an individual. Suicide is a complexly determined act, which is difficult to predict, particularly in a low base rate population, like Madeline, who is a nonpatient volunteering for an assessment. This index does not indicate anything about conscious hopelessness, perceived burdensomeness, suicidal ideation, intentionality, plans, or means. Nor does it address one's history of suicidal behavior or self-harm or potential sources of social support. Madeline's elevation nonetheless should, and did, spark a discussion with her about all the indicators of pain and distress she carries.

Several variables in the Self and Interpersonal Representation domain also are notable. This domain is more complicated than the last for considering Complexity Adjusted scores because some variables directly contribute to Complexity, such as the Contents and Determinants; others are highly intertwined with it, most notably the Vigilance Composite (V-Comp); and others are independent of it, including the Thematic Codes and proportion scores. For the variables that contribute to or intertwine with Complexity, it is optimal to focus initial interpretation on the unadjusted scores because they are part of why she has such a complex record. Madeline populated her protocol with many humans (SumH = 16, SS = 139), including many full human representations (H = 9, SS = 135). Thus, people are very much on her mind. She has many Oral Dependent Language codes (ODL% = 40%, C-Adj SS = 124), suggesting a strong implicit need for comforting support or a desire to be able to rely on others for guidance and direction. Madeline readily envisions collaborative, side-by-side cooperative relationships (COP = 7, C-Adj SS = 130), although her propensity to see combative and aggressive relationships is as strong or stronger (AGM = 4, C-Adj SS = 141). Perhaps because of these opposing views of interaction, Madeline maintains a heighted alertness and vigilant stance (Vigilance Composite [V-Comp] = 7.7, SS = 138), much like the undomesticated wily coyotes in her opening response who keep watch as observant sentinels.

Before considering variables that currently are not part of R-PAS, we briefly summarize some of the similarities and differences between Madeline's under clarified 1999 protocol and her current protocol. The absence of any clarification on 40% of her responses in 1999 leads to much less richness and complexity, as often inkblot features are not mentioned spontaneously in the response phase (Ritzler & Nalesnik, 1990). At the same time, the current administration may have prompted some excess complexity, particularly because both examiners asked clarification questions. To explore the similarity of Madeline's two protocols, we generated profile correlations using the standard scores on the Profile Pages from each protocol. These correlations quantify the extent to which the pattern of elevations and suppressions are similar.

Overall, there was moderate correspondence ($r = .66$) across all scores.[7] However, this varied by domain, with Engagement and Cognitive Processing being the lowest ($r = .60$), Perception and Thinking Problems ($r = .82$) and Self and Other Representation ($r = .83$) the highest, and Stress and Distress a bit lower ($r = .75$). The lower correspondence in the Engagement domain is due to some scores remaining similar and others differing. The variables that differed the most are ones that typically emerge during clarification (Ritzler & Nalesnik, 1990), including a decrease in form-only responses and a corresponding increase in use of color, shading, and achromatic color. Thus, there is a basic similarity in her two protocols, although Madeline was more fully engaged this time, in part due to a more complete clarification phase.

Next, we briefly note several other features of Madeline's current Rorschach protocol, referencing the variables described earlier that are not included in R-PAS. One set of variables encompasses authoritative dominance (Omnipotence = 11, SS > 140), idealized and spectacular imagery (Idealization = 4, SS = 120), and a propensity to link herself to responses in a personalized manner (Expanded Personal Reference = 19, SS > 140), although without regularly using her personal and private experience to justify a response (Personal Knowledge Justification [PER] = 1, SS = 109). Together these variables imply the kind of agentic, self-referent specialness linked with aggrandizing narcissism. These variables co-occur with a regular identification of positive affective states, playfulness, excitement, laughter, and fun (Elevated Mood States = 8, SS > 140), which likely softens the potentially adverse impact of the more narcissistically tinged variables and serves as a self-protective antidote to her depression and dysphoria.

Finally, Madeline shows many embellishments and polarized or split representations, although these variables lack good norms. Following Kleiger (2017), embellishments are seen in responses containing unseen characters (e.g., the photographer on R8), time sequences (e.g., Harry Potter finding Voldemort's castle and peeling back the darkness to bring in light on R9), or attributions of complex mental states (e.g., the rats peeing themselves in glee on R25). They also emerge in confident inferences drawn from highly specific inkblot elements (e.g., the tightness of the religious figure in R1; the closeness of the women on R6, as described in the clarification to R7). The polarized representations emerge most often in sequential responses (R3 to R4, R6 to R7, R10 to R11, R12 to R13, R23 to R24, R24 to R25, and the transformation of R20 that she describes at the end of the clarification for R23), although also in oppositely valenced objects within a response (R9, R25).

These response qualities show Madeline is vigilantly attuned to the environment but draws implausibly complex and specific inferences from subtle features or details that others either do not see or gloss over. Thus, she is prone to draw confident conclusions based on subtle gestures or cues, as well as prone to create potentially problematic embellishments in her thinking and in the information she coveys to others. Indeed, she may even use the subtle cues from another to generate what seems like a desirable or fitting embellishment at the moment, which then may make it harder at times for her to separate actual events from her embellishments about them. In addition, her mental perspective can readily shift into polarized oscillations that span extremes of good versus evil, communal happiness versus genocidal aggression, blossoming life versus entrapped immobilization, or bright and fabulous fun versus dark and murderous mayhem.\This polarized form of thinking (often called splitting) characterizes Madeline's experiential world. That is, things are unpredictable and can turn on a dime, people are either great or terrible, or they are two-faced and duplicitous. She will direct similar splits at herself, with idealized aspirational qualities countering devalued and disavowed ones. Ironically, as these oscillating shifts occur, she most likely will experience a certainty and confidence that her current view is the correct view.

After taking a break, Greg and Steve discussed with Madeline her Rorschach responses for slightly more than two hours, including many of the inferences noted above (see Chapter 7). During this discussion, she resonated strongly with the polarities in her responses (e.g., caribou versus KKK) manifesting in the polarized ways she sees others. She also noted how the "good" responses she generated often reflected ways she strives to adaptively counter the "bad" that always seems to be there in her experience; the past in the present. She also resonated with the wily coyote ("not the cartoon character!") part of herself who is always on guard against deception. Further, Madeline had a visceral reaction to the responses she gave to Card IV, when Greg and Steve reminded her of one she gave in 1999 in contrast to now. The 1999 response was of a huge fire-breathing monster annihilating a little bugger who didn't stand a chance;[8] the current response was a "definitely not fire-breathing" big galoot with the viewer further protected by a layer of ice. She readily related to the 1999 image as being a metaphor for the destructive fire rained down on her while growing up, and now, with her father dead, the current imagery reflects a safer psychological distance with that past.

Most significantly, Madeline strongly resonated with the newly developing butterfly on Card V with his wings weighed down, metaphorically both by clients at work and remnant parts of herself from childhood that she finds destabilizing. This led to a very productive discussion of how she has shut off those parts of herself in order to survive and stays hypomanically active to help keep that kind of distressing material from awareness. She also noted how she herself can turn into the fire-breathing Card IV monster that she saw in 1999, recognizing a way in which she identifies with the power of her father, perhaps as a way to be a force equal in destructive potential. Processing the interaction around the prompt Greg gave on Card X also was productive for exploring its various meanings, including her desire to end on a positive note. However, processing this did not lead to clear identifications or insights about how she might contribute to interactions in which she felt wronged or hurt by others.

TAT, ORI, and WUSCT Data and Results

Time was limited after the longer than expected Rorschach and discussion of her responses. Consequently, Greg and Steve gave Madeline just five TAT cards before ending the second day of testing. The stories were audio recorded for transcription, so regular pauses to obtain a verbatim record were not an issue like they were for the Rorschach. The previous afternoon, Madeline had completed the WUSCT. Also because of time limitations, Madeline completed the ORI in written form after she returned home, rather than in an interview format. Given that the TAT followed the extended discussion of her Rorschach responses, which Madeline found very interesting and helpful, she may have been primed to be more open and perhaps even darker and more autobiographical on her TAT than she would have been otherwise. This possibility is consistent with Madeline taking the lead in a brief post-task discussion of her TAT. She spontaneously identified how the most prominent theme in her stories was one of powerlessness versus power, which was the discussion that closed out the two days of testing. We encourage readers to review Madeline's responses to the TAT (Table 3.2), ORI (Table 3.3), and WUSCT (Table 3.4) now before turning to our thoughts about them. We first consider her material idiographically, as is typical for clinical practice, before turning to her scored results.

Some of the autobiographical elements in Madeline's TAT stories include jail time (3BM and 4) and illegal activity (1 and 13MF). The caring grandfather in her story to Card 1 has echoes of her recently deceased uncle, who provided care when her father did not; and the certainty she expresses that the main character has a brother also has an autobiographical parallel. Although the physical characteristics of the woman in Card 4 are not those attributed to her mother, her callous manipulativeness mirrors the description Madeline provided of her mother on the ORI, as does the hate Madeline expresses for that character in her story. Further, the seemingly nice enough but emotionally stunted male character's dependently repetitive need for the woman on Card 4, despite all the pain she inflicts on him, appears consistent with what one might have expected a young Madeline to experience with her mother. That is, much like we could imagine for a young Madeline with her mother, the TAT character hates what he needs from that self-centered, manipulative woman; gets in enraged fights and goes to jail because of the costs associated with it; and can't stand that all he gets in return from her is hurt instead. However, that still does not change his need for her, which feeds his wretched feelings about himself.

The alcoholism of 3BM has similar autobiographical overtones. It is not hard to imagine Madeline being one of the unnamed children who needs to get to school despite a hungover and absent parent, who could

Table 3.2 Madeline's TAT

Card 1

I'm gonna give this one a name. His name is Sebastian and Sebastian has been snooping around his grandfather's house and he's realized when he unfolded this fabric that within it was a violin and this is the violin that was stolen. So if he found it in his grandfather's house he's having a huge inner conflict about what to do. He absolutely adores his grandfather and now his grandfather he believes is a thief. Their family is very poor and he thinks that his grandfather stole it in order for him to sell it to get the money he needs to take care of his, himself and his sibling, his other brother, his little brother. He definitely has a little brother. And he's kind of mad at his dad because his dad didn't fulfill . . . What he should have done is provide for the family and now his beloved grandfather has put himself at a great risk. And he's having a huge inner struggle. The dialogue in this is with himself on what he's going to do with the knowledge, what do I do now. Now that he knows that his grandfather has stolen this violin. Do I tell? . . . He chooses to keep it a secret. That's my story. Poor Sebastian . . . You know you look at the, the way he's sitting. Elbows on the table. His hands, his head in his hands. He's got one finger up. You can see the pondering going on. The other hand all his fingers are in towards his palm. He's got both hands on his head. You know it's the anguish. The anguish of knowing . . . and he found it in his father's, his grandfather's house so he presumes that his grandfather has stolen it. Now that may or may not be the case but this is the inner turmoil that he's struggling with . . . So it's like having a sense of somebody that you believed in only to find out that they're not who or what you thought. And if it's a boy of ten and his grandfather, that can shake the very foundation of your world. As limited as it is at that age . . . (She turns card over.) (GM: Nothing too interesting on the back of those cards.) I got no happy place to go to. (GM: No. No Bern Switzerland [referring to the back of the Rorschach cards and her pleasant memories of being in Bern].)

Card 2

Oh I can't wait to get the fuck out of this place. This is what I have to look forward to. Look at her over there already knocked up. This is it. Toil in the fields. Have babies. [All said as if it was the thoughts of the young girl.] Or; oh I love it, she's carrying books. Go to school. Get an education. Get as far away from here as possible as fast as possible . . . Seems a bit disingenuous though. Just in terms of timing on this I'm having a little problem with my story. Cause women at that time would not have been afforded the time or the luxury and the expense of going to school. So she must be smart or they wouldn't have spent that kind of money in allowing her not to be working on the farm. Especially when one of the other may be her mother or maybe an auntie who's clearly expecting another child. But just get the fuck out of here as fast as possible. . . . And if she's smart, and I think she is, she will cross the sea. So not just the next county. And she's thinking to herself and with any luck I can get out of these god ugly clothes and get myself a nice pair of slacks (laugh) and maybe a pair of some fabulous high heels. I want some pumps. Get my hair out of this tight ass braid and let it flow down the back of my neck and put on some **red** lipstick. School first. Then dance. But get out of here. And she's determined. I mean look at her face. She is, her jaw is set. Chin up. Shoulders back. She'll succeed . . . . . . (long pause) . . . Any questions? (GM: I was just reviewing. I don't think I have questions. Steve did you want to ask anything? [He indicates no.])

(Continued)

Table 3.2 (Continued)

Card 3BM

Oh my God (sigh) ...... (long pause) ... Started out as a great night. Get together with friends after work. Have a glass of wine. Glass of wine turns to a couple glasses of wine. Turns to not going home for dinner ... She stayed at the bar. And I know her name but I can't think of it right now. It'll come to me. A little too woozy. A little too loose. Struck up a conversation. Had random sex in the bathroom with a stranger. Had another couple of drinks. Got into a car accident. Got arrested. Jailed and she just woke up in a jail cell hung over. And she doesn't yet know just how bad it's gonna get. And her name is Janice ... And Janice doesn't know yet about the accident. About the charges. All Janice can think of is, "What's my husband going to say? I haven't been home. Have they called him?" And Janice has two young kids who are supposed to be in school and it's a week day. And they've taken her jewelry so she can't look at her watch. She doesn't know what time it is. But she's pretty damn sure she's not going to get home in time to get her kids ready for school. And this is not the first time something like this has happened. She has really fucked up big ... Again ...... (long pause) ... And the only dialogue she's got is, "Oh lord help me. What have I done? What have I done?" She's just bathed in self-pity ... (GM: And the end?) How does it end for her? It's not good. The long end is no matter how hard she tries she just can't clean her act up. She can't stay sober. She loses her job. She loses her husband. She loses her kids. And she finds herself back in this position time and time again. She eventually dies ultimately of sclerosis [sic] of the liver. Within the decade. (GM: Ok.) Can I have a happy one?

Card 4

Oh lord this cheating son of a bitch ... "It's the second time I've caught you. You said you'd never do this again. I'm leaving you." And she says, "Don't go. Don't go. It meant nothing." But she's broken his heart. He wants to strangle her but he won't. And she's a manipulative son of a bitch who will keep doing it if he doesn't leave. But he's desperately in love with her and he's gonna stay ... This poor bastard. He's gonna catch her not necessarily in the act but he's gonna catch her cheating. At least intimately with another man but not sexually. And he's gonna lose his cool and he's gonna beat the other man. And in a fist fight the other man is gonna hit his head like on the side of a bar and it's gonna cause him to go into a coma and die. But not for, until days go by. Eight, nine, ten days and then he gets charged with manslaughter. He ends up going to jail for manslaughter all because of his, his jealousy and his rage over her cheating on him relentlessly. But he keeps taking her back. And he drives himself crazy in jail creating ideas in his head of what she's doing while he's not there. And most of what he thinks is true. She's a raging flamboyant bitch who's completely self-centered and out for whatever gain she can get for herself ... She's a miserable taker. And I already hate her (laugh). And he's a nice enough guy but he's too emotionally stunted to be strong enough on his own. He's trying to leave but she's a manipulative bitch ... With good hair. Full lips and a sultry voice ... And he's a sucker for piercing eyes. And it will be the cause of his demise (says in a dramatically low tone) ...... (long pause) ... He pulls away from her in this quarrel and he goes to the back wall and he takes the picture of her and he tears it off the wall and tears it into pieces cause as beautiful as she is he can't stand to see her. (GM: How are they both feeling?) Her? Powerful! Him? Wretched. And even though she's the cheating son of a bitch who got caught yet again ... she's begging because she knows that's what will work for him. It's a tool, a manipulative tool. It's not genuine. She's not sorry. And he's wretched because he knows he'll take her back ... And he works hard to provide everything for her ...... (long pause, hands card back) ... You can have that. I don't like her. (GM starts to hand the next card.) Happy (asked hopefully before she saw it)?

Card 13MF

Ohh shit! "Thank you my dear." I wake up, I have to stretch. "Thank you for the fabulous romp now I have to go home to my wife." I hope he gets genital warts (laugh). Except he won't because he's giving them to her. This guy's a predator. That's a child ...... (long pause) ... (sigh) This is before. She's sleeping. I don't mean a young child but like just kind of an adolescent child. He's walked in. He wants to. He desperately wants to have sex with her. He's ashamed of wanting that, but he knows he's going to, but he's not fighting the urges. But he's fighting them enough to walk out of the room. And he's going to do it. And he'll hate himself for it but he's done it before and he's gonna do it again ... And no one will believe her. When she tells her mum, her mum slaps her across the face so hard she splits her (sigh), her lip and her teeth. Calls her a fucking whore. And she can't believe it. She doesn't tell anyone else for a while. And by the time she does she is a whore. She lets all the boys sleep with her. She couldn't care less. And it continues with her dad until she gets pregnant ...... (long pause) ... And then everything explodes. There's no denying that her father is also the father of her child ...... (long pause) ... this picture should be entitled Ruination ...... (long pause, hands card over; Greg holds it) ... Any happy ones over there? Or you have a question or want to put it away? (GM: I might; I was just holding it to see if I did have a question or not.) Yeah...... (GM: I don't have a sense of how she's feeling.) You don't get to feel. (Hands card) (GM: Steve?) (SF: I think that's it.) Can I have some with daisies and birds and sunshine? (laugh).

TAT Discussion

(SF: I think we could do it without a card. I think we could find a way to end on daisies.) We need some daisies and sunshine please (laugh). (SF: Yeah.) Even a corn meadow or sunflowers. (GM: Yeah we could include a card like that.) (SF: No no no, what I wanted to see ...) But I'm teasing. Like they're all pretty black and white. They're all pretty dark like Jesus hell fire. We need some happiness in here! (SF: Well in the last 10 minutes, I think the happiness comes from talking about what we did.) Oh ok.

I don't remember them. (GM: You don't remember them?) They're awful pictures! (GM: They're pretty depressing. Yeah.) Yeah. I don't remember it being this depressing. (GM: Some of these are different from the ones you saw before, but some of them are the same.) Oh 'cause I was going to ask if I had seen these before, but I didn't want you to say yes. And then me being thrown by the fact that I don't recognize them. So that's why I didn't want to ask. (SF: You did this with Rebecca too right.) (GM: Yeah.) Oh, you know what, I did so. (GM: Yeah you remember.) (SF: It came back.) I think I did this first. (SF: Uh huh could be.) Wait a minute. (GM: I don't remember the sequence.) You're absolutely right, I did this with her. (SF: Now you remember.) I forgot about that. But yes that was where I did it. (SF: Remember anything about what it was like?) No. Nope. (GM: I was thinking you had done it last because they did fewer of these cards than they were intending to because, um, you were leaving for a flight. That was my recollection, my memory.) (SF: Uh huh, I think that's what they said. Rorschach first and then this.) I do remember this now.

(Continued)

Table 3.2 (Continued)

(GM: WAIS first I think.) (SF: Right, you did the intelligence test with her too.) Just the name of it suggests I might of failed that (laugh). (SF: Oh no you did fine.) I don't remember that. (SF: The little blocks that you had to put together.) Oh. (GM: You did fine on that.) So like a spatial test with 3-D blocks? (SF: It was a whole bunch of different ones and that was one yeah. And it was to define vocabulary words and there was. . . .) Oh I would have probably done ok in terms of vocabulary. (SF: You're smart. You did well.) (GM: Actually, you were pretty even across the board; all above average.) (SF: And with a hangover.) With a nasty hangover. Was gonna say you better get tougher tests if I did ok in that condition, you might want to raise the bar. (SF: No, I think what it means is you would have done even better.) Oh, if I had had my wits about me and a cup of coffee and maybe even some oatmeal and a banana I might have aced it. (GM: You might have.) (SF: You did so well we didn't feel like we had to repeat that.) Oh, ok. Well good.

(GM: So um, I'm just curious, this was depressing, and it was depressing pictures. Um, other thoughts, reactions?) All negative. (GM: All negative. Yeah.) Yeah. Hard to be . . . and can I point something out? (GM: Yeah of course (hands her the cards).) (Pointing to Card 1.) Powerless. Youngster. Thankfully, that's the male. (Pointing to Card 2.) But look at the power in the back and the shirt off of the male. But who knows what kind of socioeconomic power, cause he's working the fields. (Pointing to Card 3BM.) You know and again powerless. (Pointing to Card 4.) And this guy, look at the wretched look on his face, the sense of powerlessness. Where she looks incredibly confident and power**ful**. (Pointing to Card 13MF.) And you know no voice whatsoever (indicating the girl) and standing above her like that (indicating the man.) Huge power position. And she's prone and breast exposed. Like complete power differential. Like a lot of power. (GM: Vulnerability vs. power.) Absolutely. And that's . . . fuck. (SF: And you're aware of that because it came through in your stories with that kind of position.) It's shitty when you're completely vulnerable and someone's got enormous power.

(SF: Exactly. So I have a guess about a Madeline motto.) What's that? (SF: Never put yourself in a situation, ever, where someone can have that kind of power over you.) Well the thing is there's always people with that kind of power. I'm particular in not letting them exert it on me. Even when they think it's their right to do so. (SF: Right, right. Don't feel powerless.) No. And it's to my detriment. Like you know and I get into trouble for it all the time. But No. (GM: Don't tread on me.) It won't work. (SF: Never again.) Never again. Exactly. Never again. And I'll fight openly now to ensure never again.

I don't care if you're a judge who, you know they will say something, and say I don't want a reply. And it's like you don't get to say that without me giving a reply. That's why this is recorded. So I'll, don't start a fight that I can't fucking participate in just because you sit up there and you think you're better. I don't buy that shit. And that gets me into trouble all the time. You get pulled over by the police and you know they roll the window down and put their head in, you know, "Have you been drinking and driving?" "Officer that's an unlawful search get your head out of my car." And you know as soon as you question their authority like the game's on right? Fuck you. (SF: Gets you into trouble.) Fuck you. (SF: But this also saved your life.) Absolutely. Fuck you [i.e., to those trying to dominate]. (SF: It's a save your life strategy that worked. But when applied liberally it also has some downsides.) Oh detriment, like just it's a career killer. Absolutely. (SF: So are you learning to try to use that?) Moderate that? Yeah absolutely.

But you know what I have pissed so many people off in one particular arena it's kind of like, alright. A new judge will be appointed and come in and I can tell right away by how I'm being treated which camp he's been exposed to. It's the "I love her" camp or the "I hate her" camp. (SF: Right your reputation proceeds you.) And it's all that tells me is you can't fucking think for yourself 'cause you haven't made up your own mind based on your own experience, so I have no respect for you. (SF: And does this have anything to do with why you're leaving the law practice?) Oh no. Cause I kind of like the battles. But it's harder to persuade them to do something you want them to do when it's one of these (motions imbalanced 1-up, 1-down relationship). If there's animosity flowing back and forth. (SF: Right, well that's why you're learning how to moderate this.) And for me it's like they can only go so far in terms of giving a shit because if they don't do what I think is appropriate then I go to the court of appeal. And I'll say that. (SF: Exactly you don't have to fight so much because you can always appeal. Ok.) And they hate being appealed. So as much as they may not like me, they have to listen 'cause the last thing they want is the oh, you know, she did it again. And there's a couple that I don't like that you know, I'll just say, it's your job, it's your decision, do what you want. I've always got the court of appeal, which basically tells them I don't fucking care what you think. And I don't have any qualms saying that because I don't, because I've read decisions, I've been in front of them, like you couldn't be more intellectually dishonest. So I don't have any respect for you. (SF: Okay.)

So no, that's ... But the authority ... I, I get a pretty good sense of what it's like to feel vulnerable and have the monster (referring to Rorschach Card IV from 1999) and you know like no. Never again. No. Never again. I'll kill you first. Literally. That'll never happen again.

Table 3.3 Madeline's ORI

Describe your mother.
Words that come to mind to describe this person include cold, calculating, self-interested, vicious, alcoholic, greedy, violent, cruel, insular and ignorant. In terms of physical description, she is short, fat and ugly. If there is one positive descriptor that I recall it would be that she had beautiful teeth.

Describe your father.
Immediate to mind – violent and whatever you can imagine in terms of violence on a child, ramp that up to the Nth degree. Also, foreboding, cruel, cold, distant, powerful, mean, angry, physical, and drunk. Physically he was tall and handsome. In later life, outside of my experience, he reportedly sobered up and tried to be a better person.

Describe a significant other.
Sweet, loving, caring, open, nurturing, patient, cuddly, kind, powerful, funny, smart, genuinely nice, tall, dark and handsome with a protruding proboscis.

Describe a pet.
Pure love, smart, kind, warm, loving, forgiving, gentle, funny, beautiful, obedient, watchful, well-mannered and my "King". An oft used phase used over our ten year relationship was, "when we go out, he makes me look good", as in he was always so beautifully behaved and engaged. He always wanted to come with me and I was proud to have him at my side no matter where we went. He was willing to endure enormous stress and pressures in order to accompany me on many travels in a wide variety of unusual situations. He was Timex, my watchdog. He was my beloved.

Describe yourself.
Hard working, tough, smart, funny, compassionate, a loyal friend, organized, prepared, clean, reno queen, frugal, tasteful, spontaneous, sexy, social, engaging, honest, adventurous, brave, quick to judge, curious, solid and a fabulous dancer.

be either Madeline's mother or father. It was interesting how Madeline "knew" the character's name but could not draw it up. Her father's name is similar to the name she ultimately selected. At the same time, it is not hard to imagine Madeline as the protagonist in the story, as her life was on such a trajectory of alcohol abuse and reckless, selfish behavior for many years. The story Madeline creates to 13BM again features highly abusive, invalidating, traumatizing parents, as well as addiction and an inability to control sexual and aggressive urges to maintain their child's health.

Card 2 also has highly autobiographical elements, with the protagonist saving herself from a distasteful future by turning to books and education as a way to flee as far as she possibly can from the life she appeared destined to lead. Not only is the possibility of flight on the horizon, she also may be able to change her clothes, let her hair down, become alluring or even sexy, and dance. As Madeline says it, "School first. Then dance."

Table 3.4 Madeline's WUSCT (Responses in italics)

1. When a child will not join in group activities *they are smart.*
2. Raising a family *would piss me off.*
3. When I am criticized *I get angry.*
4. A man's job *can be done by a competent woman.*
5. Being with other people *can be a blast if they're my friends.*
6. The thing I like about myself is *my work ethic.*
7. My mother and I *are not compatable.*
8. What gets me into trouble is *my imagination.*
9. Education *has changed my life for the better.*
10. When people are helpless *I can be of assistance.*
11. Women are lucky because *we have strengths.*
12. A good father *is an anomaly.*
13. A girl has a right to *everything she can achieve.*
14. When they talked about sex, I *have a funny anecdote.*
15. A wife should *be a partner.*
16. I feel sorry for *people who start life with disadvantages.*
17. A man feels good when *he has a strong woman by his side.*
18. Rules are *optional.*
19. Crime and delinquency could be halted if *paid attention to their root causes.*
20. Men are lucky because *they have perceived power.*
21. I just can't stand people who *are racist, bigoted, or ~~entitteled~~ entitled.*
22. At times she worried about *the unknown.*   ⌐→ *Can't even spell it!*
23. I am *of value.*
24. A woman feels good when *the sun shines warm on her face.*
25. My main problem is *judgment.*
26. A husband has a right to *equality of housework.*
27. The worst thing about being a woman *menopause!*
28. A good mother *knows to give herself time to be herself.*
29. When I am with a man *he is one lucky bugger!*
30. Sometimes she wished that *she owned a dishwasher.*
31. My father *is dead.*
32. If I can't get what I want *I have to work harder + smarter.*
33. Usually she felt that sex *was a blessing.*
34. For a woman a career is *self expression.*
35. My conscience bothers me if *I get caught.* ☺
36. A woman should always *be her authentic self.*

We know from her history that Madeline went to an elite school for two advanced degrees and from her ORI that she considers herself a fabulous dancer.

As Madeline saw it, the primary themes in her stories were powerlessness versus powerfulness—vulnerable, young, needy characters versus those who dominate, manipulate, and subjugate them. These themes in particular resonated with her, including the ways in which her refusal to be subjugated ever again gets her in trouble, particularly at work, where she is quick to perceive evidence of it.

Other themes include core disillusionment with important elders (1, 13MF, possibly 3BM), that people are powerless over uncontrollable urges (3BM, 13MF), and that deceit is ever-present (1, 3BM, 4, 13MF). There are also themes of both abiding by and countering gendered stereotypes. On the one hand, women have babies (2), are enticing (2, 4), can be too loose (3BM), or abused and defeated enough to act like whores (13MF), while men are strong (2), prone to fight (4), and just out for sex (13MF). On the other hand, men can be caregivers (1) and manipulated (4), while women can use their smarts to overcome and succeed (2) and be master manipulators (4).

Finally, another important theme implicit in her TAT responses concerns Madeline's reliance on the environment to help her shift focus to something more positive and upbeat. She is stuck in the dark and gloomy quality of the TAT cards, unable to weave stories that go beyond their dysphoric stimulus pull. She does not like this, for it keeps her in a narrative rut of trauma, depression, and hopelessness. To right her ship, she cannot even evoke pleasant memories by flipping to the back of the card as she could on the Rorschach,[9] and thus she has "no happy place to go" after the first TAT card. Instead, she consistently asks Greg for help: after 3BM, "Can I have a happy one?"; after 4, "[Is it] Happy?"; and finally, after 13MF, "Any happy ones over there?" and more explicitly, "Can I have some with daisies and birds and sunshine?" These questions parallel the similar questions she asked during the Rorschach, "Can I have something with more color?" which she asks after Card I and again requests after Cards V and VII. She needs the environment to provide some brightness and pleasantness to aid in her affect regulation and repeatedly hopes that Greg will see that need and offer her a more optimal stimulus.

From Madeline's ORI (see Table 3.3), we see qualitatively how she provides the longest description for her dog, who was a reliable travel companion and an unconflicted source of love for her and recipient of her love in return. She describes her parents in generally one-dimensional ways, consistent with what we know from her history, although for each she makes a point of adding one positive attribute. The significant other she describes is her former partner. Madeline generally characterizes him in a one-dimensional manner, with his nose sounding as if it is an endearing quality, although the valence is opposite her parents. Madeline provides a positive self-description, noting many of her strengths as a professional and a friend, although it is not clear whether she sees being quick to judge as an asset or potential liability. We also see some humor by Madeline noting she is a fabulous dancer, as well as some wittiness with King being her Timex and with the alliterative description of her former partner's protruding proboscis.

One of the themes emerging most clearly in Madeline's responses to the WUSCT (see Table 3.4) concerns gender equality. Potential inequality emerges twice, with respect to men having *perceived* power (20) and women suffering menopause (27). However, the declaration and assertion of equality is more prevalent (4, 11, 13, 15, 17, 26, 34, and possibly 29), suggesting that opposing gender bias is a core part of her identity. Madeline provides two responses that are surprising from someone with a lifelong career as a lawyer, although less so when recognizing her lawbreaking youth and accompanying difficulty obtaining a license to practice: asserting that rules are optional (18) and—with a humorously added smiley face—that her conscience bothers her if she gets caught (35). Two other responses are noteworthy for suggesting liabilities in need of further investigation. Madeline tells us that her imagination gets her in trouble (8) and her main problem is judgment (25). These responses suggest possible consequences of the highly elevated number of Cognitive Codes in her Rorschach protocol.

We provide the formal scores for Madeline's TAT, ORI, and SCT in Table 3.5.

It is hard to compare scores across assessments. This is in part due to the very different lead-in to the TAT. However, it also is because she completed the ORI in interview format before, which allowed Rebecca Behrends to ask questions and solicit details. This produced longer and more complex replies than the written version this time, and longer replies can increase scores. In addition, Madeline did not complete the WUSCT in 1999.

Table 3.5 Scores for the WUSCT, ORI, and TAT

Madeline's WUSCT Consensus Ratings

Type of Score	E-2	E-3	E-4	E-5	E-6	E-7
Frequency	0	3	5	19	6	3
Ogive	0	3	8	27	33	36

Note: E-2 = Impulsive, E-3 = Self-Protective, E-4 = Conformist, E-5 = Self-Aware, E-6 = Conscientious, E-7 = Individualistic (not shown, E-8 = Autonomous and E-9 = Integrated).

Madeline's ORI Ratings on Conceptual Level (CL) and Differentiation Relatedness (D-R)

Narrative	CL	D-R
Mother	5	4
Father	6	5
Significant Other	6	5
Pet	7	7
Self	7	7

Note: CL = Conceptual Level (1 = sensorimotor-preoperational, 3 = concrete-perceptual, 5 = external iconic, 7 = internal iconic, 9 = conceptual), D-R = Differentiation-Relatedness (e.g., 1 = self-other boundary compromise, 3 = self-other mirroring, 5 = semi-differentiation, 7 = stable self-other in relationship, 9 = reciprocally related, moving toward integration).

SCORS-G Scores for Madeline's TAT

M for Overlapping Cards	COM	AFF	EIR	EIM	SC	AGG	SE	ICS	Global
Madeline	4.07	2.33	2.18	2.93	3.93	2.86	3.07	3.60	3.12
Clinical	3.35	3.30	2.99	3.62	3.17	3.53	3.74	4.40	3.51
College	3.36	3.33	2.97	3.70	3.21	3.64	3.84	4.72	3.58
Madeline by Card									
1	6.00	3.33	5.00	5.67	5.00	5.00	4.33	3.33	4.71
2	4.00	4.67	2.30	4.00	3.67	4.00	5.33	5.67	4.21
3BM	3.00	1.67	1.30	2.00	3.00	3.30	1.67	3.00	2.37
4	4.33	1.00	1.30	1.00	3.30	1.00	2.67	3.00	2.20
13MF	3.00	1.00	1.00	2.00	4.67	1.00	1.33	3.00	2.00

Note: All cards overlapped for the clinical sample (Stein et al., 2014), and all but 13MF overlapped for the college sample (with data provided by C. L. Siefert, personal communication, April 2, 2018). COM = Complexity of Representation of People, AFF = Affective Quality of Representations, EIR = Emotional Investment in Relationships, EIM = Emotional Investment in Values and Moral Standards, SC = Understanding of Social Causality, AGG = Experience and Management of Aggressive Impulses, SE = Self-Esteem, and ICS = Identity and Coherence of Self.

For the WUSCT, the general adult population produces scores in the Self-Aware (E-5) range, and adults in professional occupations typically produce scores at the Conscientious (E-6) stage (Loevinger, 2002). Two trained raters independently coded Madeline's responses,[10] and their joint reliability was excellent (ICC[A,2] = .86), with disagreements resolved via consensus. Her overall level of ego development was at the Conscientious (E-6) stage, consistent with what one would expect for her occupational level.

For the ORI, there are not established normative standards for Conceptual Level (CL) or Differentiation-Relatedness (D-R). However, the two raters again independently classified Madeline's narratives with excellent average reliability (ICC[A,2]; CL = .79, D-R = .97). Using the mean of the two raters and rounding up, Madeline's CL scores ranged from a low of 5 (unidimensional functional attributes) when describing her mother to a high of 7 (internal attributes) when describing her dog and herself. For D-R, her scores ranged from 4 (denigrating relationship) when describing her mother to 7 (stable relationship) when describing her dog and herself.

For the TAT, Madeline's stories were independently coded on the SCORS-G by the same two raters as for the ORI and WUSCT and a "gold standard" rater[11] with excellent reliability (ICC[A,3] from .82 [SC] to .99 [EIM and AGG], with M = .94). Madeline's average ratings for each TAT card are presented in Table 3.5 along with reference values from a clinical sample (Stein et al., 2014) and a college student sample (data provided by C. L. Siefert, April 2, 2018, personal communication). Overall, Madeline's Global rating (3.1) is lower than either of the reference samples. However, following Stein and Slavin-Mulford (2018), her *cognitive factor score* (composite of COM and SC) was about 2.7 SDs higher (4.0) than the clinical reference sample (3.3, SD = .26), while her *affective factor score* (composite of AFF, EIR, EIM, AGG, SE, ICS) was about 1.6 SDs lower (2.8 vs. 3.6, SD = .49). Thus, the cognitive aspects of her object representations in the TAT are sophisticated, but the affective elements have more maladaptive components. The latter likely reflects Madeline's open, personally revealing responses to the Therapeutic Assessment context. Scores on individual cards indicated that Madeline's stories to Cards 3BM, 4, and 13MF contained highly negatively valenced themes. Thus, normatively, these stand out as very important to understand, as we endeavored to do previously.

Summary

Integration of Findings and Observations

Madeline is a powerful force of nature. She has remarkable resources, intellect, drive, and talent, offset by an equally remarkable early history of brutalizing trauma that results in a tremendous amount of painful, disrupting, chaotic affect that she carries with her. Like the character in her second TAT story, she dealt with this history and its legacy within her by using her intellect to flee as far from home as she could, both physically and mentally, and by shutting that part of her life out of awareness as much as humanly possible. She replaced it successfully with hypomanic distractions and career accomplishments, including obtaining two advanced degrees, working "7 days a week, 20 hours a day," and partying, dancing, and reading voraciously when not at work. She also replaced it with an inner resolve to never again be a victim, adopting a tough, agentic, and defensively aggressive armor that is about as far from the traditional feminine stereotype as possible. In this context, Madeline found her brother's ability to think about those childhood events, much less talk about them, mystifying.

For Madeline, the past was too destabilizing to think about, much less discuss. We see that most clearly in her Rorschach protocol, where she produces an abundance of confused, incongruous representations when confronted with those emotionally provocative and deliberately contradictory inkblot stimuli that call on her visual-mnemonic processing.[12] These manifestations of confused and incongruous representations are closely intertwined with equally abundant markers of trauma, affective distress, and unique perceptions, consistent with the kind of cognitive disturbances seen in many traumatized individuals (Viglione, Towns, & Lindshield, 2012).

When people produce unique perceptions on the Rorschach that are not identified by others, as is the case for most of Madeline's responses, as well as most of her cognitively disorganized perceptions, an interesting neurophysiological process takes place (e.g., Asari et al., 2010a, 2010b). Seeing common or conventional perceptions on the Rorschach is associated with activation in the visual cortex of the occipital lobes and the left anterior frontal cortex. This suggests that when people give these common responses, it is a function of what they see influencing what they think. However, unique perceptions are associated with right temporal pole activation, as well as a larger amygdala and cingulate gyrus in the limbic system (the neural seat of emotionality), which suggests more active use of the latter regions in people who generate unique perceptions. Furthermore, when people generate unique perceptions, their amygdala initiates a positive, excitatory link between the right temporopolar region and the left anterior prefrontal cortex, while it simultaneously generates a negative inhibitory link from the right temporopolar region to the occipital regions. This suggests that autobiographically relevant emotional reactions inhibit general visual processing of the external environment, while simultaneously triggering mental conceptualizations. Thus, amygdala activation impairs the typical perceptual processing of the occipital lobes, while it facilitates the "perception" of personalized, unique images in the inkblots.

Although Madeline displays unique perceptual processes intermingled with disorganized and incongruous conceptual representations, she shows no notable propensity for frank perceptual distortions, an intact ability to perceive what is most obvious, and organized thought processes in the narrative stories she created to the TAT and in her ongoing discussions with Greg and Steve. Thus, the data show Madeline has a localized liability, not a generalized liability like would be seen in a psychotic-spectrum condition. The liability is localized to affectively charged traumatic recollections that color her perceptions and thinking. In February, when discussing the confused thinking seen in her Rorschach results, Madeline likened her mind at those times to the type of vehicle tire rims that continue to spin and spin after a car has stopped or like the twisting, spinning head of the Linda Blair character from *The Exorcist* (without all the vomit, she noted humorously). She also described how any interpersonal or professional action she attempts during these times of mental spinning becomes "fucked up." Her general solution is to get outdoors and walk in the woods or by water, which she finds soothing. However, that in itself often is insufficient, such that this process contributes to her consistent restlessness and inability to sleep soundly throughout the night.

Madeline's hypomanic distractions, which serve psychodynamically as an adaptive defense against trauma-tinged experience, were evident in the testing material. As she indicated, she needed brighter depictions when completing the TAT and needed color in the inkblots. However, as was evident in the Rorschach, color provides her with no reprieve.

The five colored cards generate at least as much traumatized, disorganized, and dysphoric imagery as the five achromatic cards. However, in her Rorschach responses, we see her hypomanic coping efforts in the contrast between her many positive, happy, bright perceptions and the equally numerous negative, sad, and destructive perceptions. Indeed, when discussing her responses, Madeline noted how the bright, positive images reflect her way of coping: block out the bad and replace it with its opposite. Although she was skeptical, the presence of these distancing, disavowing defenses may tie into her initial failure to recall meeting Dan McAdams in Chicago, where she talked about her abusive history to another person for the first time.

These hypomanic self-protective mechanisms encompass Madeline's propensity to see and represent experiences in a polarized manner. She herself notes this in her responses to Card III and Card X. At times, her polarized Rorschach images seemed to serve as an antidote to painful imagery (e.g., Card II). However, at other times, the process worked in the other direction, and positive images gave way to gruesome, sadistic, or destructive representations (e.g., Card III, V, IX, and X). This polarized way of thinking and experiencing the world was equally evident in her TAT stories, which, as she correctly identifies, follow a key axis of her representations—powerless vulnerability versus manipulative and destructive dominance. Similar polarities are evident on her ORI, although with slightly different interpersonal anchors, such that cold, abusive, tyranny contrasts with warm, loving, nurturance.

With many types of Rorschach imagery, and to a lesser extent with TAT imagery, it is not clear how a person responds to or feels about the imagery that is on their mind, as produced in responses to the stimuli. For Madeline, we know that she experiences herself as anything but vulnerable and powerless; indeed, states of feeling vulnerable are risky reminders that are too close to her past and will trigger the disorganizing internal "spinning" she described. Given the powerful oscillations and polarities in her representations, vulnerability and powerlessness in fact trigger an opposite, counter-dependent stance in which she seeks to achieve emotional balance by taking control. She described to Greg and Steve how rage makes her bigger than she is and how she can become a blistering incendiary force. She used this to her advantage as a youth when fighting people older or bigger than she was. In adulthood, the same axis has been a constant part of her professional life as a successful courtroom attorney who will obliterate her legal opponents as she defends powerless victims of an unfair system.

Another duality concerns dominance versus dependence. Madeline's Rorschach protocol has many Oral Dependent Language scores (SS = 133, C-Adj SS = 124). Where does this live in her daily life? She and others who know her would hardly call her dependent or reliantly needy on others for support and direction. To the contrary, dominance is more her style of interaction. We suggest Madeline expresses these opposing needs or motives in uniquely domineering ways. For instance, she told Steve and Greg that she likes to go to new places where she does not know people or the customs and to find her way without using her mobile device for aid. Often, this seems to recreate an experience of being lost and in need, but without the conscious idea of needing help. She reminds herself "I've been further from home and more scared." She had a miniature version of this kind of experience the night she arrived in Austin and made her way to the hotel. She got lost and did not know which way to go. Consequently, she stopped a bus by pulling in front of it (dominance) in order to ask the driver for directions (dependence). Thus, she enlisted her overtly dominant behavior to satisfy her dependent need for help.

Similarly, in February, on the night following her assessment intervention session and its ensuing discussion (the night of her "once in a decade" sleep), Madeline fell asleep almost immediately after returning to the hotel. She awoke hungry several hours later. Nothing on the hotel restaurant menu looked good, so she asked if the chef would make her (dominance) tomato soup and a grilled cheese sandwich (dependence). We suspect similar types of dynamics accompany many other interactions, where she assertively becomes the focus of attention (dominance) but does so to feel prized (dependence) as tough, smart, funny, sexy, engaging, adventurous, and brave, as she says on her ORI. Her social audaciousness (Wiggins, 2003) likely serves related functions, allowing her to be dominant while others dependently experience the kind of embarrassment or shame she would disavow.

Although not based on scored variables, we observed several instances when Madeline was surprised by what others thought or intended. For instance, Madeline struggled during the Rorschach administration to recognize how Greg was incapable of retaining everything she was communicating, which prevented her from slowing her rate of delivery so he could keep pace. Similarly, it was shocking to her that Greg and Steve would need any kind of clarification about her completely obvious responses. She subsequently marveled at how interesting it was to learn other people do not describe the same things she saw and to realize people genuinely see different things in the inkblot cards. These testing observations are akin to her bewildered surprise at her brother's openness to talking about their past.

These behaviors are another common consequence of early experiences of severe maltreatment (Fonagy, Luyten, Allison, & Campbell, 2017). It appears Madeline's parents, due in part to their own problematic histories and early caretaking environments, lacked the ability to engage in the kind of empathic, reciprocal social interactions with Madeline that would recognize her internal states and help her recognize the often-differing internal states of others. This social process provides the foundation for mentalization, or the capacity to recognize motives, intentions, and aims in ourselves and others, and thus to differentiate others who are trustworthy from those who are not. Without developed mentalization abilities, and while simultaneously confronted with recurrent maltreatment and abuse, it is not only adaptive but necessary to fundamentally mistrust everyone, as Madeline did. However, this fundamental mistrust of others as sources of valuable knowledge precludes learning how to genuinely recognize the mental states of others and all the ways in which they may differ from our own.

Key Psychodynamics

We opened this chapter by noting how we would use five psychodynamic principles to organize our thinking and approach to test interpretation. Madeline's openness to this assessment and to life more broadly, provided us with an excellent opportunity to do so.

The first principle is that the past, particularly early childhood experience, is important for understanding who we are in the present. Early experiences with caregivers, including those that are embedded preverbally and may not be fully accessible to linguistic expression (e.g., Bollas, 1987), viscerally shape our templates of what the world is like, what human interactions are like, and what affective experiences are like. Although Madeline spent her life attempting to shut out her past, leave it behind, and create a new and more positive present and future, her assessment data show in an experience-near and palpable way how the reverberations of the past continue now to direct her attention, structure and shape her perceptions, and organize her templates of relationships.

Her next steps, as we see it, are to accept more fully those currently disavowed (split off) vulnerable and dependent parts of her self-experience that reflexively echo her past. This is not to say she should identify with being a victim or embrace being vulnerable and helpless. Rather, we suggest she learn to have more compassion for the parts of herself that were repeatedly and traumatically hurt when she was young and less capable, and that by necessity she isolated in order to survive. Metaphoric Rorschach representations of her in relation to those parts that she is not yet fully connected with may include the tightly wrapped and trapped bodies weighing down their host as they push against its outer membrane in an attempt to be free (R11), as well as the introvert she does not understand who is *desperate* to participate and similarly attempting to push through an obscuring membrane (R23). These images of embedded objects hidden from view, but desperate for release or connection, might provide visual metaphors to guide her efforts to connect compassionately with remnants of her past. The two buddies who are so close they are zippered together and communicate by thought without the need to talk (R13) may also metaphorically embody parts striving for fuller integration.

The second psychodynamic principle is that conscious awareness is limited, and thus we carry more with us than we recognize. This principle overlaps with the first, and we could reiterate here some of the same points just mentioned. However, we recommend three primary targets for Madeline's increased awareness, with awareness then serving as the platform on which she can make a more deliberate decision about how to respond. One is recognizing when polarizing shifts in affect tone and perspective occur, toward either herself or others. These shifts are pronounced, and they likely are disorienting to Madeline and confusing to others. Learning to track these shifts will be difficult to implement on her own. However, a counselor could help her with this by exploring shifts that occur in session or by processing relevant events from work or relationships. A second but related goal concerns anger and domineering aggression. Madeline has many triggers that incite these reactions. It would be stabilizing for her to gain increased awareness of the emotional (e.g., vulnerability) and interpersonal (e.g., perceived manipulativeness) experiences that serve as triggers. The goal is not to stop her angry reactions but to increase the lead time between the trigger and the final action in order to allow her to decide whether this particular situation calls for that reaction. A final target concerns dependence. Madeline dislikes this term and state. However, dependent imagery for her is also tied to rebirth, new growth, and transformation, most prominently in her butterfly imagery to Rorschach Card V. To the extent that Madeline is able to mentally shift a distasteful view of dependence to a more tolerant, empathic view of how she might adaptively be wishing to seek help from trustworthy others to enact new growth, this also will facilitate awareness and acceptance of a part of her experience that formerly was too dangerous to consider.

Third, conflicts, coping styles, and self-protective psychological defenses influence our perceptions and behaviors. Madeline's main conflicts appear to relate to vulnerable dependence. The sustained abuse and neglect she experienced when she was a vulnerable and dependent child crystalized these conflicts, which in turn fostered internalized relationship templates and problematic coping styles. Madeline's defenses against vulnerable dependence were to take refuge in its opposite pole, preemptively asserting an agentic and aggrandizing dominance, armed with rageful fighting and scathing verbal attack as weapons when needed. These counter-dependent strategies worked; they provided a platform from which she could adaptively live, and subsequently achieve and thrive in successful work. For a time, they also permitted what for her was a deeply meaningful relationship. However, Madeline's adaptive response to these conflicts has become entrenched and overgeneralized (Fonagy et al., 2017). They pervasively color her perceptions, experiences, and behaviors along a restricted axis of distrust of others that keeps her sealed off (isolated) from reciprocal, social intimacy. They also bring along vulnerability to disorganizing thought processes that she cannot reliably quell, hypomanic surges of mental or physical action that preclude comforting sleep, and misattributions of others' actions that inadvertently leave her responding to replays of her own personal history in present day relationships with others rather than the actual behaviors of the other person.

Fourth, affects and motives ("hot" processes) are as important to mental life as cognitions and logic ("cold" processes). Madeline is a smart person. The difficulties she is encountering now, particularly in the area of intimacy and close relationships, are profitably understood as more than maladaptive cognitions or negative automatic thoughts. Rather, the affective reactions and affectively ordered relational templates she internalized in the midst of the ongoing relational trauma she experienced in childhood are important drivers of her difficulties, leaving her vigilantly on guard and self-protective, within which there is no room for weakness. Madeline's Rorschach protocol also illustrates how the nexus of affective distress markers and trauma imagery intertwine with her unique perceptions and implausible representations. Correlation does not equal causation, but we speculate that from what we know of her history, it is more plausible the first two elements (affect linked to trauma) drive the last two (unusual and implausible ideas), rather than the other way around.

Finally, the fifth psychodynamic principle is that we reenact core internal conflicts or complexes in our important relationships, including within ourselves (i.e., how we relate to our self). We did not see clear manifestations of Madeline's core conflicts in the main recent relationships she described to Steve and Greg. These included her uncle, her brother, and her male informant, as well as his wife. Madeline has a long relationship with the latter two people. Thus, she appears able to effectively manage some relationships without having her core conflicts triggered in ways that notably interfere.

However, her core conflicts did play out in other ways. We already noted her dominant-dependent interactions with the bus driver and chef. Another example was the anger she felt when she experienced Greg as spoiling her final Rorschach scene to make it become something much darker (i.e., from Paris party to London torture). Her angry effort to restore emotional balance prompted her to leave quickly for the bathroom. After she returned, she recounted Greg's behavior as very directive. She said, "It's funny. I'm sitting in the bathroom going, 'Why are you mad?!' But it's like I had such a great image and then you're like,

'Nope, there's more there' (she imitates Greg pointing to the card). And then of course you go, 'Ah shit. There's the sucky stuff. There's the bad stuff.' Cause there's always bad stuff." She thus experienced Greg as more interpersonally dominant than he was, leaving her expected to submit to his direction.

In addition, Madeline's current relationships may be relatively conflict free because they are not intimate relationships. Criterion A of the AMPD (APA, 2013) is comprised of two dialectically intertwined dimensions. The Self dimension encompasses identity and self-direction, while the Interpersonal dimension encompasses empathy and intimacy. These are fundamental dimensions of human development and experience (Luyten & Blatt, 2013; Pincus, Hopwood, & Dawood, Chapter 4). Interestingly, Madeline's current assessment questions and concerns fall more squarely along the Self dimension than the Interpersonal dimension, and thus the latter remains underdeveloped in her life. Although we do not advocate her seeking romantic relationships just to provoke conflicts, conflicts are an inevitable consequence of needing to learn how to navigate an intimate relationship, particularly when empathy and intimacy are underdeveloped. Yet, relationships are not far from mind for Madeline, and it may be helpful to her to know in advance some of the dynamics outlined above that are likely to emerge with potency as she re-enters a relationship. Having foresight about what is likely to occur will make it easier to recognize and process those experiences when they do emerge.

Finally, we note the personal reflections of Steve and Greg after concluding the evaluation. Both Greg and Steve experienced feelings of self-doubt and inadequacy after meeting with her on the first weekend. These personal reactions to her (i.e., countertransference) may have been cognitive-affective counterparts to Madeline's characteristic interpersonal ascendance and dominance during the assessment. As such, in a process of projective identification, Greg and Steve experienced feelings of personal inadequacy, which are the feelings Madeline disavows and does not yet know how to tolerate within herself.

Key Take-Home Message: Seeing Madeline via These Data and the Psychodynamic Lens

Unlike most of the other chapter authors, we had the advantage of observing and interacting with Madeline, hearing her describe the past and present, and directly checking test-based inferences with her for resonance and felt accuracy. We also benefited from Madeline's very open responses to the Rorschach, TAT, ORI, and WUSCT, which permitted us to see manifestations of her remarkably difficult and adverse history and clear successes adapting to life. We hope that from these factors, readers will gain an appreciation for seeing Madeline from a psychodynamic vantage point, as well as an appreciation of Madeline herself, including the full range of complexity and richness that is intrinsic to her as a person.

Notes

1. 1: sensorimotor-preoperational (actions, need gratification); 3: concrete-perceptual (separate but concrete, literal, appearance); 5: external iconic (functional attributes, unidimensional); 7: internal iconic (internal attributes, feelings, values, but unidimensional); 9: conceptual (integrates all previous, complexity, change, synthesis).
2. 1: self-other boundary compromise; 2: self-other boundary confusions; 3: self-other mirroring; 4: self-other idealize or denigrate; 5: semi-differentiation; 6: emergent constancy and relatedness; 7: stable self-other in relationship; 8: cohesive, individuated, empathic; 9: reciprocally related, moving toward integration; 10: integrated, empathic, attuned reciprocal relationships.
3. Impulsive (E-2), Self-Protective (E-3), Conformist (E-4), Self-Aware (E-5), Conscientious (E-6), Individualistic (E-7), Autonomous (E-8), and Integrated (E-9)
4. We thank Jessa Dmytryszyn for independently coding her protocol and resolving disagreements with Greg.
5. It is optimal to read the protocol sequentially, starting with all of the response phase and then all of the clarification phase in order by response.
6. The Critical Contents encompass two thematic variables (Aggressive Movement, Morbid Content) and five content variables (Anatomy, Blood, Explosion, Fire, and Sex).
7. Because of administration and documentation differences, we did not consider Prompts, Pulls, or Card Turning.
8. The response was as follows: "Ooh! Scary monster! Great big scary monster, getting sick. Huge feet. Small head, claws. Oh, it's like fire, burning this little person. Poor bugger. Very imposing figure! Tiny head. Not very smart, dangerous (she is very involved, disturbed about the little person being purposely burned). (E: Sick?) R: The top is his head (D3), looking down. Spraying from his mouth. First looks like he's getting sick. Then looks like fire (upper half of D5), very dark. (E: Monster?) R: The size the feet (D6) are. Closest to you. Look way up to see the head. Imposing! Not friendly at all. (E: Burning?) R: Fire from guy's mouth. He was burning him on purpose! Little bugger (D1) didn't stand a chance! (E: Person?) R: Position. Like it wasn't accidental. Back is to us. He's inside of the fire. Little arms hanging down there. (E: Poor little guy?) R: Don't you see that? God, I hope so! It's so obvious! I need to put some dancing pandas in that picture!"
9. The back of the Rorschach cards list the location of the publisher in Bern, Switzerland—a city that Madeline fondly recalled visiting.
10. We thank Emily O'Gorman for rating the WUSCT, ORI, and TAT and resolving disagreements with Mark Waugh.
11. We are grateful to Jenelle Slavin-Mulford, who co-authored the SCORS-G manual (Stein & Slavin-Mulford, 2018).
12. The Rorschach task of saying what the inkblots might be calls on visual memory, as the respondent attempts to fit images of objects seen in the past or currently imagined to some or all of the inkblot features. The stimuli also have inherent contradictions, such as a shape that roughly looks like a bat

but that has spots or holes that do not fit with such an image or a shape that roughly looks like a human but with what could be both male and female sexual characteristics. The task differs from the TAT, which also uses visual stimuli. Those stimuli have clearly recognizable figures and the task requires the respondent to embed the figures in a lexically driven narrative that has a clear structure, with a beginning, middle, and end. The ORI and WUSCT are verbal completion measures, where the task requires either a very brief (WUSCT) or slightly longer (ORI) lexical response organized by the syntactic rules of grammar and language-based communication.

Appendix

Madeline's Rorschach Responses and R-PAS Code Sequence

Respondent ID: Madeline G
Location: Austin
Start Time: ~11:15 a.m.

Examiner: Greg Meyer
Date: January 7, 2017
End Time: ~2:10 p.m. (with 10 minute break during CP)

Cd #	R #	Or	Response	Clarification	R-Opt
I	1		[02:30] [After explaining the 2, maybe 3 guidelines:) Don't go crazy. Alright. Imagination neutral (laughs). Alright. (Okay. [I hand her the card] So, what might this be?) Alright, 2 things. It looks . . . two . . . remember yesterday you said wily . . . Am I allowed to talk while we're doing this? (Steve: Yeah, but we're not allowed to talk back much.) Oh, okay. Sorry. (Steve: No, no. But you go ahead.) Yesterday we used the word wily. And if you look at this it looks like two wily coyotes [or "Wile E. Coyotes"; it was unclear how she was saying it, though in the CP she refers to it as "a word"], like bookmarks on either side. What would you call that . . . like sentinels? So these are my sentinels {EPR} on either side and here we have {OMP} like a headless religious figure	(Examiner repeats response [ERR] up to walking in the church.) (She holds up card to me.) That's not patently obvious?! (I –) Okay. Wily coyote (D7). Ears (Dd28), eyes, the snout (Dd34). Back to back (points to R and L). So you think bookends. Sentinels. . . . (She shrugs.) Figure (D4), legs (D3), it's like a big jacket or a cloak (outer D4) with a belt (strip at Dd27), headless (Dd22) with like collar (Dd22), hands in the air (D1). You know "Hands up" (demos). So either side, entrance, going in (points to DdS26, implies rest of D2 as entryway). (Pause while I type.) (Turns card so Steve and I can both see it.) How can you not see that? {OMP} (Laughs.) (Steve: It's not that we don't see it. It's that that we don't want to assume we see it like you do.) Oh! (Exactly.) I see! (Steve: Yeah, yeah.) (Yeah, yeah.) @ (So, ah, you mentioned the side entrance going in. How . . . Tell me what there makes it look like it's going in?) The orientation for me is the coyotes are on the outside (motions toward self) and because the religious type figure is behind them, the religious figure would be inside (motions away from self, past card). (Okay.) Animal out, human in. It's a wily coyote, it's not a domestic dog. Hence wily. I love that word. {EPR} (Looks at back of card.) Oh! Numbered. [I look at Steve, nodding to indicate I'm done.] (Steve: I'd . . . I would ask why coyotes. What makes them look like coyotes as opposed to . . .?) Ears, eyes, distance	

(Continued)

(Continued)

Cd #	R #	Or	Response	Clarification	R-Opt
			with hands in the air (demos by raising her arms up) like walking into the entrance into a church (motions with hand moving inward). That's probably because I don't have much respect for most religions, or dogmatic religions. ("You don't have much respect for most religions or ...?") Dog – you're writing that down? (Yeah.) Shit. Dogmatic religions. But I like the wily coyotes. v < v > ^ ...... Now you said keep it down (motions down with hand)? (Two maybe 3 things.) 'Kay.	between the two, the snout (pointing to all). You know I think like uhm, like the coyote from Roadrunner. So you know how he had that elongated snout and the short cropped ears and ... Soon as I saw it, the word wily popped into mind. Wily equals coyote. So it's not a wolf, it's not a dog, it *had* to be Wile E. Coyote [or wily coyote]. (Steve: Great, thanks.) And just the orientation on the outside. They sit like sentinels, like not the gargoyle, but just sentinels. Like keeping watch. (Steve:Yeah, yeah.) A coyote. (Steve: Good.) You know, they're very observant. (Steve: Exactly.) So they're not hunting; it's not prey. It's static. (Steve: Got it. Just again, I wanted to make sure I see it like you see it so ...) Yeah. But this is very church-like figure to me. Really *tight*. You know if you look (points) at the coat or the cloak, *tight, cinched* at the waist. *Tight* together at the bottom. And it's wholly appropriate, no head. (Laughs.) And that sense of righteousness, you know, hands in the air (throws her arms up to head height)! And it's not celebratory. It's not like 'Woohoo!' (stretches arms fully above head) way up here like on a roller coaster. It's *tight*. Hands are *tight* (demos holding hands tight at ear height). Hence the religion. (Looks at back of card as I type.)	
2		v	I have a question. Does the orientation have to stay like this or can I move it (turns to >)? (It's up to you.) Oh, cool. v If you turn it upside down, you got a boat traveling through the waters. The orientation is towards the observer (motions toward herself). [She waits for me. We both look at each other after I finish typing.] Oh, I wasn't sure if I should ... The what do you call it? The wake. So the wake coming off of the bow – the bow is the front, right? (Yeah.) The bow (points in front of her), the stern (points	(ERR through wake coming off the bow.) Okay I'm going to show you what I mean here. If you put hand like this (covers lower 1/3 of card). (Uh hum.) You see – the way I see it, this section comes to a point (points to D3 and motions outward toward self). This is very 3-D to me. This comes to a point (D3). And then on a ship, like old ships they had a section big wooden shaft that sticks out in the water (demos by pointing her arm out) and often a carving underneath of like a mermaid or a sea goddess and that's supposed to give them luck as they travel through the oceans. So you got the long wooden shaft pointing out (D3) and the bow of the boat point ... and it's in full movement (motions). You've got it pushing through the water on either side (moves hand across D2s, indicating boat and it's wake is upper 2/3 of card). (Uh hum.) Like not so much in a hurry but just powerful. {IDL} And if you ever been under water and you put glasses	

behind her), port (points to her left). And the bottom portion (motions along a line that would connect the upper boundary of the Dd34s) is where you get, like, you're wearing goggles (cups hand outside eye to demo) and you can look in the water and you can look above the water and below the water (motions with head up then down) so you can see. And here's the orientation of below the water (points DdS32), so there's our boat traveling through the water with the wake (points to upper 2/3) and then what you see below (indicates bottom 1/3). ^ And then there's our Wile E. Coyotes v and here's boat. Am I allowed to ask what you see? ([chuckle] Hang on just a second. You can ask. I, I won't –) I'm not telling you (she mimics me). (I won't tell you, but you can ask. [all laughing]) Well then (laughs). Am I allowed to ask if you can see my boat (turns card to Steve)? (Well, we'll actually talk about that more in a minute.) Cool. I like feedback. Now I do. (Steve: In short, we're going to make sure we see your boat. Yeah.) Oh, cool! Well it's impossible not to {OMP} (shows card to Steve again). (Steve: Right.) (Pause while I type.) (Shows card upright to Steve.) Like my wily coyote? First thing I looked at, it was like, yesterday – wily coyote. (Looks at back of card, asks how to pronounce Rorschach's name and I explain.) (I move the card aside and get the next one.) Can I have something with more color?

on like goggles (demos with hands cupped around eyes) and you orient yourself where the goggles hit between say the bridge of your nose (holding hand flat in front of nose at bridge) would be under and then the rest above (motions with hand moving up). And you can move your head up and down on the surface of the water (moving head up and down, moving arm back and forth to indicate the water's surface) and you see a different dimension under as above (moves cupped hands from below to above). Then if you look here, it's you're, your nose is there (puts hand perpendicular to card in a line from top of Dd34s). This is above the water (upper 2/3) and this is below the water (lower 1/3). And you can see the rock surface (Dd28) and the open water areas (DdS32) on either side (S below and outside D7). And it's a powerful boat {IDL} traveling through. (Pause for me to type.) Again, patently obvious {OMP} (laughs)! (Steve: I can see it now that you explain it.) (Uh hum.) You didn't see it before?! (Steve: I didn't see it as well as you explained it.) Oh. Really?! I want to ask both you gentlemen what you see in these! (Steve: After we're done.) Oh, okay. I bet everyone sees something different don't they? (Uh hum. They do.) Isn't that fascinating? (Steve: And like some people might see boats but not see it the way you saw it. So, that's why we're asking. I don't want to assume your boat is the one I see. So ...) Okay. What's that section at the front of the boat (prow-like motion with her hands together), you know where it's long ... (Steve: I don't know what it's called.) ... almost like a timber that tapers. (It's not really the prow, but there's a name for that.) There's a name for that, isn't there. (Yeah.) And then there is always like a mermaid or ... (A figure of some sort) ... or even a head carved underneath and that leads the way and protects them. There's a lot of myth and lore and superstition attached to that. [I ask for the card and check in with Steve about questions and he has none.] [~11:00 into CP]

(Continued)

(Continued)

Cd #	R #	Or	Response	Clarification	R-Opt
II	3		Ah! Beautiful! (What might this be?) Easy. {OMP} A woman's – she's singing, voice wide open, crying, sad. (Hang on, I'm catching up with you.) …You're stifling me by making me stop (laughs)! (Sorry. Sorry.) This is a very sad one. I'm going to have to say opera. Like a lament.	(ERR) (Holds card to face me.) Face. Open face. Eyes (D2). See even in the orientation of the eyes the sadness, dripping like tears coming outside the eyes. This like sadness because of the black (D6) coming out of either side (motions hand coming out of the card toward viewer). Open. Like powerfully open (motions at DSS coming out). So not like a hum or anything. It's operatic. Like powerful, pushing it out (motions toward ceiling). {IDL} See right into her tongue (D3); the sadness is even dripping off her tongue. Very much female. (Pause while I type.) I'm astounded that's not what everybody sees {OMP} (laughs). Very big. Very 3-D. (What there makes it look very 3-D?) Being able to see right inside (DSS). It's like an emptiness right inside of her (points to DSS). Pushing that lament out (demos with hand arching up and away from the card). And you just look at her eyes. They're so … they're not vacant, they're sad. But she's singing it out. Like very operatic. Like Mimi in La Bohme. Like Carmen. [EXH] Like big and bold. (You mentioned it looked like sadness dripping off her tongue; what there makes it look like sadness?) What there makes that looks like sadness? … Because it ties in with the eyes, both in terms of color and displacement. You know the dripping eyes, which I equate to fluid or crying. And then you got the tongue is wet but … You ever get that expression, "You're just dripping with sadness?" So the expression associates appropriately to the tongue and the eyes. And just moist and dripping. (Steve: And what makes it look like a tongue?) Oh come on! Because it's at the bottom of the mouth, the mouth is wide open (gestures); you can see in. So orientation. Color. Appropriateness with the rest of the picture. Everything. (Steve: Again, just want to make sure I'm seeing it like you.) Everything! (Steve: Yeah.) Eyes, tongue, mouth wide open. Like big sound, big. But it's painful, like it hurts. (Steve: I get it.) Yeah. And the hurt – with all the outside darkness, the hurt is bigger than the sadness. Like it really hurts. And that's why I think opera. You know it's big, it's loud, it's powerful and there's always a heartbroken lament. Poor Mimi. You've seen La Bohme? (I have not.) Okay, well	

4 v (Laughs) Okay, I can't help this. We have a very robust, Rubenesque again woman. Flamboyant. And that the upside. That's the turned orientation with the legs at the bottom (shows card to me so it's clear I see how she was holding it). ... Lot of anger.

> (ERR) Oh yeah! Okay. So here you go. Think of this as the legs (D2); I mean Rubenesque. Chunky, chunky thighs. Like big cape (D6), wide open (demos throwing hands wide). Consider that (D3) the personality, in the head orientation. Almost like a flash, like "Woohoo!" {EXH} (laughs; demos throwing open a cape to expose body), right. Here the cape looks polka dotted (points to interior of D6), so not a plain type of fabric; like big and bold and ... bright red stocking on her chunky thighs; exposed. Loud. But playful! [EMS] Maybe a little dirty. Not so much sexy, but dirty. (Pause as I type.) (She holds up card for us to see.) Do you get it? (Mhm.) (Steve: I do.) You know the fun part too? It's just the way her hands (Dd22) — it's not like this (demos hands up and out with fingers forward), it's like her hands are thrown back (demos hands up and out with fingers back) like wide, wide open. That to me is one of the most interesting characteristics, is the orientation of the hands. (Steve: What makes them look that way in the blot?) I think it's like the way the darkness changes (pointing to Dd22) (Steve: Oh.) Like instead of having it like this (demos arms up and out with palms facing forward) it's almost like back behind her shoulders and her hands back like that (demos arms stretched back and out with palms facing back). (Steve: The change in the color —) Palms up it just — it even orients the direction. Yeah. Like "Woohoo!" (Laughs.) You dirty bird! (Laughs.) I want a glass of wine with her. {EPR} ^ Oh,

(said like then I couldn't get it). (Steve: I have.) Exactly, right?! (I do have one more question. You said it looked wet. What there in the inkblot makes it look wet?) The tears. The sadness in the tears. You know how you cry and just gravity; the tear will come down the bottom of your lid or the side of your lid. Well, it's like you cried and it splashed (motions out with hands over card). Like it's really ... she's really sad! (Thank you.) And you sing and your mouth is ... you know, you got, not me right now because I'm out of water. When I say fluid, I don't mean just water. When you're singing you salivate kind of and the sadness, it's wet; it's fluid, like sad and dripping. Dripping in and of itself. It's wet. (Thank you.) And it sure as hell not like you laugh so hard you cry; it's sad so hard you cry. If you look here (inner D2) and it's like the eyelids are heavier on the top. Like weight, it's the weight of it. [~18:30]

(Continued)

Cd #	R #	Or	Response	Clarification	R-Opt
				and isn't that awful. And you turn it around and it's so sad. {SPL} Just – (We'll get to that in a second.) Just the head. (Yeah.) Just the head. And then this one v is the entire body. Like head to toes and beyond. ^ Isn't that funny. v ^ And definitely not the same person. [She asks if she can go fill her water; Steve does it for her.] So, what else do we have. (So I did have one other question on this one.) This orientation ^? (Actually, I'm sorry; this v orientation.) 'Kay. (And you mentioned polka dotted. And I was wondering if you could tell me what makes it look –) Oh! (…polka dotted.) The colors (points in D6). Like even though they're muted here, see how it goes a lot of grays, then you've got a red in here, red in here, red in here. To me I see this as black and bright red circles, so like really lady bug-ish. [Steve returns with water. She feels better after a drink. Steve wonders if I asked about dirty. I explain that I asked about polka dotted and summarize what she said.]	
5	>		^ …> Oh my god. 'Kay. I have a third. Can I go ahead? (Uh hum.) So, turning it this way > The first thing I see is two guys in hats playing patty cake {EMS} (laughs). ^ And it's funny how I don't see it in the appropriate orientation; only when I turn it sideways >. Isn't that weird how they change from a woman ^ to a man >. < > < > And that patty cake guys <, they work both ways (shows me). > (Okay.) v ^ Cool. (Looks at back of card.) (We look at each other.) (Okay?) (She hands card back.) Well you said two or three. (Uh hum. Is that good?) Well, I don't know if it's good or not. It's just what's there. You get to decide what's good.	(ERR) How can you miss that? {OMP} (And again, I'm interested in you explaining to me where you–) 'Kay. They're sitting down, hands up (D4), chest level. But that's the most boring. Like two guys playing …, like who cares? I find it boring. {EPR} But you said tell me what you see. (Uh hum.) (Thanks.) Yeah. I like the opera singer. (Uhm.) And the dirty bird. (And the dirty bird. Uh hum.) [~24:30]	

| III | 6 | (And this one here [hand her card].) Oh, this is lovely. We've got 2 women working together. I can't tell if they're cooking something or doing the laundry. This one is a hell of a lot happier. Communal. | Oh this one's great. {OMP} (ERR) Oh yeah....... (We look at each other.) Oh. Oh, like show you? (Please.) Oh. Okay. Two women (D9s), clearly women. They have breasts (Dd27); they have hips (Dd21 and below); the way they're standing. And over a center (D7), I can't tell if it's a stone where they're rubbing clothes on or a stone where they're making – pounding corn. But it's absolutely working together. Just the unity between the two of them. And what I love {EPR} is they're sharing a heart in the middle (D3) like they're sisters or community members or wives of the same tribal prince or whatever. But they're very close and they're working on a shared task. And they're happy doing so. {EMS} (Pause while I type.) In my head anyway (laughs). They looked happy. (And what about it makes it look like a heart?) The shape! You know, where is your heart; in your chest. Right. So where are their hearts? Right outside their chest. And they're mirroring one another. So to me, closeness. Like sisters or wives. Friends. Like close, tight friends. *Connected*. It's the sense of connectedness. (Thank you.) You're welcome. That'll be 20 bucks. (We laugh.) (Steve: And again, you know, someone else might see it as a heart for a different reason, so we want to get your reason. That's why he's asking. Okay?) It's just, you look at something and you see it is what it is. (Steve: Right, right.) So it's hard to understand how you can't not see it. (Steve: Exactly. But as you say, people see all different kinds of things.) Oh I'd be fascinating [sic] to know what other people saw and then have them of course explain it to me. (Steve: Right, right. So –) And see if that's ... (Steve:... we're just trying to make sure we're getting in your shoes as you see it. That's why we're doing that.) Makes sense. (Steve: Yeah, yeah.) I'm not challenging it, I'm just surprised. (Steve: Right, right, right. Yeah.) Yeah. (Steve: Then we have to ask.) Yeah. (Steve: Right, right, yeah.) (Uh hum.) |
| | 7 | > v You turn it upside down and the happiness has absolutely disappeared. More like warriors (points to D7). Isn't that funny; on the same card, very much pain and suffering. And loss. And the complete opposite of that ^ is the community and the working together. | (ERR up to warriors, when she jumped in.) Okay. So here (Dd31s), look at shape of head and this is like African American, and I don't mean United States of America, I mean like Congolese. You know what I saw this, I went in my head, Hutus and Tutsis. {EPR} Like a horrific genocide. And angry, bearded (points to lower part of Dd31 adjacent to Dd30). (Okay, hang on a second. I don't mean to slow you down, but I'm trying to catch up.) Okay. [I repeat what she said; she |

(Continued)

(Continued)

Cd #	R #	Or	Response	Clarification	R-Opt

{SPL} > v < ^ This is the most interesting card so far. (Uh hum.) By far. (Hands card back.) That one stands out as my favorite. So far. (Uh hum.) I don't remember ever seeing that before. (Hmm.)

Clarification:

confirms.] Hutus and Tutsis. Like a horrible genocide. Names like that, how do you kill each other. Hutus, Tutsis. Can't help that. Fuck that was a mess. [Redacted; relates to Rwandan peacekeeping effort.] (And you mentioned there was pain and suffering and loss.) Oh, terrible. (And what there makes it look like pain and suffering and loss?) What was a heart to me in the other orientation (D3) and it's arcing, tying them together, the oriented here and it's like pulling apart. Like literally tearing your heart out. This (D2) had no role, but for color and warmth, in the first orientation; here it's like literally death. Blood spot. Like just shot, bleeding, done. You notice here ^ they're face to face and connected; here v back to back and apart. Again more tearing apart above their heads (points to upper D8). And armed (points to D5). (Armed?) Oh absolutely. Armed. Like rifle armed. Or knives. But armed. Like dangerously armed. And very tribal to me. And it literally polar opposite ^ v ^ See how the leg is here, like one leg down (main D5) and then portion of the other leg (Dd26). (Uh hum). It's like you know if you put your feet together (demos) and take somebody's hands (stretches arms out and crosses them at the wrist) and lean back. (Uh hum, Uh hum.) If you let go you're gonna fall. So you can see they're trusting each other enough in that staying jointly connected without fear of falling. Like they're *really* close. (Uh hum, Uh hum.) And then you do this v and everything about them is tearing apart. So literally *polar opposites*. (Pause while I type.) I feel really strongly about this one. (Uhm. Uh hum.) And I mean like all of it. Not the card itself but the the contrast between opposing good and evil (laughs) and I like that the good is the women. {EPR} And I didn't create it but the bad is clearly male. (You mentioned that they were African American, not U.S.-like but Congolese-like; what makes them look Afric–?) The shape of the head, see the really high forehead and just the darkness changes like literally everywhere where the face is, the forehead comes out, indent for the eyes, no comes out, nose comes out, indent for you know the face and then a arc for the chin and neck, then a little bit of facial growth on the

IV	8			

(And this one?) (laughs) Okay, big galoot walking on ice (she demos lurching gait with arms to side). The perspective of the picture is being below the ice looking up (holds card above self and motions up with hand across card). So the photographer's safe but this is the image that's coming from above. (Still holds card at arm's length slightly above sightline.) And given my size 10s, I have a lot of respect for the big feet (laughs). {EPR} Hard to say if it's harmful or harmless, but the person taking the picture is safe.

(I might have misheard you on this one, but I thought you said, "Big galoot walking on the ice.") Yeah! (Okay.) You know what a galoot is? (No, I don't.) (Steve: Oh, I know that word.) Yeah! [We discuss its meaning and Madeline likens him to a Sasquatch that is not a monster, or a big dog who is not graceful and loves you to pieces.] (So this one is walking on the ice.) Yeah! You can see the orientation is you're underneath the ice taking a photograph. These are beautiful. If you've ever seen photographs where you're under the ice and you can actually take a picture and the water is so clear that you can capture the image above (demonstrates all this with hand motions, being below and seeing above). They're beautiful pictures. But this what got captured. See the bottom of this feet (D2) are flat and so it's on the ice. And can't really tell … and it's definitely a he. But you can't really tell if he's surprised or not. But he was good enough to stop and let the picture be taken. So he's a galoot and not a monster. A monster may have like banged his foot on the ice and crashed it and hurt the person taking the picture, but he just stopped to get his photo taken! I like 'em. I keep showing you this (motions with card). (Yep.) Don't you see what I see (laughs)!? (I think I'm seeing, yeah. Uh hum.) And see how tall he is, look how small his head gets (D3). Like he's a big one. But not scary. (Pause while I type.) And definitely not fire breathing. Too cold. (You mentioned the bottom of his feet are flat on the bottom of the ice.) Yeah. See the difference in coloration and the outline. It's the outline you can see so clearly. It's like uhm, what are they called on dogs where they have that extra

bottom of the chin, back of the head (identifying contour for all). All of that area there (inner part of Dd31) is darker, suggesting to me hair, short-cropped but hair. And same on the other side. High forehead, arc, nose, mouth, chin, and neck, neck. All the orientation is correct. Not to mention the ink is black. But besides that it's the shaping. ^ And it's hard for me not to miss, but the women look like what they have those neck rings in certain areas. It's a, I think it's a sign. You do something of distinction and I think that's awarded to women in certain cultures. But the elongated neck with the rings for the women. (Steve: Do you need to ask about the blood?) (Uhm. I don't think I do.) (Steve: Okay, great.) (Uhm, yeah, no we're good.) (Steve: Good.) [35:37]

(Continued)

Cd #	R #	Or	Response	Clarification	R-Opt

| 9 | v | | v < ^ > v Turn it upside down or upside right, whatever your perspective. This one is complex. So I'm going to have to … (sets card on table in front of us, leaning it against mic so we can see it). I'll slow down but I'll explain it to you. And you'll have to forgive me because this is like a Harry Potter moment. (Okay. I'm trying get down | little claw. (Uhm, dew, dewclaw.) Dewclaw. That's right. So you see how he has like a dewclaw at the back (lower appendage on D2), flat; completely clearly outlined. Everything is flat, like literally standing on the ice. (Uh hum.) And then you … (shows me card above her head) you look up and he's looking down. Perfectly flat surface (she rubs hand along bottom edges of D2s and D1). (Holds card above head again.) Get it? (Yeah, I get it. Thank you.) Okay. I'm confused! (Laughs) How do you (smacks card against her leg for cadenced emphasis) not (smacks card again) see these (smacks card again; laughing)?! (Steve: We do!) Okay! (She holds card above her head, as far as she can.) Especially if you hold it up like that. (Steve: Again, the questions are not that we can't see it, it's just to make sure we're getting it exactly as you see it.) Well, I'm just not used to being in this position. (Steve: I know.) I find it really … frustrating I think. (Frustrating; yeah.) I want you to see it right away! (Yeah.) Cause I see it right away. (Sure) (Steve: Actually, you know what? We do sometimes but again we have to make you say it so we can check –) Confirm. (– to see we're seeing it like you do.) (Ah hum. Thank you [said to Steve]). (Steve: Do you get it?) Yep. And even though you might have to tell me again. Because I'll still get frustrated. (Yeah.) (Steve: It's okay. No, it's a very frustrating process.) (She holds card high.) I love you big galoot {EPR} (points to him). Now you know galoot. (Now I know galoot. [smiling]) That's good. (Yes.) [Brief discussion of where the term "galoot" originated.][~41:00] (So this time you said –) Ah, Voldermort! (… upside down or upside right this one is complex.) Yep. (And you wanted to set it down and you said "This is a Harry Potter moment.") Yeah. (And you said "You have to know Voldermort" and "This is not a happy place.") No. ("The top section looks like a castle." Uhm, and "Harry Potter is good vs. evil so Harry peeling back to expose the castle." And then you mentioned "the chicken-shits" –) The cowards, jumping. (And so maybe we'll just start there; 'cause that's a fair amount already.) Okay, can I explain something to you? (Sure). In the Harry Potter series Voldermort does not have a home. Harry | |

Potter lives at Number 4 Privet Drive when he's with his Muggle family, but for the most part he lives at Hogwarts. So this is just a bit of a backstory. Voldermort doesn't have a home. If Voldermort had a home it would be in that castle. Just so you know. And Harry Potter is struggling to be good. And he is good. There's good vs. evil; it's him and Voldermort. And they're all big – It's a complex story. There's a little bit of Voldermort in Harry. So this is Harry finding Voldermort's place. (Pause while I type.) And I find it frustrating having to slow down when I'm really excited about trying to explain something to you. (Sure, sure. No, I understand that.) Okay, can I go? (Yes.) 'Kay. You see how this here (points to D2 and D6) has got a peeling back effect (motions to demo image coming out of the card) on either side? If you think of this as a circle (motions circularly with hand above and card as card faces me), like in 3-D, all the way around the castle (i.e., in front of it and behind it). It's like he was able, Harry was able to break through and peel enough to make like a seam (D5), and then peel from behind, peel this (D6) back down (D6 away from and in front of D1) to expose. And once, you know, it's like anything, once you're exposed, then there's the true you, right? So he found where Voldermort – and that then brings in all this light (points to DdS24), because it all got, the blackness got torn away. So once the light goes in, the cowards book it. They jump ship. And look, there's a lot of them (points to dots on left below Dd28). (Mmhmm.) It's very dark. (It is very dark.) But exciting too, because I'm a big Harry Potter fan. I like the books, so it's exciting, to go "Whoa! We should show this to J. K. Rowling" (laughs). But, you know, Voldermort's gone now. So this is all pre-Voldermort's death. What an imagination there. Have you ever read those? (I have not.) Oh you got to; they're fun. They're so much fun. (Steve: I read them all.) And did you love them? (Steve: Mmhmm.) Me too. [Pause as I type.] [[Nodding to Steve] Sounds good [i.e., to move on].] [I should have queried the V "peeling back effect" at D2 vs. D6 because V was suggested by the contrasting shades.]

everything that you're saying, so I'm catching up with you. [Pause while I type.] "This is like a Harry Potter moment …") Yeah. So you won't get the reference unless you're familiar. You got to know who Voldermort [sic] is. And just by saying that, this is not a happy place. (Okay.) So top section, castle {IDL} (points to upper part of D1). Now Harry {MAG}, peeling back to expose the castle (demonstrates peeling D2 toward us and away from D1). The chicken-shits (points to tiny strings of dots on the left side of D1 below Dd28). What do you call that when you jump to save yourself but you don't save others? You know like jumping ship kind of thing. Save them … These ones are leaving (points again) to save themselves. Because they are getting pulled back (demos pulling D6 away from D1 and toward us) from where Voldermort lives or stays or … Black (points to D1). Dark. But by peeling away (demos peeling again) letting the lightness in (points to DdS24), and that's why they're booking it. And because – (Hang on a second. Sorry.) There's an important final piece. (Okay.) [pause] "That's why they're booking it …") Well, they're cowards. That's why they're so small. ^ v (And that was the last piece?) Yes. The cowards. So the tiny cowards. (She hands card to me

Cd #	R #	Or	Response	Clarification	R-Opt
			and I pass it back, forgetting this was her second response already.) (Take a moment and look a bit longer.) Which orientation? (Whatever you like.) Whatever I like? ^ I like this guy because he's just "Do to do to do" (singing). It's like he just belongs there. It's like someone captured a picture (she demos holding a camera pointing up). (Oh, I'm sorry.) (Steve: We have two, right?) (Yeah, we do. My mistake. I'm sorry.) Did I fuck up? (No, you were totally fine. [I pat her arm and look at her] I did. [we all laugh]) You're forgiven. Because we don't [inaudible (know what you?)] did wrong.		
V	10		(And this one?) Oh sweet. I don't know how you can look at this and not think blossoming cocoon {OMP} (demos expansive opening). Just opening (motions). Whew. These brand new wings (points along D4s).	Oh yeah! I remember this. (ERR) Initial. And then it got shitty fast (laughs). (Let's do this one first.) Okay. If you look at this, it looks like, you know when a caterpillar in cocoon you see it, if you've ever watched it, like a Monarch butterfly, they're really popular. And you literally can see it open up and change from caterpillar cocoon, to literally pushing out, and boom butterfly wings (throws her arms out). Like you open this up (points to card). When you handed it to me and you just turn it and open it up; it looks like brand new heavy wings (points D4). Like "Boom" (demos opening her arm up). Like they haven't even … what's a word to describe the motion of waving (raises her arm). You know. flapped. They haven't even flapped yet or taken flight, like they're just, wow (throws arms out), brand new heavy, whomp. Like you almost could hear it, the unfurling (makes sound effect; slow "whomp'") and hit the floor kind of thing. Like they're that heavy. Like, wow! Like boom, you're, brand new. Baby wings. And then you go holy shit (laughs), there's a lot inside. You want me to continue? (No. I'm sorry. Just hang on just a second. [pause] I'm just reviewing.) Okay. (To Steve: I was going to move on to Steve. [He nods.])	

II

Well, so far most have been a picture; now within this, unfortunately you got considerable sadness on either outer side. Like being trapped in here. Like people; bodies being trapped in here (points to lower part of Dd35). But if you look at it as a whole, a blossoming cocoon. But if you look at it closer, not so nice. And more trapped on the inner area of the wings at the bottom (points to area around Dd25). More profiles trapped on the top (points to Dd33). But if you look at the dark line (points) down the center; you can unzip that and they can all just be free (arm out motion) and not trapped. And then you look away (holds card far off to the right) and then you look back (brings card in front of her) and initially you got that nice pretty blossoming opening cocoon to butterfly. But then you look closer (looks intently). Whew (moves blot as far outstretched to the right as she can). Shew (motioning sound; moves blot in front of her). < v . . . ^ I'm so stuck on this orientation. I'm absolutely stuck on that. > v ^ No matter where I put it, it still stays. So that to me is the only orientation that works (meaning upright; leans card against mic on table . . . picks up again). There's a lot of weight to this. (Hands card back.) (Thank you.) I don't like that one very much {EPR} (looks serious). I'd like some more color please (laughs).

(ERR to "profiles at the top.") OK, see how you got, this to me, like a hunched, like you can feel the shoulders hunching here (she demos by scrunching down, points to lower part of Dd35 on left), and the body and legs coming out (D10). But it's stuck inside and like pushing against the outside (motions on card). So there you've got someone hunched over, like just, you can feel the tightness, the restriction. And then just above that (points to Dd33) is like the hair here, and literally you can see the eyelashes, the eyes, the nose. And here's another person pushing their face against the outside of that (she looks up and pushes face forward). And another one stuck down here (Dd25 and surrounding area). You can see the head, you turn it (turns to v to show me more clearly), but the head, the eyes, nose (points along contours). ^ So you've got this whole person's body, you can see. This guy (protrusion in contour interior to Dd25) stuck in behind him and you can see his head and his face. The profile of it. And this guy is wrapped in here (1st guy on bottom) and he's got his face sticking out. And then double down (points to right side, indicating the same over there). And they're all *tightly wrapped*, stuck in here and stuck in here and here and here (points to each). Like *shitty!* But the worst is this little bugger (points to D7) is carrying all that weight (i.e., its wings are D4). Can't fly, can't move. Cause all of this is inside (points). Like grounded – and not in a good way. Like if an eagle was grounded. Not good. Can I go on, because this is important? (Hang on just a second. Ok.) So the neat thing about this is see how it's all pushing from the inside out (points and motions pushing above and then below wings)? If they can get their hands and unzip this seam (points to center line), and peel this off, then maybe they can come out of this. But they're not going to be a butterfly. So, possible for a transformation, but it will require a totally new identification (said slowly). (For this one, I'm not sure if these are two different things or if this is all part of the initial percept of the . . .?) Well the first one, when you handed it to me was like, "Wow," absolutely obvious. It wasn't until the closer inspection that it was something else. {SPL} So I kind of treated it like we did the other assessments. It's like, what's the first thing that pops into your head. Trust that. I couldn't because it was something else going on (laughs). But it started looking like a brand new baby butterfly, like just weighted down by new wings, but it's... (Steve: But there's

(Continued)

Cd #	R #	Or	Response	Clarification	R-Opt
				like a comma in between.) I think there's a colon in between. Okay, great.) Yeah. (Okay.) Or a semi colon, like, there. So it's both. (I think I understand that now.) Okay. (Ok, thanks. [Extend hand for the card.]) You're more than welcome to have that back (laughs).	
VI	12		I'm working hard not looking at what you're writing. (Is it distracting?) Yeah. (I'll turn it away more.) No, no. It's the noise [from the keyboard]. (Ahm.) And it's the limiting. I look at something and I want to say the first thing that comes to mind and you're like 'Hold on please.' And I'm like, ach (motions like 'What? You have to be kidding.') I *can't*. OK I got to tell you this is kind of weird. This looks like – the top half looks like profiles of a cat and then the bottom looks like one of those animal skins where something's been skinned and is laying flat (motions side-to-side with arm) on the floor (motions in front with hand flat, palm down). This is very 2-dimensional to me (holds card flat in front of her at arm's length). That's weird. Everything looked 3-dimensional till now, but this just looks like it should sit like that (holds card flat on top of her hand). Not even up [i.e., not even upright]. So I wouldn't even hang it on a wall. I can say this one looks ugly (holds flat at arm's length).	[Steve asks how she doing. Says okay but would like tea. Steve goes to get a cup.] (ERR to "laying flat.") See this here (D3) to me it's like the head of a cat if you're above, looking down and just see the top of it (motions with hand above her head to illustrate vantage point, looking down on crown). (Okay.) Not the rest of it, like that's all you see. (Just a second. Okay. That's all you see ...?) Yeah. (Uh huh.) It's just, this whole thing for me, like this (points to D1), completely flat and 2-dimensional. I think this is the one I find the least interesting. {EPR} (Uh hum.) And then just, you know, nothing interesting to me other than you know, you see sometimes it's cowhide, sometimes it's deer. You know, it's just a hide. (Uh hum.) Like something dead, skinned, cured, on the floor. Like a carpet. Not my tastes in carpets {EPR}, but just a flat skin. Excuse me, a flat hide. Boring. (Steve returns with tea and she thanks him "I'm not used to being catered to so I gotta tell you I'm loving this ... It's nice and hot, perfect, thank you very much.") The boring one (shows card to Steve). And my regards to anyone who sees something interesting here (laughs). (Hmm.) Because I'd sure like to know. (And what about it makes it look like a hide? What there makes it look like a hide?) The edging on this, you get a sense of like, legs here (Dd24), legs here (Dd25). So two per side. The orientation is right. And I hate to say it like this because it's an animal, but the *cut* (points to D12). The fact that it's split open (edge of hand at D12) and flat (motions both hands flat). And the coloration (motions across card). But you have to do this (puts hand over D3), you have to cover the top of the cat's head. So this would be the back end (at Dd31), smaller legs (Dd25), where the head would have been (Dd33), arms on both sides (Dd25), back legs (Dd25), both sides,	

(Continued)

indentation for the head (contour at Dd33). Just the flattening out of it. If it didn't have what would, to me, look like legs, to me that would then look like a piece of fish, sliced open, filleted. But fish don't have legs (says in a laugh). So it has to be a hide (said laughing)! You have to account for what's there. Oh that's so good (referring to tea). [I start with the next response.] And then turning it this way, you said –) (Steve: Can I ask a question?) (Sure.) (Steve: The coloration, can you say more about that?) On the top, see how it's dark (motions all along D5). On the very top, much like when you see, uhm … You ever see a dog that gets, like, pissed off or on guard. And they have that strip of hair (motions a strip in space). Like mine will literally go from between her ears to her tail {EPR} (motions left to right in space). It stands straight up like a Mohawk (motions hands moving together and up). When that happens, there's a change in color underneath (motions hand going lower in space). And that's what that reminded me of. (Steve: Thought that's what it was, but just wanted to make sure. Yeah.) And then the coloration, there's stripes here (vertically in Dd24), spots here (in D1 outside of D12), so I can't say if it's a cat, like it's definitely not like a leopard or that kind of thing, but a mammal with – that you would find on a hide, not really a lynx. (Steve: Got it.) It's bigger than that.

(ERR to "party going on" [she talks over me].) Know where I get that? Er, do you wanna finish? (No, go ahead.) Here, like … You know when you're really close to something [sic], you can say something and the other person, you know, knows what you're thinking, and you'll burst out laughing and not even saying it. So like it's in your head, not verbal. And these two have a party in their head (points to Dd33 area). Like you see how high the arms are (motions with arm above her head, mimicking arms at Dd28 of characters residing at Dd27 in their heads). Like before that religious figure had the hands right here (holds hands next to her head), these guys are like "Woohoo!" (raises arms up and down above head). It's on either side, look (shows card and points, indicating each half of Dd27 and each Dd28, meaning two guys). There's a party going on in their head. They don't have to say it out loud, they know it, they're laughing. {EMS} They're tight, they're really close friends. I like that one. And it's funny because this is anything but two

13   v   v Well that's better. (Okay, hang on a second). Okay. (Sorry.) I'll hold my thought (holds hand up by head). (Okay.) (You said 'Well that's better.') Turning it this way (v). This is the correct orientation. {OMP} 'Kay, this one's easy. {OMP} Two buddies back-to-back. They are so close they are like zippered together. And if look at it from the top down here (points to Dd27 and 28) they got a party going on. That's fun. {EMS} So you should show them this orientation (v) first. {OMP} ^ That's ugly. v That's fun. [SPL] (Starts to hand card back but I'm typing so she sets

(Continued)

Cd #	R #	Or	Response	Clarification	R-Opt
			it against mic on the table.) I'm giving you the party side back (v). (Okay.) You know, the exciting part is waiting for the next card. (Yeah? The exciting part?) So far. The unknown. What's coming. (Ahhah.)	dimensional now. Just by changing it upside down. (Uh hum.) It's funny. I like the little voices in their head {EPR}; they're like "Rock on!" (demos one fist pumping, laughs). [Pause while I type.] (You mentioned they were zippered together. How are you seeing that?) Ok, so see these 2 hooks at the top (Dd21), if you were to do this (circles hand above edge of card) and wrap them around, like . . . (moves hand to large microphone on the table) So, cut this in half (demos cutting mic in half, top to bottom), but we're going to put it back. This here (returns to card; points up D12) zipper would come together, that would attach (the Dd21s) and you would pull these in (upper quarter of each D4), and they'd become one (motions hand cupped, to indicate top folding over behind the card). You see the connection? (Aha.) You just have to roll it around (motions to top). I don't want to screw up the card. (Okay.) But if I were to take the card and turn it (imitates making a cylinder) it would be together. This here (D12), continue this as a zipper. (Uh hum.) That (DdS30) would close up, these two (Dd21s) would kind of latch together, this (upper quarter of each D4) would wrap around and connect (demos a cylinder). (Uh huh.) Like they're . . . See how the hand is there (Dd24). So (stands up to imitate) it's like you're laughing really hard going "Ha ha ha" (holds one hand to stomach to indicate bulging contour below Dd24 and one hand out to indicate Dd24) and that section (bulge below Dd24) is the hand sticking out, like on top of the belly (demos). (Uh huh.) Right here (points to card). (Uh huh.) They're both laughing hard, holding their bellies (demos on self; then sits down). So you can take this (D12) and continue up and zipper them (motions going above card and down the backside of it). (Okay.) There's just so . . . They're that close. But you need to turn the card (demos cylinder). (Uh huh.) You'd need to wrap it around this bottle (picks up bottle and places it behind card). (Wrap it around the bottle, uh huh, okay.) And then follow the zipper up and there's a little clasp (Dd21). "Click" (shows card to us). "Zing" (demos zipping up and over card to back). But instead of zippering it this way (circular motion	

VII	14		Oh that' is so cool! So two little girls, kinda like fairies, pixies. They're planning trouble. They're going out. They're very excited {EMS} about going out. They're just confused on where they're going. And they're very close. The one on the left is a little bossier than the one on the right.	indicating horizontal plane) you're going to zipper it this way (motion indicating vertical plane, from front to up and over card). You with me? (I think so [said confidently].) Well I don't want you to think so, I want to make sure you're with me Greg {OMP} (laughs). That's what I think. I think of my friend [Name 1] and [Name 2]. {EPR} That's what I think. And they're big guys. They're both really big guys. So when they laugh it's, it . . . it has a good effect. And they're close like that (points to card and then leans it against mic). To me the zipper's the most obvious thing there. (Uh hum.) It's the bringing them together all the way around (motions). Now (addressing Steve) can I ask an unrelated question? (Steve: I'll let him decide.) (Um, can we hold off for just a minute? Of course. ('Kay. Until we get through this. If that's alright with you?) Sure. (Thanks.... Okay. I didn't have anything else Steve.) (Steve: Me neither.) (Okay.) [~106:00]
				Oh this one is fun (as I hand her the card). (Yeah.) Pixies! (ERR through "confused on where they're going.") Yeah. ('Kay.) And one's bossier than the other (we both laugh). I think his one (L) is the going to be the one that gets to decide (laughs). (Okay. Again, I'm interested in where you're seeing things and what makes it look the way that it does.) Okay, [redacted phrase] you would understand this reference, Pocahontas, you get that? {OMP} (Uh huh.) Pixies (D9), feathers (D5), like fairies. Very cute little noses (points), like really cute features. Hair (D8). Facing each other. This one (L) is pointing in that direction (points L), this one (R) is pointing in this direction (points R). Dressed up (D4), very connected (points to D6), tightly connected, closeness, playful. {EMS} (Points to the one on left:) "Let's go this way" (in falsetto) (points to one on right:) "No let's go here." (points to one on left:) "No let's go here." She's (L) going to win because she's a little darker. A little more powerful. And she (R) wants to go. So she'll go no matter what. ('Kay. Let me catch up with you.)
	15	> v	> v (laughs) Oh, Ok (laughs) Can I describe this in motion instead of in words? 'Kay, cause check this out (stands and sets card on table against mic). Do you know what twerking is (laughs)? (Ah, I do.) Okay (laughs). So we got	(And then you asked if you could describe it in motion instead of words. And you mentioned and also showed how it was twerking.) (Steve and I near simultaneously say upside down.) Oh, that's this! (turns v) Well look at that! {OMP} [Shows card and laughs.] Little legs, butt sticking out, tiny waist, the hands forward (pointing to both sides). You know the only thing that came to mind

Cd #	R #	Or	Response	Clarification	R-Opt

Response column:

us (demos twerking posture; laughs). {EPR} (Uh huh. Okay.) You got that (laughs; sits back down)? This is a fun card {EMS} (shows to me). So (turns card ^) maybe that's what these two are getting up to. They are going to (turns to v) end up getting into a little bit of fun (laughs, seems kind of strained). (turns to ^) "Now remember girls, (turns to v) safe sex. And enjoy it." (turns to ^) This is a fun card (props against mic; laughs; picks card back up, turns to v). Well, whoever designed these had a sense of humor anyway (shows Steve the card). Now I know you're not allowed to talk to me, but seriously we got some twerking going on (^, sets card against mic; laughs half-heartedly). I like that side better (turns to v). These braces are killing me (pulls at teeth; drinks water). Now you don't have to take down that kind of stuff do you? (Uhm. Yeah, I'm trying to get a record of what we're saying.) Everything? Like even if my … braces hurt? (That I did not write down. [Though I have now since transcribed it.]) Okay. Good…. You could always transcribe the video. {OMP} …I find it hard to behave in between. (Uh huh.) I gotta tell ya I'm getting antsy. (Sorry.) That's okay. It's part of the process. But it's like "C'mon!

Clarification column:

was when you shake your ass a little bit in the back, in that pose, I think that's called twerking. (Uh hum.) It's got a real Betty Boop feel to it to me. Like an old fashioned, kind of "Boop boop be doop." But in now a days they call it twerking. I don't think Betty Boop did that. But she had that, you know, butt out, hands forward, on your tippy toes kind of thing. Or heels. I don't remember if it was on her tippy toes or wearing heels. But that's what it – Like as soon as you turned it upside down, it's like "Holy smokes!" (Uh hum.) And there was something else in here but it was just kind of weird and I wasn't sure if I was supposed to say it or not. But the white space in between. Darth Vader {SPL} (laughs). That might be because there's a new Star Wars movie coming out. (Hmm.) Or come out, or whatever. (I didn't have anything else Steve.) (Steve: Yep.) [She hands card back.] (Thank you.) No Problem. [~110]

Let me have another one." (Momentarily.)
Preferably one with color.... And the more
I talk the worse it is, right? (Steve laughs.)
Fuck. And you think I could help myself? No!
(laughs) That's probably why my braces hurt;
'cause I'm *dying* to say something. (We look
at each other; smile; I get next card.)

VIII 16

Oh thank goodness! Here we go. Alright, two
bears on outside of what looks like doing
their laundry. They're young, they're playful,
they're okay. Even though it's tasks, they're
having fun. {EMS} And I don't think it's
their laundry they're doing but they're still
enjoying themselves. (All said in a sing-song
manner.)

(Okay [hand card to her], here we –) Oh, this is the multiplicity one! (Yes, ERR)
Yeah. I'm quite familiar that bears don't do laundry. But that's sure what it looks
like. And standing up on their hind legs, just, if you need me to point this out to
you (points to D1; laughs). (Pause while I type.) Is there any questions, er ...? (I
was just –) Okay, sorry. (– reviewing and catching up.... What about it makes it
look like laundry?) I guess cause to me they are folding it over (points to each
side of D6, motions across central line). Top something (points to D4). And that's
what came to mind. (Okay.) Backstory? [Two sentences redacted; content relates
to national parks and wildlife.] {EPR} And bears are always stealing food and I just
thought, well wouldn't it be nice if they helped out instead of taking – to me it
was just like, well, people are camping in the woods – do their laundry (laughs).
You'll get a better rap, and you won't get killed. And it was playful. (Uh hum.)
You have Yogi bear here, don't you? (Yeah, yeah.) Smoky the bear? (Smoky the
bear too. Yep.) Yogi wouldn't be in this much trouble if he did laundry (laughs).
(Steve: Madeline, you said they looked young and playful. What about the card
made them look young and playful to you?) Well body shape mostly, because
when you're old you're way more lumbering and you wouldn't be standing up on
your hind legs unless you were angry. That's kind of an attack pose. This is more
activity based than – They're not attacking anything. And – So body shape. The
size of head suggests like they're older than cubs but younger than adults. More
teenager-like. And I think because there's so much color in this. That after seeing
all the darkness, darkness, darkness, this just presented to me as very playful.
The color really helps. The color's important to me. As I look at my socks {EPR}
[which are colorful] (laughs). (Hmm. [Pause as I type.] I was going to go on Steve.
[He nods.]

(Continued)

Cd #	R #	Or	Response	Clarification	R-Opt
	17		It also kinda looks like a fish with its mouth wide open that's died and you kinda end up with just the skull. But I like the skull. But I like the bears better. {EPR, SPL}	(ERR) Skull, yeah. You ever seen like a shark, like the jaw (motions jaw opening with both hands at her head), you just, sometimes you'll see a fish head and then the mouth is open (demos with hands held out) and a lot of the thin bone from the head just falls to the side (motioning falling in space). That's what that looks like to me. Open mouth of the fish (motions opening with one finger at D8 and one at D2), bit of the head bone (S between D4 and D5), and then the rest (D1s) just falling to the side. (And I'm not sure what there makes it look like an open mouth.) Oh. Here's the maw. There's the whole exterior (D4, D2). What you see here (DdS32) is just the inside into nothingness. So this here is the outer section, mouth open (demos by stretching fingers wide). So you're looking in (motions inward at DdS32). So I consider this (DdS32) just background; through the skull (makes sound effect; motions through the card), other side. (Pause while I type.) You're very serious when you do this. (Mmm. Yeah. I'm thinking through what it is you've said, what I have here, and whether or not I need to ask you another question.) I'm patient. (Okay. Thank you. And I do have another question on this one.) Okay. (So you mentioned it was a skull and I'm —) Fish. (Yeah. Fish skull. And I'm wondering what makes it look like a fish skull. Or you mentioned the jaw. And I just wanted to ask you about that.) The points at the top, the way it's shaped. (Okay.) The orientation of it being open, so like this is the fish looking at you (holds card up to me). (Yeah.) If it was a real fish. But now that it's dead all you got left is the outer section, the maw (D2 and D8), where the sides (D1s) would be falling away. So I think, too, the size. This would be like a real, um, what do you call that, life-size. Like a fish this big. (Uh hum.) Like, "Oh, that's a fish head." (Uh hum. Okay.) But just the skeleton. Whereas everything else is a completely different orientation in terms of size [meaning other percepts], that struck me just by the actual physical life-size presentation. And I think too the coloration, particularly up here (D5) and all the grays (D4) and the tinting. The shape. I can't account for why I see it, I just do (laughs). (No, I appreciate you explaining that, thank you.) [The Q about the skull and jaw was not optimal and it would have been better if I focused specifically on the phrase "head bone" to more directly target C'.]	

| 18 | < | (Pause as I type.) Can I show you an orientation so you know what I mean? (Uh hum.) (Holds card to me, <.) You know what comes to mind. Shot through the heart (motions along central line from D2 to D4 and then off card). (Uhmm.) | (ERR) Oh that, < now you have to orient it now length wise. (Yes, I meant to mention that.) It was just when I went to hand it back to you. And I went like this (motions turning the card to sideways) and it was gray on top (^) and then when I went to hand it to you (turns to <). See on the side (points to D2) it's literally heart-shaped now. It's almost like "heart on fire" and then like a like a spear or a bullet (Dd21; makes shooting sound effect ["pih-chew"] and motions trajectory) shot through the heart. So that was kind of a weird, spontaneous, didn't expect that (demonstrates turning the card to sideways as she was in process of handing it to me). (Uh hum.) (Pause.) (And what there makes it look like a heart or on fire?) See, okay, I will put it back to the orientation where I first saw that, <. Color (points to D2), starting with the pink, dark pink at the top, heart shaped, you can clearly make out the shape of the heart [outlines Dd33] and then near the bottom [even though card is sideways, talks about D2 as if it was still upright] is all the orange mixing in with the pink and a little bit of red. Just gives it a sense of flame. And the fact that it's been shot through (motions along Dd21, going from D4 to D2), so that it heated up. Like either a spear or bullet goes in, it's hot, heats it up, changes (pointing at center line in D2 [Dd99+23]). But I have to admit the Bon Jovi song comes to mind, (starts singing) "Shot through the heart and you're to blame, you give love a bad name." (Laughs.) Not a big fan, but the song came to mind. {EPR} [~1:22:30] | |
| 19 | > | > Oh my god. Different orientation (holds card for me to see). Day of the Dead. (Turns card to look at it and then toward me again.) I'm going to be careful not to ask for color again (laughs; looks at card). ('Kay.) This didn't turn out the way I thought (laughs). So we're going back to the happy bears {OMP} (turns card ^). (Okay, I'll take that from you.) Thanks. (Pause to type.) (And just a reminder. We're looking for two, maybe three on each of these.) I thought there was three | (And then in this orientation, v −) Day of the Dead. (Day of the Dead.) Instantly. And that's the reiteration of that skeleton. Like the fish head. But this is like the whole head. Very Day of the Dead to me. (And what about it makes it look like Day of the Dead?) I guess the way at the top, I see this as the skull (W), the orange turning into the pink as the eyes (Dd33), the green where across the face (D5), the white space (DdS32) for the nose, and then the jawline (D4) is in this macabre ... almost grimace slash smile. Mocking. Like a mocking expression. This is like a realistic skull presentation. (Uh hum.) And a lot of the Day of the Dead – sort of culturally, they're very colorful. So I think the color really attached to that notion as well. (Pause.) (Good. I was going to move on Steve.) (She hands card back.) Bathroom break gentlemen? (Ah −) (Steve: Absolutely.) (...if you'd like. | Pu |

(Continued)

(Continued)

Cd #	R #	Or	Response	Clarification	R-Opt
			on that one. (Well, maybe I miscounted.) (I pick up Card IX and hand it to her.) Shot through the heart, the dancing bears, and Day of the Dead. (She takes card but doesn't look at it.) Each orientation was different. (Ahh, the fish, with its mouth.) Yeah, but it was dead. It was just skull. I'm not sure if that one was . . . (laughs). (Okay.) That's four. Oh look at me not following instructions. Couldn't help it; there was a lot there. {OMP}	Sure.) I do like. And a bit of a stretch (stands up). [We all discuss the challenging nature of the task and decide to break.] [125:30]	
IX	20		(She looks at card; sighs.) (Steve: You did fine.) (Thanks Steve.) [She laughs.] A little positive reinforcement so I'm nice through the rest? (Steve: No!) Got a couple of caribou. In the woods, very cold. But safe.	[We return from break; Steve and I express appreciation for her helping us see what she's seeing and getting in her shoes. She says it's not easy, we assure her we know it's not.] (ERR) Yeah. The caribou to me, everything in the orange. This is very wildlife-ish to me, outdoors, it looks very geographical, very outside, right away. First instinct is just thinking . . . out. And out, I mean by nature out. (And what makes it look that way?) I get this orientation of like horns (Dd34) and big and powerful {IDL} (motions to D3) and . . . First impression. Caribou. Strong. (You mentioned "in the woods;" what makes it look like woods?) Overall coloration. The greens (D11) and the blues (D8) mixed together (points to center of card) looking natural to me. Like it looks very natural.	
	21		Can I section this one? (It's up to you.) 'Kay, I want to do this. And cover the pink on the bottom with my hand (she does). That literally looks like a map I'd see in an atlas {EPR} (turns card to face me with hand covering D6; turns card back to look at it). But not with the pink (removes hand).	(Then you mentioned that if you cover the bottom with your hand, that the —) The pink. (Yeah, cover the pink. Literally it looks like a map I'd see in an atlas.) When you look at an atlas and it shows, ah . . . I'm gonna use Canada specifically because of the greens. When you look at . . . each province will be ascribed a different color (motions with hand in space to designate segments). If you cover the pink, right away, the green looks to me like Quebec (holds up card and shows it). (Hmm.) The outline. Like not literally. But that's what popped into my head, "Oh, Quebec!" It's not prominent but the edging on all of that (points) is . . . turns from green to blue, so land to water.	

| 22 | v | > v ...... Bottle (points to D8), flowers (D6), and stained glass art on the outside of the bottle (D11 and D3s). ^ The orange in here is beautiful. v The color itself. No matter where you put it < ^ the orange is beautiful. (Pause while I type.) | (And then you turned it upside down. Or the other way, I should say.) Or upside right. (Or upside right.) [We both laugh.] (ERR) For me, you look at this and it's like a vase (D8); sits in behind the stem (D5) of the flowers (D6). I don't know, I'm stuck on a nature theme here {EPR} (laughs). And if you've ever seen someone blowing glass, and ... as you apply oxygen and the glass is malleable, the color changes as it expands. It goes from dark to light as it expands out. I have a girlfriend who is a glass blower so I've seen some of the things she makes where she'll start with a piece of glass that's one color and then blow something and as it's hot, she can attach it. So you can literally attach a piece of colored glass to the vase and give it a new shape. So all of this at the bottom as the base (D3s). And then the vase in the center (D8). And then more blown glass (D11) attached near the neck and the top, and then the flowers (D6) in the vase blooming out of it (motions with hand opening gesture). (You mentioned that the vase was sitting in behind. How are you seeing that?) You see how the orange and the green overlap (points to Dd28 area)? (Uh huh.) And attach onto the glass. So it's like ... (I see.) It's not hiding the glass, it's complementing it. (Got it.) [~7:35] |
| 23 | | I have a third one, but I'm not sure if that's three or four. (Uhm, I've actually got you down as having three already.) I have an important one. {OMP} May I have four on this one? (Okay.) In the back here you got an introvert (shows me card) desperate to participate. But can't. [We look each other in the eye.] v And that works in both orientations, which is interesting. ^ [We look at each other again; I reach for card.] I feel bad for that one. {EPR} (Uh hum.) [She takes off her glasses and looks at the card stack in the chair.] Oh shit we're running out. Uh oh. [Both smiling.] [I did not give a reminder about the number of responses because she clearly was cognizant of the guidelines.] | (And then you said that you have an important one. You said in the back here —) [She turns card to v.] (I think you were holding it —) Back in the original orientation (turns ^). (Yeah.) It works in either. (You said that. Yeah. I think when you were saying it initially you were holding it in that direction though.) With the caribou on top. (I believe so, yeah.) Okay. (And uh, you said in the back here you got an introvert desperate to participate, but can't.) That's a weird one and it works in both orientations. (You mentioned that. Uh hum.) I don't understand introverts. I don't know how you couldn't want to be a part of your surroundings, an active part, not a passive part. {EPR} And if you look at this, and this is hard to describe ... (Okay, hang on just a second. Sorry.) That's alright. See, this is where I get antsy (laughs hard). (Yeah.) Because it's exciting. (Ok, you said they don't want to participate in their environment.) And I mean actively participate, like being there is a sense of participation. But I mean like talking or responding, like actively participating. Like I've never really understood introverts. Like if you're in a room with people how can you not be thrilled? So can I show you what I ... (Please.) Okay. So, to me these are like flaring nostrils (Dd22). Like a |

(Continued)

(Continued)

Cd #	R #	Or	Response	Clarification	R-Opt

desperation. Like a heavy breathing in. Like "OhAhhhh." And no matter what the orientation, you notice no eyes (points in D8) but wanting to push through (points to Dd22). And there is a sense of clinging. See the green down here? (Okay, hang on just a second. Sorry. [I type.] "See the green down here …") It's like literally clinging to push through and the nostrils are flared and like desperate to be in there but can't. Like just can't. And it works whether the orientation is with, in this direction (^) and then if you turn it like this (v) you see it all as like desperate because now they're clinging from the top, but you still have the flared nostrils and you still have the … Either being kept back but a sense of wanting to push through and not being able to (makes pushing motion with both hands). Like in behind it all. And it's the lightest color. So the more dramatic, the more powerful colors are in front of it (shows card). And can't push into that. (Looks at card; pauses.) But really wants to. [Pause; review.] (Okay, I don't think I have any questions on that. Steve? [He does not.]) I do. (Yeah? What's your question?) I'm not sure if it's because of the sign I saw [reference to a "No Guns Allowed" sign outside she noticed during the break], but immediately when I saw this (^), this is like caribou, you know; head in the air, horns sticking out, like a sense of you know, pride; outside. It just seemed really comfortable and nature-like to me. I gotta tell you, now I look at, and I'm specific to the orange (D3), it's like two fat fucks. With like Klu [sic] Klux Klan hats on it. Shooting at each other. The line going up it (D5) like a border. And I'm kind of pissed off that they've screwed up my caribou (laughs). {SPL} You know and I mean like big guns a-blazing. And it's hard to shift back to caribou and not see that. So I'm a little bit choked that I actually read the sign outside now (laughs). And this (motions to D11 and D6) is like the mess they've left behind in their wake. And that's (D5) like a border in between them and they are now shooting at each other. (Okay, thanks. [Hold out hand for card.]) You're welcome. It's what I'm here for.

24

Oh wow! Look at you! This is Paris (throws open arms and head back, showing 'it's obvious')! This is fabulous. Fun. Playful. Travel. Exciting. Food. Booze. Dancing. Music. {EMS} This should be a tattoo (shows me card). With those colors. This is a blast. My dear, this is a party (shows me and laughs)! {SPL} v > And it doesn't matter where you put it or how you put it. ^ > ^ This is not a house party; this is a party party. I love this. {EPR} (Her stomach growls.) That's my stomach. (Hmm.) (We look at each other and smile.) Noisy beast. > v ^ No, this one's fabulous. Whoever made this one I like them. {EPR} (Pause as I type.) (She looks at the back of the card.) Did Hermann come up with these? (He did.) Way to go Hermann. This is my favorite. (Hands card to me; I don't take it.) (No, take your time; try to see something else.) Oh! There's ... You want more?! (Uh hum.) Don't be greedy! This is the party picture! (Uh hum.) (She looks.)

(So this it's Paris –) Paris! Party! (Party. Fun. Playful. Travel. Exciting. Booze. Dancing. Music. This should be a tattoo.) This should be a tattoo! At first! And then it got ugly. But look at that! Like don't you immediately in the background go, "Oh my god, Paris!" When you're in Paris you dance, you sing, you eat, you kiss – you hope. This is fun. {EMS} Initially. You know what, and ... that's (D10) almost mustache-y to me. You know, Parisian, like little twirl on the end (motions around her mouth, like twirling a mustache). It's colorful, it was playful. (Said to Steve: I actually don't have more on that one.) (Steve: Could I ask? How did you know it was Paris, not some other city?) Oh, my Eiffel Tower straight off in the background. (Steve: Uhmm.) That was like, soon as it was passed to me, it was like the first ... reference. And it all played well together. (And you mentioned that it's in the background?) Yeah, right off the top. The size in association to everything else. So it's like Paris. And you have music. It just looks like you have music and food and dancing and alive and "Woohoo" (laughs). Party! (Steve: I think I know, but what about the blot makes it look like the Eiffel Tower?) (She turns card to him.) Right here! (points D11) Right at the top. (Steve: That's why I said I think I know, but ...) The center, right in the center; right at the top, place of prominence. "Ba-ding" here you are (singsong). What does that make you think of? I know that's kind of funny because you got that with the mustache and then the whole thing just explodes with fun.

25

Holy. Alright (sets card against mic on table) ...... Shit you blew it for me.... 'Kay, you know in London where they have police, they refer to them as guv; governor; guv is for short. But they have those bobby hats (points to D8). Look at this. This just went from the party piece to now it's all nasty {SPL} (said quietly; sitting forward). Bad cops (D9). Detained. ... But not by other cops.

(ERR through "they're going to get killed.") Oh yeah. 'Kay. See the way the hat works here (D8). And the police in London don't carry guns, they're typically unarmed. They even have kind of a term of endearment. If you interact with the police you say, "Yes guv." You know, like short for governor; which is a term for a bobby or a policeman. Whether it's a man or a woman. It's almost used as a term of endearment. They're not vilified or treated badly in my experience in traveling in Europe. {EPR} But these guys are like, the way the body looks (D9) is like they've been captured and detained. By detained I mean like almost wrapped up, like you would – not mummify, but you know when you're in handcuffed or your hands are

(Continued)

(Continued)

Cd #	R #	Or	Response	Clarification	R-Opt

This is like by criminals (moves hand from bottom to top over areas outside of D9). And they're going to get killed. (Picks card up.) v ^ And the people who are doing it are going to get away with it (sets card against mic again). (Sighs.) Ah! (Throws up hands in exasperation.) My party picture turns into murder and mayhem. (Picks up card.) v (Set's card against mic; stares for ~20 sec; picks up card to turn ^; sits forward and stares again for ~15 sec; she turns slowly toward me; I look inquisitively.) I'm pissed at you for giving that one back to me {EPR} (hands card to me). (Hmm.) I have to go to the bathroom now. (Steve: Okay.) (Do you? Okay.) Yes. And I'm using it as an excuse to leave (laughs). I loved the last one! (She leaves.) [50:40]

cuffed behind you, you got no sense of mobility. So they're not mobile; they're clearly detained. And afraid. And hurt. And they're all, I know it looks pink, but to me it's very red now. So they've been cut. And even like the location (points to D6), like they've been emasculated. And that's outside of them (referring to D6). And what looked like fun and explosions of fun ... now look like crabs (D1) ready to beat them, armed (points to D12). So the blue and the green change from fun to very menacing. Blue as in cold. And if you look at the back of the legs (lower D9), these now look like rats (D7) that are literally biting them in the ass. And angry rats. See the squinting eyes (points to S within D7)? (Uh hum.) And they're so excited about doing this, it's like they're pissing themselves in glee (D15). That's what I mean by they're criminals; like rats, and crabs and you know, pinchers and sharp and... They're (D9) dead; if they're not dead yet, they're (D1 and D7) going to kill 'em. So the first one's the tattoo, not the second one (laughs). The fun party one. And I just get the sense that they're not bad cops, but they're bad people doing this. {SPL} Ironically it's kinda like my favorite card and my least favorite card all in the same one. {EPR} (Uh hum.) (Pause while I type and review.) (I think I'm set Steve.) (Steve: Me too.) (Thank you Madeline.)

Note: Curly brackets indicate supplemental non-R-PAS scores.

(After returning from bathroom following RP.) It's funny, I'm sitting in the bathroom going, 'Why are you mad?!' But it's like I had such a great image and then you're like, 'Nope, there's more there' (she imitates me pointing). And then of course you go, 'Ah shit. There's the sucky stuff.' 'There's always bad stuff.' (Steve: We'll talk more about that. But there's a second part of the test first before we can do it.) [I pick up and give instructions, adding that I'm going to be trying to see it from her perspective and asking questions to help me do that.] I'm going to have to point out what's patently obvious?! (Laughs.) (Uhm, perhaps.) Okay. (Laughs.) (Steve: Just so we can make sure we're seeing it like you do.) Oh. Okay. [Steve continues, explaining it's not a challenge, not indicating we can't see it, and not indicating it's a weird thing. Just want to get into your shoes. See the world from your eyes.] (As much as we can.) You lucky buggers. Here we go! (All laughing.)

(After thanking her at the end of the CP.) Is that it? (That's it. Did you want more [smiling]?) (Steve laughs.) How disturbed am I? (We all laugh.) (I think you've been very spontaneous, very open with us. In telling us how you see things. I think this leaves us with a lot of things we can helpfully talk with you about. And that would be our plan for this afternoon.) (Steve: Yeah we're going to. After lunch we'll talk more about this. Yeah.) (Steve: What was the overall experience?) Frustrating! (Hmm →) (Steve: Yeah, yeah.) (...having to wait?) Yeah. (Yeah.) (Steve: Right.) [She goes on to describe being spontaneous and having her natural train of thought interrupted and the frustration of waiting.] (Yeah, it cuts up your experience.) It does. (Yeah.) It slices it very cl- it slices it just like a pair of scissors. Stop. Start. Stop. (Steve: It gets you out of the flow.) It does. [We continue to discuss the process, the frustration, and her ability and willingness to stick with it despite the discomfort and difficulty of having to pause. Says it was the hardest part of the assessment so far. When asked, she describes how this time she felt less challenged than the last time; as if we wanted to understand what she was seeing rather than doubting her veracity. Says she felt irritated last time as opposed to frustrated this time.]

R-PAS Code Sequence

C-ID: Madeline **P-ID:** 1460 **Age:** 51 **Gender:** Female **Education:** 19

Cd	#	Or	Loc	Loc #	SR SI	Content	Sy	Vg	2	FQ	P	Determinants	Cognitive	Thematic	HR	ODL(RP)	R-Opt	Text
I	1		W		SI	Hd,Ad,Cg,NC	Sy		2	o		Ma,FMa,mp,FD	FABI	COP,AGC,MOR	GH			*
	2	>	W		SI	NC	Sy			u		ma,FD	DVI		PH	ODL		*
II	3		W		SI	Hd				o		Ma,mp,FC,C',FD		MOR	GH	ODL		*
	4		W			H,Cg,Sx	Sy		2	u		Ma,CF,C',V			GH	ODL		
	5	>	W			H,Cg	Sy		2	o		Ma			GH	ODL		
III	6		D	1,3		H,An,NC	Sy		2	u	P	Ma	DVI,FABI	COP,MAH	PH			*
	7	>	W			H,Bl,NC	Sy		2	u		Ma,ma,CF,C',Y	DVI,DRI,FAB2	COP,MAH	GH			*
IV	8		W			(H)				o	P	Ma,Y,FD		AGM,AGC,MOR	PH			*
	9	>	W		SI	H,NC	Sy			u	P	Ma,ma,C',FD	DVI,PEC	AGC	GH	ODL		*
V	10		W			A				o	P	FMa		AGC		ODL		
VI	11		W			H,A	Sy		2	u		Ma,FMa,C',FD	DRI,FABI	MOR,MAP	PH	ODL		*
	12		W			Ad				o	P	C',V	DVI,FABI	MOR,MAP				*
VII	13	>	D	1	SI	H,NC	Sy		2	u		Ma,FD	DVI,DRI,FAB2	COP,MOR,MAP	PH	ODL		*
	14		W			(H),Cg	Sy			o		Ma,C'	DRI	COP	GH	ODL		
	15	>	W			H,Sx	Sy		2	o		Ma		COP	GH			
VIII	16		W			A,NC	Sy		2	o	P	Ma,CF	DRI,FABI	COP,MAH	GH			
	17		Dd		SI	Ad,An				u		FMa,mp,FC,C',Y,FD	FABI	MOR				
IX	18	<	Dd	2,99		An,Fi,NC	Sy			u		ma,CF,Y	FABI	AGM,AGC,MOR,MAP				*
	19	>	W		SI	Hd,An				u		Ma,CF	INCI	AGM	PH		Pu	*
	20		D	2		A,NC	Sy		2	u		CF,Y						*
	21		D	2		NC				-		CF,Y						
X	22	>	W			Art,NC	Sy			u		mp,CF,Y,FD		PER				
	23		W		SI	Hd,NC	Sy			u		Ma,CF,V	DVI,DRI		PH	ODL		*
	24		W			Hd,Ay	Sy			o		Ma,CF,FD			PH	ODL	Pr	
	25		Dd	21,1,12,7,15	SI	H,A,Cg,Sx,NC	Sy		2	-	P	Ma,CF	DRI,FABI	AGM,AGC,MOR,MAP	PH			*

Chapter 4

A Contemporary Interpersonal Reassessment of Madeline G.

Aaron L. Pincus, Christopher J. Hopwood, and Sindes Dawood

This chapter presents the results of a contemporary interpersonal reassessment of Madeline G., conducted about 17 years after her initial assessment (Pincus & Gurtman, 2003). It is a reassessment in that we include the identical self- and informant-report measures used in the original assessment. It is also contemporary in that it extends beyond the original assessment, exemplifying two major advances in interpersonal assessment.

Advances in Interpersonal Assessment

Interpersonal assessment employs multiple models, measures, and methods at varying levels of specificity and combines these with theories of development, motivation, and regulation to examine the interpenetration of personality, psychopathology, and psychotherapy (Pincus, 2010, p. 467). Since Madeline's initial evaluation, several advances have evolved that enhance the assessment of interpersonal dispositions and interpersonal dynamics (Dawood, Dowgwillo, Wu, & Pincus, 2018; Pincus, Hopwood, & Wright, in press; Pincus et al., 2014; Zimmermann & Wright, 2017). In this chapter, we focus on two of these advances. One examines Madeline's self-ratings on a range of dispositions using the Multisurface Interpersonal Assessment approach (MSIA; Dawood & Pincus, 2016), and the other examines moment-to-moment behavioral exchanges between Madeline and Dr. Stephen E. Finn during the first and the final assessment meetings using Continuous Assessment of Interpersonal Dynamics (CAID; Sadler, Woody, McDonald, Lizdek, & Little, 2015).

Multisurface Interpersonal Assessment (MSIA)

Empirically derived and psychometrically sound measures are available to assess a variety of interpersonal dispositions based on the Interpersonal Circumplex (IPC) framework. Normal-range interpersonal traits can be assessed using the Interpersonal Adjectives Scales (IAS; Wiggins, 1995) or the International Personality Item Pool—IPC (IPIP-IPC; Markey & Markey, 2009). A popular clinical measure is the Inventory of Interpersonal Problems-Circumplex (IIP-C; Alden, Wiggins, & Pincus, 1990), which assesses distressing behavioral excesses and inhibitions. Additional IPC measures assess the value the respondent ascribes to certain interpersonal experiences or behaviors (Circumplex Scales of Interpersonal Values [CSIV]; Locke, 2000), the respondent's confidence in enacting specific interpersonal behaviors (Circumplex Scales of Interpersonal Efficacy [CSIE]; Locke & Sadler, 2007), and the respondent's endorsement of adaptive interpersonal behaviors (Inventory of Interpersonal Strengths [IIS]; Hatcher & Rogers, 2009). Other measures capture the way the individual responds to others. For instance, the Interpersonal Sensitivities Circumplex (ISC; Hopwood et al., 2011) assesses the behaviors of others that the respondent finds aversive, and the Impact Message Inventory-Circumplex (IMI-C; Kiesler, Schmidt, & Wagner, 1997) assesses covert reactions to others' behaviors. Each IPC measure differs in the disposition assessed via use of different item stems and targets (e.g., self versus other).

An advantage of using multiple IPC-based measures that have the same eight-scale/octant structure is that it offers a multisurface perspective on the individual's interpersonal functioning that adds to standard IPC profile interpretation for a single measure (Dawood & Pincus, 2016; Hopwood et al., 2016). This multisurface method was first suggested by Kiesler (Van Denburg, Schmidt, & Kiesler, 1992) and was employed in a limited way in Madeline's original interpersonal assessment. MSIA offers a unique approach to identifying and understanding coherence and conflict within and across different interpersonal dispositions characterizing an individual's personality. This is especially important because conflicts in multiple domains of interpersonal functioning can impact a person's psychological well-being and quality of life (e.g., Leary, 1957; Pincus & Wright, 2011). A number of case studies (Dawood & Pincus, 2016, Hopwood, Pincus, & Wright, 2019; Hopwood et al., 2016; Pincus et al., 2014; Pincus & Gurtman, 2003) show how MSIA batteries can provide a context to better understand an individual's symptoms and problems (e.g., depression, anxiety, anger, substance use, suicidal ideation) and relational difficulties beyond psychiatric diagnoses and demonstrate how MSIA results can inform case conceptualization and treatment planning. Specific guidelines for interpreting MSIA batteries are now available (Dawood & Pincus, 2016).

Continuous Assessment of Interpersonal Dynamics (CAID)

MSIA of interpersonal dispositions provides a lens on an individual's general functioning and conflict areas. However, important interpersonal dynamics are also revealed in the moment-to-moment unfolding of a social interaction. As an interaction unfolds, an observer can perceive and reliably code various entrainments and temporal patterns, which crucially link the two interactants. Computer-based CAID methods [Girard & Wright, 2017; Lizdek, Sadler, Woody, Ethier, & Malet, 2012) allow assessors to follow and rate the unfolding interaction in the same way that they experience it and to record their moment-to-moment impressions of each person's agentic and communal stance within the context of the larger interaction. CAID uses the IPC as a parsimonious framework in which dynamic changes in interpersonal behavior are represented as time series for both interactants, coordinated in time such that various patterns of entrainment that link the interpersonal behavior of the interactants can be modeled (Dermody, Thomas, Hopwood, Durbin, & Wright, 2017; Sadler, Ethier, Gunn, Duong, & Woody, 2009). Thus, the data produced from CAID are inherently dyadic with the interpersonal behavior of each person in the interaction providing an inseparable context for the interpersonal behavior of the other.

Several studies demonstrate the promising nature of CAID. In initial work (Sadler et al., 2009), observers recorded the moment-to-moment levels of agency and communion for 50 previously unacquainted mixed-sex dyads working on a collaborative task. Results revealed that many dyads developed interesting rhythmic patterns that were distinguishable from overall shifts in interpersonal behavior. CAID has since been employed to examine associations between moment-to-moment interpersonal dynamics and speed and quality of task collaboration (Markey, Lowmaster, & Eichler, 2010), intervention techniques, change processes, and alliance formation in psychotherapy (Altenstein, Krieger, & Gross Holtforth, 2013; Sadler et al., 2015; Thomas, Hopwood, Woody, Ethier, & Sadler, 2014), parallel processes in clinical supervision (Tracey, Bludworth, Glidden-Tracey, 2012); and quality and outcomes of parent-child interactions (Klahr, Thomas, Hopwood, Klump, & Burt, 2013; Nilsen, Lizdek, & Ethier, 2015). CAID was also used to examine how depression impacts conflictual marital interactions (Lizdek, Woody, Sadler, & Rehman, 2016) and how interpersonal behaviors and affects are linked within and across spouses during conflictual interactions (Ross et al., 2017). This method can help investigate a variety of questions about moment-to-moment interpersonal dynamics across assessment contexts.

Contemporary Interpersonal Reassessment of Madeline G.

We employed MSIA (self-reports on interpersonal dispositions), informant ratings on interpersonal dispositions, and CAID to assess Madeline's interpersonal dispositions and dynamics.

Measures and Procedures

MSIA Measures (Madeline's Self-Reports)

Madeline completed a battery of self-report measures including five IPC-based measures of interpersonal dispositions: IAS (traits), IIP-Short Circumplex (problems), CSIV (values), CSIE (efficacies), and ISC (sensitivities). Madeline also completed the IAS and Inventory of Interpersonal Problems-Short Circumplex (IIP-SC) during her original assessment.

Informant Ratings

A male friend also rated Madeline on the IAS and IIP-Short Circumplex. For her original assessment, Madeline's male romantic partner at that time also provided ratings of her on the IAS and IIP-SC.

CAID

The initial and follow-up meetings between Madeline and Dr. Stephen E. Finn[1] were video recorded, and Dr. Finn selected brief (~10 minutes) interactions during those meetings that he felt were clinically resonant. Those interactions were coded by three individuals who had been trained previously using CAID.[2]

Scoring Self-Reports and Informant-Ratings

First, we discuss the basic scoring and interpretation of the individual IPC measures, and then we present interpretative guidelines for MSIA.

Structural Summary Method for Circumplex Data

Each IPC-based measure used here generates eight octant scales reflecting blends of agency (dominance–submissiveness) and communion (warmth–distance). Once these scale scores are standardized based on available norms, they form an eight-point profile that can be examined using the Structural Summary Method for circumplex data (Gurtman & Balakrishnan, 1998). This method takes advantage of the geometry of the circle, decomposing an IPC octant profile into four structural parameters: elevation, angular displacement, amplitude, and prototypicality (Figure 4.1).

These parameters reduce the complexity of eight scales down to four parameters with substantive interpretations. Elevation (e) captures the average scale score for a profile; for many measures, this has a substantive interpretation (e.g., IIP-C elevation is generalized interpersonal distress; ISC elevation is generalized interpersonal sensitivity). Angular displacement (Θ) indicates the principal interpersonal theme or style of the profile, and amplitude (a) indicates the degree of differentiation or distinctiveness of the theme. Finally, an R^2 statistic (i.e., goodness of fit) provides a measure of the prototypicality of the profile relative to the predicted circular pattern (a sinusoidal curve). An R^2 value (≥ 0.70) suggests adequate prototypicality, and a value of (≥ 0.80) suggests good prototypicality. Although the elevation parameter can be interpreted regardless of profile prototypicality, amplitude and angular displacement are interpretable only when a profile is prototypical (Gurtman & Balakrishnan, 1998). Conversely, a lower R^2 value (< 0.70) indicates that a profile is complex and should instead be interpreted at the octant level. In the current case, five IPC profiles were created based on Madeline's responses to the IAS, IIP-C, CSIV, CSIE, and ISC, and two IPC profiles were created based on informant ratings of Madeline on the IAS and IIP-SC. In addition, Madeline's original assessment provided two additional self-report profiles (IAS, IIP-C) and two additional informant-rating profiles (IAS, IIP-C). Structural summaries for all 11 profiles were then computed (see Table 4.1).

Table 4.1 Circumplex Profiles and Structural Summaries for All Interpersonal Measures in the Original and Current Assessments

Year	Standardized Scale Scores								Structural Summary			
	PA (90°)	BC (135°)	DE (180°)	FG (225°)	HI (270°)	JK (315°)	LM (0°)	NO (45°)	e	R^2	Θ	a
Interpersonal Problems–Informant												
2017	1.88	0.66	0.41	−0.84	−1.55	−1.04	0.65	−0.03	0.02	0.78	94.29°	1.31
2003	3.55	4.76	2.72	−0.71	−1.32	−1.71	−1.18	3.26	1.17	0.93	115.00°	3.37
Interpersonal Traits–Informant												
2017	1.89	−0.98	2.03	0.23	−2.30	0.97	−0.79	0.40	0.18	0.17	114.26°	0.81
2003	2.00	4.00	3.70	0.20	−2.10	−3.30	−4.00	−0.20	0.04	0.97	146.00°	3.98
Interpersonal Problems–Madeline												
2017	0.36	−1.15	−1.05	−1.11	−1.55	−1.62	−1.17	−0.66	−0.99	0.60	93.03°	0.64
2003	−1.56	−1.27	−1.28	−1.53	−1.90	−1.37	−1.42	−0.02	−1.29	0.34	60.00°	0.43
Interpersonal Traits–Madeline												
2017	1.76	−0.08	−0.66	−1.76	−2.77	0.83	0.17	0.69	−0.23	0.70	60.34°	1.62
2003	3.00	1.90	−1.20	−1.70	−2.40	0.20	1.80	2.40	0.50	0.94	64.00°	2.65
Interpersonal Efficacies–Madeline												
2017	1.35	0.79	0.18	−1.45	−2.16	−0.01	0.08	0.15	−0.14	0.75	84.78°	1.31
Interpersonal Values–Madeline												
2017	−0.64	−0.36	−1.04	−2.13	−2.03	−2.36	−1.02	−0.75	−1.29	0.88	96.51°	0.95
Interpersonal Sensitivities–Madeline												
2017	−0.04	0.07	−0.77	−0.70	−0.24	0.60	0.88	−0.06	−0.03	0.70	6.65°	0.62

MSIA Guidelines

We followed the interpretative guidelines for MSIA (Dawood & Pincus, 2016) to examine the five interpersonal disposition profiles (or surfaces) generated by Madeline's current self-reports. First, we interpreted prototypical profiles ($R^2 \geq 0.70$) using the structural summary parameters. Second, we interpreted octant scores and conflicts in "complex" IPC profiles ($R^2 < 0.70$). Finally, we made cross-surface comparisons aided by graphical representation. More specifically, whereas in Step 2 the assessor is interested in identifying conflicts or discrepancies in interpersonal themes within the same surface, Step 3 involves identifying conflicts or connections in interpersonal themes across different surfaces.

CAID

CAID assessments record data points every half second for both interactants on both warmth and dominance as an interaction unfolds. The resulting data can be interpreted via examination of the warmth and dominance time series graphs and in terms of summary statistics and cross-correlations between time series. Basic summary statistics include the mean (range = –1000 to 1000), standard deviation, and coder interrater reliability for each time series. The mean indicates how warm or dominant the person was during the interaction on average, and the standard deviation indicates how much the person tended to vary from that average. Reliability indicates the degree to which observers agreed about the individual's level of warmth and dominance during the interaction. Reasons for disagreement could include coder error, low behavioral variance, and ambiguous interpersonal behavior. We computed three sets of time series cross-correlations. First, we computed the correlation between the individual's behavior and time to indicate the degree to which the person became warmer or more dominant as the interaction unfolded. Second, we computed the within-person correlation between warmth and dominance. This correlation indicates the degree to which the person's IPC structure diverges from the nomothetic expectation of orthogonality. For instance, whereas warmth and dominance are uncorrelated for people on average, it can be interesting to know when a person tends to be dominant mostly when they are also being warm or cold (e.g., Roche, Pincus, Rebar, Conroy, & Ram, 2014). Finally, the cross-correlation between individuals for warmth and dominance indicates the complementarity in their behavior. The general expectation is that as one person becomes warmer, the other will, too, whereas dominance will be correlated inversely across interactants (Sadler et al., 2009).

Results

First, we present a comparison of self-reports and informant reports of interpersonal traits and interpersonal problems from the original and current assessments and focus on similarities and differences in the results. Second, we extend the results by presenting an MSIA based on Madeline's current full battery of self-reported interpersonal dispositions. Third, we examine Madeline's moment-to-moment interpersonal dynamics in two interactions with Dr. Finn.

Madeline Then and Now

First, we compare Madeline's self-reported interpersonal traits and problems from the original assessment and the current assessment (Table 4.1, Figure 4.2).

Both the trait and problems profiles are quite similar across the two assessments, with some notable differences. Both trait profiles are prototypical, suggesting Madeline generally sees herself as warm and dominant (Θ values differ by less than four degrees). Although her current trait profile is somewhat less differentiated than the original due to less extreme ratings on warm, gregarious, and dominant traits, its essential information is quite consistent. Results from the current assessment suggest Madeline

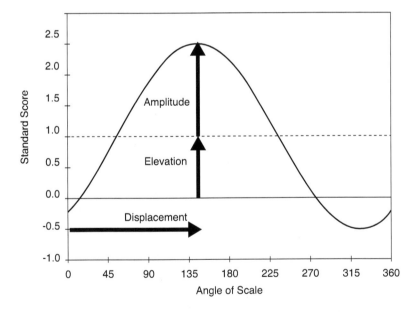

Figure 4.1 Structural Summary for Circumplex Data

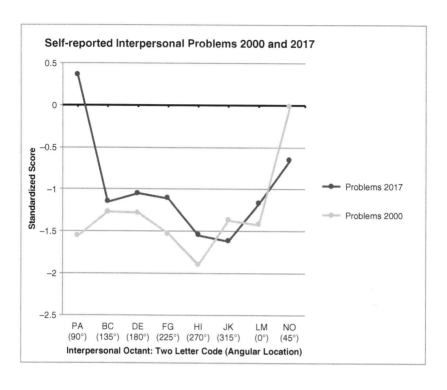

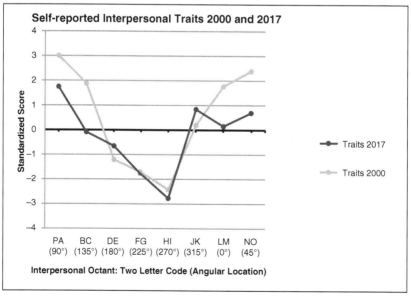

Figure 4.2 Comparisons of Madeline's self-reported interpersonal problems and traits across two assessments

continues to see herself as dominant and warm, but somewhat less warm and gregarious than during the original assessment.

Madeline's interpersonal problems profiles exhibit some similarities and a notable difference across assessments. Neither profile is prototypical, but what is most prominent for Madeline's self-report is not prominent or conflicting problems but very low-profile elevation. Consistent with her original assessment and the major information conveyed in the IIP-SC profiles, Madeline reports she is less distressed about her interpersonal behavior than the average person (*e* values about one standard deviation below the norm). The most noticeable change across assessments is that Madeline now reports distress regarding her domineering interpersonal problems, whereas she was not distressed about these behaviors at the time of her original assessment.

Next, we compare Madeline's self-reported and informant-rated interpersonal traits and problems from the current assessment (Table 4.1, Figure 4.3).

Whereas Madeline sees herself as prototypically warm and dominant in terms of traits, her informant sees Madeline as both dominant and cold (but not arrogant or vindictive) and not particularly warm. Regarding interpersonal problems, the informant's profile is prototypical for highly domineering interpersonal problems and an average level of overall distress, whereas Madeline generally denied experiencing interpersonal problems and distress. Looking back to the original assessment (Table 4.1), it is notable that although the informant differs and time has elapsed, the same general patterns of agreement (dominance) and disagreement (coldness versus warmth; interpersonal problems/distress versus denial of problems/distress) are evident. When comparing the two informant profiles, those from the original assessment have very high amplitudes compared to the more moderate amplitudes found for the current informant profiles. Also, the current informant sees Madeline as much less distressed (IIP-SC) than the original informant. It is not possible to be sure whether these differences reflect moderation in Madeline's behavior or the perspectives of very different informants (friend versus lover).

MSIA Results

We next present the MSIA based on Madeline's current self-reports on interpersonal traits, problems, efficacies, values, and sensitivities (Table 4.1, Figure 4.4).

Following MSIA guidelines (Dawood & Pincus, 2016), we first examine Madeline's structural summary profiles from her 2017 assessment and identify prototypical profiles. Four out of five profiles are prototypical ($R^2 \geq 0.70$), and one profile is a little complex, namely, problems (IIP-SC:

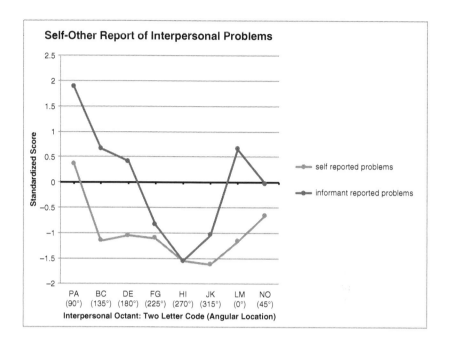

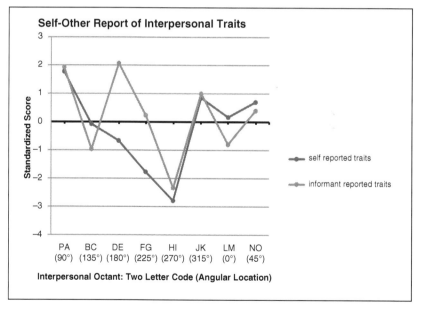

Figure 4.3 Comparisons of Madeline's self-reported and informant-rated interpersonal problems and traits from the current assessment

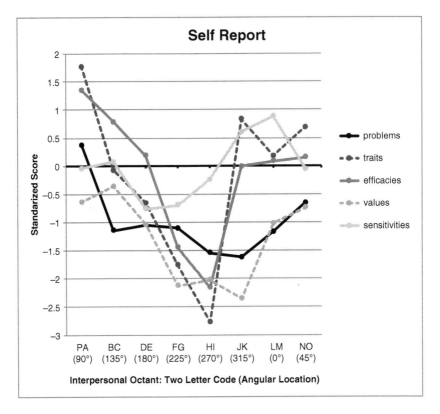

Figure 4.4 Madeline's multisurface interpersonal assessment results

$R^2 = 0.60$). Prototypical profiles are interpreted via the structural summary approach, whereas "complex" profiles ($R^2 < 0.70$) are interpreted at the octant level aided by graphical display (Figure 4.4). Although Madeline's problems profile shows a small amount of complexity, its essential information is low *e* (denial of problems/distress). As its deviation from prototypicality is minor, all five of Madeline's profiles are interpreted using the structural summary method for the MSIA.

As can be seen in Table 4.1 and Figure 4.4, Madeline's trait profile suggests that, in general, she views herself as a dominant and gregarious person. Her problems profile suggests that she can be a little too domineering and controlling with others; however, her low elevation suggests that, overall, she sees herself as having fewer problems and less distress than the average person. Madeline's efficacies profile suggests she feels distinctively confident in being dominant, but her elevation suggests she lacks interpersonal confidence more generally, particularly in her abilities to be submissive and reserved when relating to others. On the values surface, Madeline's elevation indicates she does not value interpersonal goals as much as the average person, but to the extent she does, it is most important that she be seen as self-confident and in charge when interacting with others. Madeline's sensitivities profile indicates she has an aversion to others expressing affection toward her, but generally, her elevation suggests that the behaviors of others do not bother her more than the average person.

Next, we follow the third step of the MSIA approach, examining whether there are any conflicts or connections across different surfaces on the same octant (Figure 4.4). Indeed, there appear to be conflicts with dominance (PA). Although Madeline sees herself as an assertive person and is confident, she can be dominant with others, does not value this behavior, and thinks her domineering style is her main problem when relating to others. Additionally, although she sees herself as average on trait warmth, she finds affection and dependence from others aversive and does not value warm connections and cooperation herself (JK, LM).

CAID Results

Dr. Finn began the first meeting by asking what Madeline would like to learn from the assessment. Madeline described the stresses related to being under-resourced and overburdened at work, which were compounded by the need to take care of a family member who was ill and eventually passed away. She had not worked for some time prior to the meeting and felt that it was a good time for this assessment because it could help her re-evaluate her life. Figure 4.5 depicts the warmth and dominance time series for this interaction, and Table 4.2 summarizes these data.

The time series are relatively flat and show that in general, Madeline was colder and more dominant than Dr. Finn (as indicated by means in Table 4.2). Dr. Finn listened warmly and did not vary much from that position (SD in Table 4.2). This modest variance likely contributed to the relatively low reliability for Dr. Finn's warmth. Time series correlations show that Madeline became colder and more dominant over time, which probably explains why her warmth and dominance were negatively correlated. This may relate to the content of the meeting, in that Madeline focused on expressing her dissatisfaction with certain themes in her life. In contrast, there was a modest positive correlation between Dr. Finn's warmth and dominance. This suggests that when he asserted himself more, he did so warmly. Complementarity correlations suggest relatively strong entrainment for dominance. The somewhat weaker value for warmth is likely due, again, to the relatively low variability in Dr. Finn's behavior on this dimension.

During the second coded interaction, Dr. Finn and Madeline discussed the test results. The scene begins with a lighthearted joke about the possibility that the assessment might suggest Madeline's "vulnerability," which was an apparent allusion to an earlier moment when this possibility had been raised.

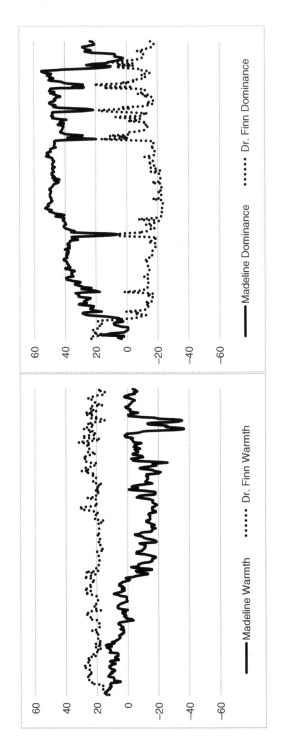

Figure 4.5 Continuous Assessment of Interpersonal Dynamics from interaction during first meeting

Note: Y-axis is scaled from −100 to 100 on this figure

Table 4.2 Continuous Assessment of Interpersonal Dynamics Summary Statistics

	Madeline		Dr. Finn	
	Warmth	Dominance	Warmth	Dominance
First Meeting				
Mean	−41	358	215	−105
SD	107	141	36	112
Reliability	.79	.87	.40	.90
Time Series Correlations				
Time	−.66	.32	.09	−.12
Structure	−.70		.20	
Complementarity	.16	−.70		
Second Meeting				
Mean	199	161	248	−42
SD	146	131	133	152
Reliability	.71	.60	.77	.74
Time Series Correlations				
Time	−.30	−.30	−.55	.19
Structure	−.32		−.19	
Complementarity	.66	−.66		

Note: Inter-rater reliability computed as consistency ICC across three coders. All time series correlations were computed after covarying linear trends. Structure indicates the correlation of warmth and dominance within person. Complementarity indicates the between-person correlations for warmth and dominance.

The spike in warmth for both Madeline and Dr. Finn reflected their shared laugh about this joke, which carried on for some time but dissipated somewhat uneasily. Madeline then described how she had learned a lot during the assessment but did not necessarily want to go "too far" at this time (e.g., into the vulnerability). Dr. Finn and Madeline agreed that she had already gone pretty far and could go even further in the future. This led to a more extended discussion of vulnerability, sprinkled with light-hearted humor but also with serious undertones. At one point, Madeline wondered aloud why she can cry at a movie but cannot cry about herself. She also referenced an earlier moment during the interaction when the subject of the "little girl" inside her comes up. She acknowledged being afraid of talking about the little girl, who could not feel vulnerable. Dr. Finn responded empathically that it would have been dangerous for that little girl to feel vulnerable. The interaction ended with a series of sarcastic comments from Madeline, such as "it's your fault this was hard," "those are just tears of laughter," and "I didn't even want to come to Austin for this—it's too cold here."

The richness of this interaction is indicated by the complexity of the time series in Figure 4.6.

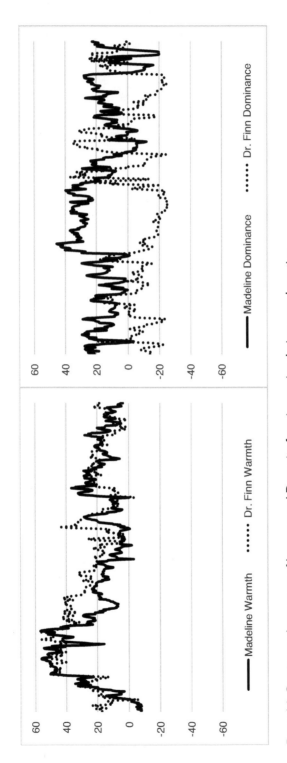

Figure 4.6 Continuous Assessment of Interpersonal Dynamics from interaction during second meeting

Note. Y-axis is scaled from −100 to 100 on this figure

Dr. Finn and Madeline are closely matched on warmth and dominance, as indicated both by their similar averages and by their complementarity correlations. Both of them become colder over time, which is primarily a function of the spike in warmth while they laughed at the initial joke. Madeline becomes somewhat more submissive during the interaction, perhaps indicating a shift from this joke to a more vulnerable position. Both Dr. Finn and Madeline have modest negative IPC structures, signifying that they are somewhat colder when they are more dominant but closer when they are more submissive. These values seem to highlight the dialectic in this scene between warm, genuine, and close vulnerability and cold, superficial, and defensive sarcasm.

Interpretation

In this section, we provide a general summary of the results, discuss their links with the original assessment, Madeline's life since then, and her presentation at the current assessment. Finally, we consider the results' implications for Madeline's four questions.

Madeline's Agency and Communion

The results of the dispositional assessment suggest that Madeline is a dominant, assertive woman who may see herself as warmer than others see her. She feels well equipped to lead, be in control, and compete with others. She generally sees herself as lacking interpersonal problems and distress but acknowledges some concern that she can be too domineering at times. Additionally, she has difficulties being submissive, cooperative, and loving or even seeing the value in doing so. These results are quite consistent with the results of her original assessment. What appears different now is a growing awareness that her dominance is not always experienced positively by others and a general trend toward less extreme self-ratings and informant ratings. New information gleaned from the current assessment suggests that although Madeline and her informant disagree on her level of warmth, Madeline is not necessarily a hostile or vindictive person. Rather, she finds others' affection and reliance aversive and does not value warm and cooperative relationships. In fact, she does not value interpersonal experiences nearly as much as the average person, suggesting she moves through life without strong interpersonal goals for her relationships. These results may relate to her traumatic developmental history (McAdams, 2003). There were no secure attachment figures in Madeline's childhood, warmth was neither given nor modeled, and she tended to fend for herself.

In Madeline's original assessment, one converging result was a sense of underlying vulnerability and unresolved trauma that she tended to avoid and defend against through a variety of means (Trobst & Wiggins, 2003). One way she did so was in her management of agency and communion in her life. Pincus and Gurtman (2003) suggested that Madeline was identified with her ideal self (or redemptive self—see McAdams, 2003), in that she tended to describe herself in ways that failed to incorporate her history of violence, criminality, and alienation, instead favoring her agentic strivings and goals after release from prison. They also suggested that Madeline expressed and satisfied communal motives through her agentic actions (e.g., championing native people's legal rights). Ultimately, they concluded that her adaptation, redemption, and reformation was "a work in progress" and "the interpersonal domain of communion may be where Madeline's most difficult future challenges will be encountered" (Pincus & Gurtman, 2003, p. 261).

These conclusions appear to still be an accurate part of the present picture. But now, Madeline is also taking on some communal challenges and is aware she can come on strong and create negative impressions. We also emphasize that it is important to contextualize our findings with the most important observation: Madeline has overcome significant disadvantage, has exhibited a sustained history of success, and continues to be successful moving forward in life. Madeline's tendency is to assert agency and pursue agentic motives (which give her a redemptive identity as a warrior for justice) while avoiding submission, closeness, and communal motives (which elicit vulnerability associated with her toxic developmental history).[3] Several examples have played out since the original assessment. First, it is notable that Madeline initially claimed to have forgotten the initial assessment, the results provided to her, and the previously published book (Wiggins, 2003). This immediately reminded us of her extremely low elevation on the CSIV, suggesting that the nature of her relationships and how others experience her (and presumably the original assessment itself) are not particularly important. Of course, this could be for self-protective reasons. Second, after the jarring ending of her long-term relationship following the original assessment, Madeline has rarely pursued a dating or intimate relationship and reported not having kissed anyone since 2007. This is a challenge of communion that she has yet to take on. Third, Madeline initially left her practice to care for her dying uncle and reconnected with some family members over that time. This a challenge of communion that she did take on and it certainly impacted her. However, agency is still what provides Madeline self-cohesion and identity. For example, although she experienced an early career setback when she was terminated from her initial position as a junior member of a large law firm, she went on to thrive in private practice. More recently, she arrived for the current assessment at a time of career and identity upheaval after closing her practice. Yet, she returned only weeks later having secured a high-paying consultant position training legal advocates for Native Americans and feeling her initial questions for the assessment were no longer relevant.

This assessment also included examining Madeline's moment-to-moment interactions with Dr. Finn using CAID. Several themes were evident in these data, which seemed to offer a representative thin slice of her personality more generally. A general finding is that while she tends to be relatively dominant, on average, she has considerable interpersonal range. This points to the value of using techniques such as CAID to get beyond cross-sectional depictions to capture Madeline's interpersonal flexibility, which may have helped her adapt to challenging situations in her past. Variability was also observed between meetings. Her mean values suggest that Madeline was relatively disengaged and dominant during the initial interaction whereas she was more engaged during the second. This pattern may reflect that her main motivations were self-protective initially but that during the course of an interaction with an empathic, understanding, and interested clinician, she became close and even vulnerable. In this regard, the second interaction was perhaps richer than the first. During that interaction, her data suggest that she was more "in tune" with Dr. Finn, and in terms of content, she vacillated between the gruff and sarcastic exterior that is typical of her and a more exposed version of herself. Overall, this brief interaction seemed to offer a kind of microcosm of her general interpersonal style: she leads by asserting her agency and denying a need for connectedness, and while she can become close and vulnerable for brief moments within an attachment relationship, she returns quickly to baseline.

Madeline's Four Questions

In this section, we discuss the four questions Madeline developed during her second visit with the assessors.

Why Am I Not so Driven Right Now? Where Has That Gone?

We think it is perhaps obvious for us but more difficult for Madeline to acknowledge that we all have our limits. Years of effort and self-sufficiency are simply exhausting. Madeline has been in "warrior mode" for a long time. A second hypothesis involves Madeline's choice to leave her practice to care for her uncle, ultimately until his death. This is a very communal interpersonal situation and to prioritize it over career is a new emergent capacity in Madeline. If Madeline can see more value in being close and connected to others and reduce her aversion to others' affection and reliance, she may have less drive toward the agentic goals that are so familiar to her. That is, she is no longer exhibiting unmitigated agency

(Ghaed & Gallo, 2006; Helgeson & Fritz, 2000) but rather a more balanced approach to managing agency and communion in life. Ten years is a long time to go without a kiss.

How Do I Get Judges I've Alienated Before to See the New Person I'm Becoming and Believe It's Authentic?

We thought this question converged with the change in Madeline's IIP-SC since the original assessment, suggesting she now has some concern over coming across in a domineering way that can negatively impact her relations with others. It also suggests she may be seeing the need to develop her interpersonal efficacy to defer and cooperate in relationships, as well as put more value in communal aspects of relationships. Of course, there is no easy way to repair soured relationships, but they can be repaired. If the "new person" Madeline is becoming is one who focuses on agency a bit less and focuses on communion and cooperation a bit more, the principle of interpersonal complementarity (Sadler, Ethier, & Woody, 2011) suggests that the natural unfolding of her judicial relationships will likely improve over time (Altenstein et al., 2013; Hopwood et al., 2016, Markey et al., 2010).

What Tools Do I Need to Effectively Remain Inspired?

We would again suggest that balancing agentic and communal goals would help Madeline remain inspired. If she could gain respite from her role as solitary warrior and receive the social and emotional support, love, and help shouldering the physical and financial burdens that close relationships provide, risk of burnout would lessen. But this would require facing her unresolved trauma, tolerating her vulnerability, and increasing her trust in others. Although Madeline exhibits an emergent capacity for communion, the obstacles to its full development are very real. Madeline reported she had recently begun counseling because of concerns about her drinking. We encourage Madeline to seek additional treatment to finally address her traumatic past and its impact on herself and her relationships. This would promote greater capacity to make close, authentic connections with others, which would in turn help to inspire her agentic efforts.

How Do I Deal With the [Inner] Chatter and the Typical Rumor Mill? How Do I Address All That?

Inner chatter can torment us if we have no way of processing it other than rumination (e.g., Johnson et al., 2016). The hurtful actions of others are generally outside of our control. However, if Madeline can learn to tolerate vulnerability and can increase her capacity to be close to others, she will have options other than rumination available to her. Additionally, rumors often fill the information gap, and this gap might be reduced if Madeline is able to share more of herself with others.

Conclusions

Madeline appears to be at a potential turning point in her life. Although she has been successful and self-sufficient (i.e., agentic) for many years, it has come with the costs of not working through her developmental trauma nor forging close bonds with others (i.e., communion). The results of this assessment suggest that while Madeline's interpersonal dispositions have remained stable, she now has emerging awareness of how she comes across to others and emerging capacity to prioritize communal motives and goals. If she can address her traumatic development and related vulnerability, decrease her aversion to the affection and reliance of others, increase her efficacy to defer and cooperate with others, and increase the value she places on closeness and connection with others, she is on the way to a more balanced and perhaps fulfilling next chapter in her life story. Consistent with the interpersonal paradigm (Bakan, 1966; Horowitz, 2004; Pincus & Ansell, 2013; Sullivan, 1953; Wiggins, 2003), we anticipate continued growth and change in Madeline's agentic and communal dispositions and dynamics in her interpersonal relations as a naturally challenging and ultimately rewarding step in her ongoing adult development. We would expect to see continued positive growth and change should we have the honor of conducting a third assessment in a decade or so.

Notes

1. Dr. Gregory J. Meyer was also in the room during these meetings.
2. We thank Evan Good and Xiaochen Luo for coding these interactions. Dr. Hopwood was the third coder.
3. Madeline also satisfies communal motives through her agentic efforts.

Chapter 5

Madeline G. and the Five-Factor Model

Thomas A. Widiger and Cristina Crego

The "multivariate" paradigm within Wiggins' (2003) original text concerned dimensional trait model descriptions of general personality structure. "Our interest here is identifying the significant dimensions along which individuals differ from one another and in capturing the structure of these differences in terms of the covariation among personality attributes" (Wiggins, 2003, p. 125). As illustrations of the multivariate paradigm, he referred to historically important and influential models and measures of personality, such as the Personality Research Form (Jackson, 1984) and the Eysenck Personality Questionnaire-Revised (Eysenck & Eysenck, 1993). However, he emphasized in particular the "lexical paradigm."

A traditional approach to identifying the basic dimensions of personality has been to review the vast body of previous theoretical, clinical, and research literature and from that derive an opinion as to the predominant personality trait domains. This has been essentially the approach taken by Jackson (1984), Millon (1994), Cloninger (2000), and many others throughout the history of personality assessment. In contrast, the lexical approach is more purely empirical. The lexical approach rests on the compelling premise that what is of most importance, interest, or meaning to persons when describing themselves and others will be naturally encoded within the language. The most important domains of personality are those with the greatest number of terms to describe and differentiate their various manifestations and nuances, and the structure of personality will be provided by the empirical relationship among these trait terms (Goldberg, 1993). The language is essentially a sedimentary deposit of the observations of personality made by all persons using and transforming that language over the thousands of years of its existence. The most useful and naturally compelling structural model of personality will then be evident from the inherent structure of the trait terms within a respective language. The lexical research of the English language, and all other languages considered, have converged well onto what has been referred to as the "Big Five," consisting of the broad domains of surgency (or extraversion), agreeableness (versus antagonism), conscientiousness, emotional instability, and intellect (or openness).

The multivariate assessment of Madeline was provided via the heavily researched and well-validated NEO Personality Inventory-Revised (NEO PI-R; Costa & McCrae, 1992). The NEO PI-R provides an assessment of the Five-Factor Model (FFM) of personality, consisting of neuroticism, extraversion (versus introversion), openness, agreeableness, and conscientiousness, which are clearly closely aligned with the Big Five (i.e., neuroticism with emotional instability, extraversion with surgency, openness with intellect, agreeableness with agreeableness, and conscientiousness with conscientiousness). Each of the five broad domains of the Big Five can, of course, be differentiated into more specific facets. For example, the facets of agreeableness (versus antagonism) identified by Costa and McCrae (1992) are trust (versus suspiciousness), straightforwardness (versus deception and manipulation), altruism (versus exploitation and self-centeredness), compliance (versus oppositionality and aggression), modesty (versus arrogance), and tendermindedness (versus callousness). The NEO PI-R provides, hands down, the predominant measure of the FFM (Samuel, 2013; Simms, Williams, & Simms, 2017; Widiger & Trull, 1997).

It is worth noting, though, that Costa and McCrae did not begin with the intention of assessing the Big Five. They began with just a three-domain model of personality (Costa & McCrae, 1980), assessed by the NEO Inventory (e.g., McCrae & Costa, 1983). Soon after the development of the NEO Inventory, Costa and McCrae became aware of the Big Five lexical model as described by Goldberg (1982). They quickly appreciated the compelling premise of the lexical paradigm and immediately extended their instrument to include the domains of agreeableness and conscientiousness, eventually publishing the NEO PI-R (Costa & McCrae, 1992).

Much of the early research with the NEO PI-R were demonstrations of how it could account for pretty much all of the meaningful individual differences within any of the alternative and competing trait models currently and historically within the literature (Costa & McCrae, 2017; McCrae & Costa, 1990), including, for instance, the measures and models of Jackson (1984), Eysenck (Eysenck & Eysenck, 1993), Millon (1994), Cloninger (2000), and many others. This was not always well received. If your research, teaching, or clinical career was devoted or closely tied to a particular theoretical model or measure of personality, you may not appreciate being absorbed into a broader trait model with which you were not particularly familiar. It was comparable to the Borg of Star Trek, a juggernaut absorbing or assimilating anyone and everyone into a common collective. Nevertheless, as was often the case with the Borg, resistance was indeed futile. The FFM has become the predominant dimensional trait model of personality structure (John, Naumann, & Soto, 2008; Widiger, 2017).

The robustness of the FFM has been compelling (O'Connor, 2002, 2005, 2017). O'Connor (2002), for example, conducted integrative factor analyses of previously published findings from approximately 75 studies involving FFM scales along with the scales of 28 commonly used self-report inventories of personality. He concluded that "the factor structures that exist in the scales of many popular inventories can be closely replicated using data derived solely from the scale associations with the FFM" (O'Connor, 2002, p. 198). O'Connor (2002) further suggested that "the basic dimensions that exist in other personality inventories can thus be considered 'well captured' by the FFM" (p. 198). The robustness of the FFM is a natural result of its lexical foundation. To the extent that the Big Five includes all of the trait terms within the language, then it would very likely include virtually all traits. There would not seem to be many, if any, traits for which persons have not yet developed words to describe them.

The FFM has also amassed a considerable body of construct validity support (Widiger, 2017), including a strong documentation of childhood antecedents (Caspi, Roberts, & Shiner, 2005; Mervielde & De Fruyt, 2002), multivariate behavior genetics with respect to its structure (Jarnecke & South, 2017), temporal stability across the life span (Roberts & DelVecchio, 2000), and cross-cultural replication (Allik & Realo, 2017). The FFM is also associated with a wide array of important life outcomes, both positive and negative, including diverse forms of psychopathology (Bagby, Uliaszek, Gralnick, & Al-Dajani, 2017), mortality, divorce, and occupational attainment (Roberts, Kuncel, Shiner, Caspi, & Goldberg, 2007) and subjective well-being, social acceptance, criminality, and interpersonal conflict (Ozer & Benet-Martinez, 2006).

Madeline in 2000

Costa and Piedmont (2003) were provided the NEO PI-R (Costa & McCrae, 1992) results completed by Madeline in 2000 and an informant version of the NEO PI-R completed by her common-law husband. The completion of both a self-report and an informant report proved to be quite informative and intriguing. Figure 5.1 provides the NEO PI-R FFM profiles of Madeline by herself and her husband.

Visual inspection alone suggests a good deal of agreement with respect to the elevations and the shape of the profile (e.g., high in openness and extraversion, and, with notable exceptions that will be discussed below, low in agreeableness). Indeed, these two FFM descriptions correlated .51, which suggests a compelling convergence across self and informant reports (Piedmont, 1998).

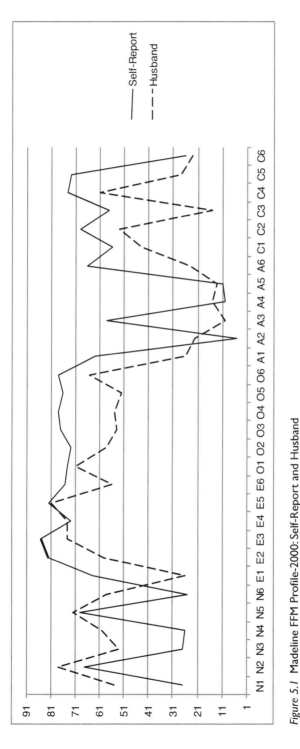

Figure 5.1 Madeline FFM Profile–2000: Self-Report and Husband

Note: N1 = Anxiousness, N2 = Angry Hostility, N3 = Depressiveness, N4 = Self-consciousness, N5 = Impulsivity, N6 = Vulnerability, E1 = Warmth, E2 = Gregariousness, E3 = Assertiveness, E4 = Activity, E5 = Excitement-Seeking, E6 = Positive Emotions, O1 = Fantasy, O2 = Aesthetics, O3 = Feelings, O4 = Actions, O5 = Ideas, O6 = Values, A1 = Trust, A2 = Straightforwardness, A3 = Altruism, A4 = Compliance, A5 = Modesty, A6 = Tendermindedness, C1 = Competence, C2 = Order, C3 = Dutifulness, C4 = Achievement, C5 = Self-Discipline, C6 = Deliberation.

However, there are some notable exceptions to this convergence. Whereas Madeline described herself as being high in trust and altruism, her husband described her as being very low (they both agreed though that she was very low in straightforwardness, compliance, and modesty). Whereas she described herself as being very low in self-consciousness and vulnerability, he described her as being high on these facets of neuroticism (they both agreed she was high in angry hostility and impulsivity). Whereas she described herself as being high in warmth, he described her as being very low. Whereas she described herself as being high to very high in competence, dutifulness, and self-discipline, he described her as being low to very low on each of these facets of conscientiousness (they agreed she was high to very high in achievement-striving and very low in deliberation).

In sum, there are striking discrepancies on 8 (out of 30) FFM facets. These fundamental differences in how each of them perceived Madeline did not bode well for a successful relationship (Piedmont & Rodgerson, 2017). As suggested by Piedmont (1998) and Piedmont and Rodgerson (2017), strong differences in how one (or both) of marital partners are perceived often reflect sources of significant marital dissatisfaction and perhaps even conflict. Madeline's common-law husband perceived her as being very low in warmth and tendermindedness, whereas she would have considered herself to be quite warm and empathic. He apparently considered her to be quite vulnerable, as well as irresponsible, undependable, and negligent. He clearly had an unfavorable view of his common-law wife, which did not bode well for the strength or future of their relationship. In addition, if her common-law husband's perceptions of Madeline were correct, particularly with respect to her low conscientiousness, then this did not bode well for Madeline's professional future. Low conscientiousness is strongly related to problematic employment (Ozer & Benet-Martinez, 2006).

At the time of the first assessments, Madeline was a very successful civil rights lawyer, newly employed within a prestigious law firm. She was living with her common-law husband, in what she felt was a strong, secure, and satisfying relationship. In sum, the future of Madeline's career and romantic relationship appeared, at least to her, to be very positive.

Included within the American Psychiatric Association's (APA) Diagnostic and Statistical Manual of Mental Disorders (DSM-5; APA, 2013) are disorders of personality. Wiggins (2003) and Costa and Piedmont (2003) referred to an understanding of these personality disorders from the perspective of the FFM in the original text but did not offer any explicit suggestions as to the presence of a personality disorder for Madeline. However, there now exists a scoring algorithm for the DSM-5 personality disorders on the basis of FFM elevations (Miller, Bagby, Pilkonis, Reynolds, & Lynam, 2005). If one is guided by her common-law husband's description, Madeline was well above threshold for narcissistic personality disorder. His FFM profile of her correlated .80 with the profile of a prototypic narcissist (Lynam & Widiger, 2001). His FFM profile of her correlated as well with the prototypic profiles for the borderline (.68) and histrionic (.61) personality disorders but well below the correlation with the narcissistic. She was elevated on scales suggesting arrogance, selfishness, manipulativeness, lack of empathy, and dominance—key narcissistic traits. Trobst and Wiggins (2003), in their peer review of Madeline, had indeed described Madeline as being "boastful and self-aggrandizing" and "a master of manipulation" (p. 314). Madeline's husband even elevated her on traits of vulnerable narcissism, including self-consciousness, angry hostility, and vulnerability (Glover, Miller, Lynam, Crego, & Widiger, 2012). As suggested by Trobst and Wiggins (2003), "Madeline is proud of who she is . . . but these tendencies also belie an underlying insecurity" (p. 314).

It is possible that Madeline's husband overstated Madeline's negative traits. However, it should also be noted that Madeline did herself acknowledge some key traits of narcissism, including arrogance, manipulativeness, and dominance. Her own self-description correlated .59 with the FFM profile of a prototypic narcissist (Lynam & Widiger, 2001), the highest for any personality disorder, albeit her self-description correlated almost as highly with the histrionic personality disorder (.53), reflecting in large part her elevation on all of the facets of extraversion (Lynam & Widiger, 2001), perhaps to the point of a histrionic exhibitionism and attention-seeking, which was quite evident in the description of her interpersonal relatedness by Trobst and Wiggins (2003). "Madeline is an extremely extraverted and exhibitionistic woman. She is audacious, brash, and brazen, and being out in public with her can be highly embarrassing for the weak of heart" (Trobst & Wiggins, 2003, p. 313). Inconsistent with her husband's description, though, she did not consider herself as having the traits of vulnerable narcissism, with low scores on self-consciousness and vulnerability (Glover et al., 2012). Her self-portrait correlated weakly with borderline personality disorder (.18) due in large part to her low scores on facets of neuroticism (as well as high scores on conscientiousness).

The negative personality traits identified by her husband and herself were perhaps prescient. At the time of the assessments, Madeline was clearly very self-confident, glowing in her occupational recognition and rising fame as a successful civil rights attorney. However, subsequent to the assessment, "Madeline and her boss apparently agreed that Madeline wasn't capable of being an employee" (Trobst & Wiggins, 2003, p. 317). Further details regarding why she wasn't capable of being an employee were not provided. In addition, approximately 1.5 years after the assessment, Madeline's husband left her, much to her surprise and substantial dismay. Madeline did not appear to have a clue as to her husband's critical view of her. She suffered a substantial depression in response to his sudden departure (Trobst & Wiggins, 2003). In sum, the traits of narcissism and rash impulsivity evident within the initial assessment, were likely to have been contributors to her loss of relationship and employment.

It must also be emphasized, however, that Madeline's personality is not well described by simply a reference to a DSM-5 (APA, 2013) personality disorder. A significant limitation of the DSM-5 personality disorder nomenclature is that very few persons who meet the diagnostic criteria for a respective personality disorder have all of the features of that disorder and many will have additional maladaptive (as well as adaptive) personality traits not included within the respective syndrome (Clark, 2007; Krueger & Eaton, 2010; Widiger & Trull, 2007). For example, many of Madeline's traits of extraversion were clearly adaptive and even admirable. Even her husband agreed that she was quite engaging, gregarious, outgoing, sociable, and active, experiencing a very stimulating and exciting life.

Equally notable are her traits of openness. Madeline considered herself to be very high on all six facets of openness, and her common-law husband considered her to be high to very high on three of them. These traits have nothing to do with a narcissistic personality disorder, yet they are also very integral in appreciating Madeline's personality. As expressed by Trobst and Wiggins (2003), "There is no question that Madeline lives life fully, and her energy and engagement in all that life has to offer can be wonderfully contagious" (p. 212).

Finally, one should also acknowledge, if not emphasize, Madeline's traits of conscientiousness. She described herself as being high to very high on five of the six facets of conscientiousness, including competence, order, discipline, dutifulness, and achievement-striving. Only the trait of achievement-striving would typically be evident within someone diagnosed with a narcissistic personality disorder (Miller et al., 2005), and they are all very inconsistent with a person who is said to be histrionic (Lynam & Widiger, 2001).

It is true that Madeline's husband agreed with her for only one trait of conscientiousness, achievement-striving, the one trait of conscientiousness evident within narcissistic persons (Glover et al., 2012). However, perhaps in this instance, Madeline's self-description is more accurate. There is no evidence that Madeline was trying to portray herself in an inaccurately positive manner. She honestly believed that she had all of the traits of conscientiousness. Indeed, she could not have become such a successful lawyer without a good deal of competence, discipline, and dutifulness, as well as achievement-striving.

On the other hand, she and her husband both agreed that she was low to very low in deliberation. She could be quite rash in her antics, actions, and exploits. As expressed by Costa and Piedmont (2003), Madeline "often speaks and acts in a hasty fashion without considering the conse-quences" (p. 268). As expressed by Trobst and Wiggins (2003), "to some [her] antics are amusing; to others, they are highly offensive" (p. 313).

Madeline in 2017

Approximately 17 years after Madeline and her common-low husband provided their FFM descriptions, Madeline again completed the NEO PI-R, and a close confidant and friend completed the informant version. These FFM profiles are provided in Figure 5.2.

It is rather remarkable how consistent her 2017 self-report is with her original 2000 self-report. There are some shifts in elevation for some scales, but the profile shape and elevations are for the most part very consistent, correlating .79. This shows considerable temporal stability in self-description over a 17-year period. Madeline continues to describe herself as being low to very low in the neuroticism facets of anxious-ness, self-consciousness, and vulnerability; continues to describe herself as being high to very high on all six facets of extraversion; high to very high on all six facets of openness; low to very low in the agreeableness facets of straightforwardness, compliance, and modesty, as well as high to very high in the facet of tendermindedness; and again high to very high on five of the facets of conscientiousness but again as low in the facet of deliberation. Pretty much everything that was said about her in regard to her 2000 self-description would again be said on the basis of her 2017 self-description. There is very little change and/or inconsistency, despite the substantial amount of time that has passed and the signifi-cant developments that have occurred in her life. She even continues to acknowledge the maladaptive traits of antagonistic oppositionality and immodesty (or arrogance). This attests well to the temporal stability of personality traits and an FFM assessment.

There were, however, a few changes that are worth noting. Whereas Madeline originally described herself as being very high in angry hostility, she now describes herself as being only average, consistent perhaps with the fact that she is no longer the hard-driving civil rights advocate and lawyer. Such a shift is also consistent with longitudinal FFM research, which suggests some decrease in facets of neuroticism as one gets older (Roberts & DelVecchio, 2000). Madeline also originally described her-self as being very low in depressiveness but now describes herself as just being average on depressiveness. This shift is inconsistent with longitu-dinal research and may reflect that she is suffering a number of setbacks and defeats, although it should also be emphasized that she is not describ-ing herself as being high in depressiveness (and she continues to describe herself as being low to very low in anxiousness, self-consciousness, and vulnerability).

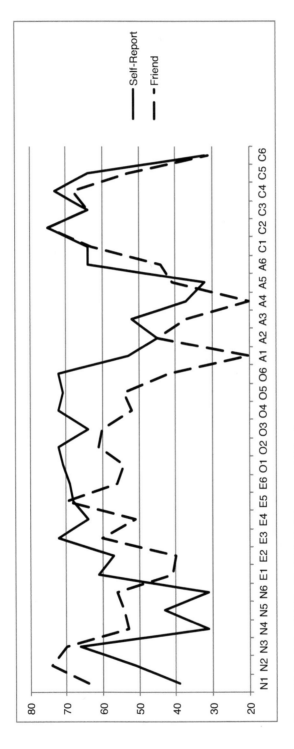

Figure 5.2 Madeline FFM Profile-2017: Self-Report and Friend

Note. N1=Anxiousness, N2=Angry Hostility, N3=Depressiveness, N4=Self-consciousness, N5=Impulsivity, N6=Vulnerability, E1=Warmth, E2=Gregariousness, E3=Assertiveness, E4=Activity, E5=Excitement-Seeking, E6=Positive Emotions, O1=Fantasy, O2=Aesthetics, O3=Feelings, O4=Actions, O5=Ideas, O6=Values, A1=Trust, A2=Straightforwardness, A3=Altruism, A4=Compliance, A5=Modesty, A6=Tendermindedness, C1=Competence, C2=Order, C3=Dutifulness, C4=Achievement, C5=Self-Discipline, C6=Deliberation.

Perhaps the biggest and most notable shift was with regard to impulsiveness. Whereas Madeline originally described herself as being very high in impulsiveness, she now describes herself as being low in impulsiveness. This is again consistent with longitudinal research to find a decrease in the negative urgency and impulsivity as one gets older, and it may indeed reflect a significant decrease in the more harmful and risky behaviors that were so predominant at the time of the original assessment. On the other hand, she does still consider herself to be very low in deliberation, suggesting a continuation of potentially rash, hasty decisions.

The only other shifts were with regard to three facets of agreeableness. Whereas in 2000 she described herself as being high in trust and altruism, in 2017 she describes herself as being just average in trust and altruism. Whereas in 2000 she described herself as being very low in straightforwardness, she now describes herself as being just low in straightforwardness. It should be noted though that the changes on some of these scales were quite minor with respect to raw scores (i.e., shifts from 27 to 24 and 27 to 25). Perhaps one should not make too much of these particular changes. Nevertheless, most persons experience somewhat of a increase in trust and altruism as they get older (Roberts & DelVecchio, 2000), and these changes for Madeline may also reflect a true decrease in feelings of altruism (e.g., no longer pursuing a career as a civil rights lawyer) and trust (e.g., no longer naïve or as confident about the strength of her relationships).

Perhaps even more noteworthy are the consistencies across time and person with respect to the informant reports. Madeline's close friend and confidant completed the informant version of the NEO PI-R, as had her common-law husband years ago. This is not just a potential change in the views of the same informant over time; this is an entirely different informant who has a different relationship with Madeline. Yet, his views are, for the most part, remarkably similar, including with respect to a number of negative personality traits. The correlation across informants and across time of the common-law husband NEO PI-R profile with the recent NEO PI-R profile by her close friend and confidant was .59. Informants do tend to have very similar perceptions of a respective target person (Oltmanns & Turkheimer, 2006), but in this case, the nature of the relationship was quite different and a considerable amount of time had passed, yet the perception was very congruent.

Madeline's common-law husband and her current friend consider her to be high to very high in the extraversion facets of assertiveness, activity, excitement-seeking, and positive emotionality. They also both consider her to be high to very high in an openness to aesthetics and fantasy, as well as achievement-striving. They also both agreed with respect to a number of maladaptive, negative traits, including being high to very high in angry hostility, self-consciousness, impulsiveness, and vulnerability;

low to very low in warmth; and low to very low in all of the facets of agreeableness. Both Madeline's past husband and current friend consider her to be mistrustful, manipulative, self-centered, brusque, oppositional, immodest, and tough-minded. On the other hand, Madeline's friend is more in agreement with her with respect to the facets of conscientiousness. Unlike her past husband, her current friend considers her to be high to very high in most of the facets of conscientiousness, including competence, organization, dutifulness, achievement-striving, and self-discipline. They both consider her to be low in deliberation, but, as noted earlier, this is also in agreement with Madeline's self-description.

It is worth noting, however, that Madeline's close friend does not perceive her nearly as narcissistic as did her husband; the correlation of his profile with the profile for a prototypic narcissist was "only" .55. This is still a convergent correlation (the correlations with histrionic was only .04), but it is not nearly as strong as it was for her prior husband (i.e., .80). Indeed, the friend perceives her as fitting almost as well the profile for a borderline personality disorder (.50).

Madeline in the Future

Madeline is currently working through another transition in her life, having recently retired from her career as a lawyer. She had taken a leave as a lawyer to help a very ill uncle, whom she had cared for deeply. Sadly, he eventually succumbed to his illness, and she no longer felt that she wanted to return to her law career, feeling exhausted by its many demands. She was feeling a little unmoored, ungrounded, and uncertain. We are, though, perhaps more sanguine about her future than she is herself.

Madeline asked, "Why am I not so driven right now? Where has that gone?" We would suggest that her drive has not gone anywhere. That has not changed. Madeline's conscientiousness score from 2000 to 2017 was remarkably consistent. Indeed, high achievement-striving was the one facet of conscientiousness that everyone, including her common-law husband in 2000 and now more recently her friend in 2017, were all in agreement. Madeline's concern about losing her drive to succeed is perhaps itself a reflection of her being so high in achievement-striving. She would not be so concerned about her future life path if she was not indeed so high in achievement-striving.

Indeed, apparently it was not too long before Madeline was able to obtain another high-paying job as a consultant for a position that she had helped design: training legal advocates for Native Americans. Madeline's very high score on achievement-striving combined with her high score on competence and self-discipline (traits recognized as well by her friend) suggests that she not only still has very high aspiration levels and works incredibly hard to achieve her goals but that she is also capable, skilled, effective, and able to begin tasks and carry them through to completion, which will likely be an asset in whatever direction she may choose. It is natural to have some doubts as to one's future success when making major changes in one's career, but her concerns are themselves an expression of her high aspiration levels. Now that Madeline has found a new career path, she is likely to again approach it with considerable diligence, discipline, competence, and conscientiousness.

What is perhaps of more concern is the continued elevations on traits of antagonism, as perceived by her husband and still to this day by her close friend. She had asked, "How do I get judges I've alienated before to see the new person I'm becoming and believe it's authentic?" This may be a tall order. Her current friend is probably very much on her side, yet he also considers her to be mistrustful, suspicious, brusque, and oppositional, as well as somewhat deceptive, self-serving, immodest, and tough-minded. She continues to consider herself to be very tenderminded, but she would agree that she is oppositional, deceptive, and immodest. Her self-description does at least suggest a decrease in her angry hostility and she is less prone to rageful bursts of temper, but her friend does still consider her to be high in angry hostility. In sum, her relationships are likely to continue to be somewhat strained and at times problematic.

An additional point of concern is that her husband and her friend both consider her to be high to very high in self-consciousness and vulnerability, traits that Madeline does not identify within herself. Self-informant agreement is typically least strong with respect to the FFM domain of neuroticism (relative to agreeableness and extraversion), but this typically reflects the fact that the target persons are generally more aware of their emotional instability than their peers (Miller, Pilkonis, & Clifton, 2005; Oltmanns & Turkheimer, 2006). In Madeline's, case, her peers perceive her as significantly more troubled and vulnerable than she perceives or is aware of herself. She is currently in some form of counseling or therapy to manage her drinking. Perhaps she will become more aware of her emotional vulnerabilities. Boding well for her is that she is now questioning and reflecting upon herself.

Madeline's FFM description though should end on her strengths. Everyone would agree that she is a very active, alluring, interesting, and lively person. She lives a very rich and engaging life. She is generally very high in positive emotionality, assertiveness, and excitement-seeking. Madeline is not a passive wallflower, drifting into the background and shadows of relationships and events. Madeline is not particularly cautious or careful, but she is otherwise highly competent, effective, and capable. She is very dutiful and disciplined and will likely always achieve whatever tasks or career she pursues.

Conclusions

A reviewer of Wiggins' (2003) original text had declared, "Madeline G. may go down in history as one of the best case studies ever published" (Strack, 2005, p. 106). We could not agree more. Madeline is a fascinating person and personality. It was particularly intriguing for this "multivariate" assessment to consider not only the stability of her FFM profile over time but to also consider the self-informant agreement over time. The congruency over a 17-year span of time was really quite striking, as well as the agreement with the informants and the agreement across the informants over time. There were, of course, some notable disagreements between the self and informant descriptions, which added to the interest and richness of this multivariate assessment.

Chapter 6

The Empirical Paradigm and Madeline G.

Yossef S. Ben-Porath

A response to a personality inventory is an interesting and significant bit of verbal behavior, the non-test correlates of which must be discovered by empirical means.

Meehl (1945, p. 297)

One cannot help noting the contrast between Hathaway's (1972) earlier pessimistic assessment of the future of the paradigm—"So, in summary, we are stuck, I think, with the MMPI . . . for a dreary while longer" (p. 40)—and Ben-Porath's (1994) optimistic challenge to those who would develop instruments intended to augment or replace the MMPI-2: . . . tests that are intended to replace the MMPI-2 are faced with the daunting challenge of matching its empirical and experiential data base, whereas instruments designed to augment the MMPI-2 must be shown to possess incremental clinical validity in the assessment of clinically relevant phenomena.

(p. 389)

These contrasting opinions were expressed by individuals representing widely separated generations within the highly "inbred" empirical paradigm. As an obvious heir apparent to a guiding role in the future development of the empirical paradigm, Ben-Porath has a gratifyingly deep appreciation of the history and significance of that remarkable endeavor.

Wiggins (2003, p. 192)

The quotes above bookend Wiggins' (2003) chapter on the "empirical paradigm" of personality assessment. The first, taken from Meehl's

Author Note. I thank Auke Tellegen and Beverly Kaemmer for their feedback on an earlier version of this chapter.

Disclosure. Yossef S. Ben-Porath is a paid consultant to the MMPI Publisher, the University of Minnesota Press, and Distributor, Pearson. As co-author of the MMPI-2-RF, he receives royalties on sales of the test. He also receives research funding from the University of Minnesota Press.

"empiricist's manifesto," is the epigraph to the chapter. It sets the stage for Wiggins' elaboration that by "empirical," he was not limiting his definition of the paradigm to measures constructed with the contrasted groups methodology used to develop the original MMPI Clinical Scales. The second quote includes the final two paragraphs of Wiggins' (2003) chapter. It conveys his optimism that the final word on the empirical paradigm had yet to be written and reflects Jerry's personal generosity toward me. At that time, I was an early career psychologist whom he had first noticed when reading my chapter (Ben-Porath, 1994) in Strack and Lorr's (1994) *Differentiating Normal and Abnormal Personality*. I did not know him well, but in our correspondence, he was invariably gracious and supportive. I was honored by his invitation to contribute to the original *Paradigms* volume and by his positive appraisals of my early contributions. Such encouragement from one of the giants of personality assessment, on whose book *Personality and Prediction: Principles of Personality Assessment* (Wiggins, 1973b) I had cut my assessment teeth, played an important role in my professional development. I never had the opportunity to thank Jerry personally and appreciate the opportunity to do so here.

This chapter is divided into two primary segments. The first updates the paradigm; the second updates the case of Madeline G. In the former, I first revisit Wiggins' description of the empirical paradigm and my interpretation of Madeline's 2000 MMPI-2; in the latter, I turn to subsequent developments of the paradigm and to Madeline's 2017 MMPI-2-RF.

The Empirical Paradigm

In this section, I summarize Wiggins' (2003) description and analysis of the MMPI and MMPI-2 (the latter was released a dozen or so years before the chapter was written) as exemplars of the empirical paradigm, followed by a review of subsequent developments.

Wiggins (2003)

Wiggins (2003) traced the MMPI's origin to Kraepelin's (1896) taxonomy of mental diseases, noting that the inventory was developed to provide differential diagnoses between categorical Kraepelinian syndromes. Although acknowledging (in reference to the DSM-IV) that Kraepelin's descriptive nosology remained "the system basically adhered to by the American Psychiatric Association (1994)" (p. 164), he noted that critics of the DSM-IV approach (e.g., Widiger & Frances, 1994) had advocated replacing this categorical nosology with a dimensional one, reflecting the proposition that psychopathology could more readily be conceptualized and assessed from an individual differences framework. Wiggins (2003) went on to observe: "The reasons why an instrument that was constructed on such shaky foundations became the most widely used inventory in the world is one of the more intriguing stories in the history of personality assessment." (p. 165).

Paradigm Shift #1: The Move Toward Correlate-Based Interpretation

Commenting on the utility of the original Clinical Scales as differential diagnostic indicators, Wiggins (2003) noted:

> [I]t soon became evident that they were subsequently rather unsuccessful in discriminating pathological groups from normal control groups (Benton, 1949). For example, Morris (1947) found that the MMPI profiles of patients diagnosed as having psychoneurosis, constitutional psychopathic state, and schizoid personality were "markedly similar" to one another and concluded that "the Minnesota Inventory cannot be regarded as a practical clinical tool the results of which can be accepted as valuable diagnostic aids to the psychiatric member of the clinical team" (p. 374).
>
> (p. 160)

Wiggins (2003) went on to note that:

> As a consequence of these findings, the original emphasis within the paradigm on properties of single scales shifted to an emphasis on the *correlates* of diagnostic patterns (Gough, 1946) and on clinical scale configurations (Meehl, 1950). In keeping with the empirical philosophy, there was also a shift of emphasis from the scale labels (e.g., Sc for Schizophrenia) to the more neutral characterization of scale numbers (e.g., "Scale 8" for Schizophrenia).
>
> (p. 170, emphasis added)

The transition from a measure to be used for the direct differential diagnosis of psychopathology to one that classifies individuals into groups on the basis of Clinical Scale score patterns and (an important change!) on the empirical correlates of the resulting "code types" (code here referring to the numeric code that replaced the original scale labels) represented the first major shift in the empirical paradigm. In leading this movement, Meehl (1950, 1956) "salvaged" the original MMPI. Commenting on this and subsequent shifts within the paradigm, Wiggins (2003) noted:

> To understand the 60+-year history of this instrument is to understand the history of objective personality assessment for the same time period. As Craik (1986) put it in his historical survey of personality research methods, "the MMPI came to serve as the centerpiece of this

period's [post-World War II] predominant or mainstream agenda" (p. 21). Within that agenda, one can discern the operation of two separate dialectical processes over time: (1) ongoing disputes *between* the developers of the MMPI and their critics, and (2) bipolar shifts in conceptualization that have occurred *within* the evolving conceptual and interpretive frameworks of the developers of the MMPI. The ongoing disputes reflect the fact that, because of its prominence, the MMPI came to be associated with such contentious issues as clinical versus statistical prediction (Meehl, 1954) and response styles (Wiggins, 1962). These shifts in conceptualization reflect the virtuosity and intellectual flexibility of members of the empirical paradigm, who were able to shift from typological categories to continuous trait dimensions; from discriminative validity of differential diagnoses to the construct validity of scales and profiles; and from denigration of self-reports to the canonization of item content (Ben-Porath, 1994).

(p. 176, emphasis in the original)

The last point, pertaining to the role of item content in MMPI scale construction and interpretation, reflects the second major shift in the empirical paradigm, marshalled by Wiggins himself.

Paradigm Shift #2: Incorporation of Item Content

The original MMPI authors rejected the use of item content in scale construction and interpretation. In his empirical manifesto, Meehl (1945) responded to criticisms of rational or content-based item selection or interpretation by noting that the MMPI relies exclusively on empirical correlates for both purposes. Wiggins (2003) noted that consideration of item content nevertheless began to seep into MMPI scale construction through introduction of Clinical Scale subscales as early as the mid-1940s. Incorporation of item content in scale construction and interpretation gained both empirical support and legitimacy with Wiggins' own development of a set of content scales for the original MMPI. When providing a rationale for this effort, Wiggins (1966) commented:

> The viewpoint that a personality test protocol represents a communication between the subject and the tester (or the institution he represents) has much to commend it, not the least of which is the likelihood that this is the frame of reference adopted by the subject himself.
>
> (p. 2)

He went on to acknowledge that:

> Obviously, the respondent has some control over what he chooses to communicate, and there are a variety of factors which may enter

to distort the message. . . . Nevertheless, recognition of such sources of noise in the system should not lead us to overlook the fact that a message is still involved.

(p. 25)

Wiggins (1966) set the standard for rigorous construction of content-based scales for the MMPI. He offered cogent arguments favoring development of such scales, citing research that had demonstrated equivalence, if not superiority, of content-based measures over empirically keyed ones and the desirability of developing psychometrically sound dimensional means of gauging the information conveyed by the test taker. He began his study by examining the internal consistency of the 26 content-based groupings of the MMPI item pool presented originally (for descriptive purposes) by Hathaway and McKinley (1940). He found some to be promising for further scale-development efforts, whereas others, for a variety of reasons, including a dearth of items, clearly were not. He then set about revising the content categories on the basis of a rational-intuitive analysis followed by additional empirical analyses that yielded a set of 15 content dimensions promising enough to warrant further analyses. Empirical analyses of the entire item pool of the MMPI eventually yielded a set of 13 internally consistent and relatively independent content scales. It is critical that Wiggins (1966) provided empirical correlate data, which served the dual purpose of both demonstrating the validity of his content scales and identifying empirical correlates that could guide their interpretation.

The significance of Wiggins' (1966) contributions to the empirical paradigm cannot be overstated. His methods served as the prototype for all subsequent efforts to develop content-based scales for the MMPI. The psychometric effectiveness of his endeavor provided much-needed empirical support for the still-fledgling content-based approach to MMPI interpretation in particular and for personality assessment generally.

Importance of Validity Scales

As just noted, Wiggins (1966) was well aware that test takers do not always respond to items veridically. Incorporation of content-based scale construction and interpretation highlighted further the need for and advantages of having a comprehensive, well-functioning set of Validity Scales for the MMPI. The original MMPI developers were cognizant of this:

One of the most important failings of almost all structured personality tests is their susceptibility to "faking" or "lying" in one way or another, as well as their even greater susceptibility to unconscious self-deception and role-playing on the part of individuals who may be consciously quite honest and sincere in their responses.

(Meehl & Hathaway, 1946, p. 525)

It is telling that Wiggins (2003) began his description of the original MMPI with the Validity Scales. Critical for any self-report-based assessment, scales that can alert the interpreter to various threats to the validity of an individual test protocol are vital to the utility of measures that rely, at least to some extent, on the accuracy of test-takers' responses. A detailed description of the evolution of MMPI Validity Scales, which is beyond the scope of this chapter, can be found in Ben-Porath (2012).

Wiggins (2003) on the MMPI-2

Commenting on the need to update the original MMPI, Wiggins (2003) observed that by the 1970s:

The MMPI developed in the 1940s was, by more contemporary standards, based on inadequate and outdated norms, replete with offensive and anachronistic items, and unsuited in many ways to the diagnostic task for which it was devised. Pressures to (1) restandardize, (2) revise, or (3) replace this relic had existed almost from its inception, culminating in a historically important summit meeting in which the third option was seriously considered (Wiggins, 1973a). Butcher's (1972) *Objective Personality Assessment: Changing Perspectives* contained invited addresses to the Fifth Annual Symposium on Recent Developments in the Use of the MMPI.

(p. 152)

In a review of Butcher's (1972) edited volume, which Wiggins (1973a) titled *Despair and Optimism in Minneapolis*, he commented:

While the introductory chapter by James Butcher provides a sketchy survey of the field of personality assessment, it hardly prepares the uninitiated for the conceptual and technical fireworks that follow. This book is a splendid collection of truly first-rate papers, geared, for the most part, to the level of the assessment specialist. It should be read by those who wish to be exposed to the new ideas and second thoughts of some of the major figures in personality assessment.

(p. 605)

Following this rather dramatic introduction of the topic, Wiggins (2003) went on to provide a more neutral description of the MMPI-2;

the exception being his discussion of the newly developed MMPI-2 Content Scales:

> The development of "official" content scales for the MMPI-2 signaled a final shift in conceptual perspective-from the original "dustbowl empiricism" to a construct-oriented perspective, to the even more substantive view of construct validity first proposed by Loevinger (1957). This extended view of construct validity has been discussed earlier in this chapter (see "Contrasting Views on the Meaning of Test Responses"). Interest in the content of patients' communication of complaints via the MMPI remained minimal until the appearance of the Wiggins (1966) MMPI content scales. In terms of Loevinger's (1957) distinctions, these content scales appeared to provide (1) representative coverage of the universe of content of the MMPI item pool (see Johnson, Null, Butcher, & Johnson, 1984); (2) psychometrically sound measures of 13 self-report dimensions that were interpreted with reference to previous studies of the factorial structure of the MMPI (Welsh, 1956); and (3) empirical evidence of convergent and discriminant validity with reference to psychiatric diagnostic categories (Wiggins, 1966; Payne & Wiggins, 1972).
>
> (p. 186)

Here, Wiggins (2003) observed that with the introduction of a formal set of Content Scales, the MMPI-2 authors (some perhaps unwittingly) embraced Loevinger's (1957) expansion on Cronbach and Meehl's (1955) definitions to include consideration of item content, internal structure, and extra-test correlates in the appraisal of construct validity. Left undiscussed was Wiggins' view of the MMPI-2 authors' decision to leave the Clinical Scales essentially intact, thus carrying over to the MMPI-2 the many challenges that were the focus of Butcher's (1972) volume.

Wiggins' (2003) Concluding Thoughts About the MMPI-2

In closing his chapter, Wiggins (2003) noted:

> Ben-Porath (1994) has provided an excellent historical summary of the "reinvention of the MMPI" following the failure of the empirical strategy and its subsequent evolution into an omnibus measure of personality within a construct-orientated perspective. The highlights of this shift over a 50-year period of unprecedented research and clinical work include emphases upon (1) MMPI profile configurations, rather than on single scales; (2) normal correlates of profile types; (3) additional empirically and substantively derived scales that have broadened the nomological network of MMPI investigation

(e.g., Morey, Waugh, & Blashfield, 1985); and (4) actuarial prediction systems based on configural profile types.

One cannot help but wonder whether Wiggins viewed the disjointed product he described as an optimal way of reinventing the MMPI.

The Empirical Paradigm Post-Wiggins (2003)

Much has transpired with the empirical paradigm during the years since Wiggins (2003) wrote his concluding comments. The MMPI-2 Restructured Clinical (RC) Scales were released the year his original *Paradigms* book was published. Unfortunately, as a result of a disabling stroke in 2002, Wiggins was unable to comment on this development and the subsequent introduction in 2008 of the MMPI-2-Restructured Form (MMPI-2-RF), which are described next.

Paradigm Shift #3a: Restructuring the Clinical Scales

Soon after the MMPI-2 was published, Auke Tellegen, a member of the committee that developed the restandardized inventory, began to explore ways to address long-recognized problems with the original MMPI Clinical Scales. Many of these challenges were identified and discussed at the previously mentioned *Fifth Annual MMPI Symposium* and in the resulting edited volume by Butcher (1972) but were left unaddressed in the 1989 revision in an effort to maintain continuity with the original MMPI code-type literature. Approximately ten years after Tellegen initiated his project, the resulting set of Restructured Clinical (RC) Scales was added to the MMPI-2. This turned out to be the first phase of a comprehensive effort to modernize the test, which ultimately generated the MMPI-2-RF. Development of the RC Scales played a critical role in this process. The procedures Tellegen designed for revising the Clinical Scales were later implemented in the construction of many of the additional measures included in the MMPI-2-RF. RC Scale development is recounted in detail by Tellegen, Ben-Porath, McNulty, Arbisi, Graham, and Kaemmer (2003), and Ben-Porath (2012). Following is a brief description of the rationale for and the methods used in this work.

A primary shortcoming of the Clinical Scales was limited discriminant validity, which resulted from excessive correlations between the scales, magnified by considerable item overlap. Discriminant validities of Clinical Scale scores were particularly problematic. This shortcoming was in part the product of how the empirical keying technique was applied. Items were assigned to each Clinical Scale primarily on the basis of discriminating the targeted patient groups from a common "normal" comparison sample. As a result of this approach, each of the eight original Clinical Scales included not only items that characterized the designated patient group but also items that reflected a generalized common (across-disorders) factor distinguishing patients from nonpatients. A second critical limitation of the Clinical Scales was the heterogeneous composition, including items both statistically and conceptually unrelated to the targeted constructs, which diminished convergent validity. Finally, a near-total absence of theory to help guide their interpretation made it almost impossible for MMPI users to rely on construct validity in their interpretation.

Tellegen's goal was to develop restructured Clinical Scales that would directly address the limitations just noted and make available measures with improved discriminant and (in some cases) convergent validities that could be linked to contemporary theories and models of personality and psychopathology. Scale construction proceeded in four steps. The first was to develop a marker of the MMPI common factor, which, as noted, was overrepresented in the Clinical Scales as a result of how the scales were constructed. Tellegen et al. (2003) labeled this factor *Demoralization* and conceptualized it within the framework of Tellegen (1985) and Watson and Tellegen's (1985) two-factor model of affect as the MMPI-2 as the equivalent of pleasant versus unpleasant or happy versus unhappy mood. Ben-Porath (2012) provides a detailed discussion of this construct as it applies to the MMPI-2-RF. The second step was to conduct a factor analysis to identify a major distinctive core component of each Clinical Scale. In Step 3, these core markers were refined further to yield a maximally distinct set of *Seed* scales. In Step 4, correlational analyses were conducted on the entire MMPI-2 item pool. An item was added to a Seed scale and included on the final Restructured Clinical Scale derived from it if: 1) that item correlated more highly with that Seed scale than it did with the others; 2) the correlation exceeded a certain specified value; and 3) it did not correlate beyond a specified level with any other Seed scale. The specific criteria varied across scales as detailed by Tellegen et al. (2003).

The result of this four-step process was a set of nine nonoverlapping scales representing Demoralization and a major distinctive core component of each of the eight original Clinical Scales. Restructured Scales were not developed for Clinical Scales 5 (Masculinity-Femininity) and 0 (Social Introversion) because the focus of the RC Scales was on assessment of psychopathology. Further development efforts, described later, identified the distinctive core components of these two scales. The final set of nine RC Scales consisted of 192 MMPI-2 items. Research reported initially by Tellegen et al. (2003), and later in the peer-reviewed literature, demonstrated that the RC Scales had successfully met their developer's goals, showing substantial improvement in discriminant and convergent (and therefore also construct) validity.

Table 6.1 includes a list of the RC Scales and a brief description of the constructs they assess.

Table 6.1 The MMPI-2-RF Scales

Validity Scales

VRIN-r *Variable Response Inconsistency*—random responding
TRIN-r *True Response Inconsistency*—fixed responding
F-r *Infrequent Responses*—responses infrequent in the general population
Fp-r *Infrequent Psychopathology Responses*—responses infrequent in psychiatric populations
Fs *Infrequent Somatic Responses*—somatic complaints infrequent in medical patient populations
FBS-r *Symptom Validity*—somatic and cognitive complaints associated at high levels with over-reporting
RBS *Response Bias Scale*—exaggerated memory complaints
L-r *Uncommon Virtues*—rarely claimed moral attributes or activities
K-r *Adjustment Validity*—avowals of good psychological adjustment associated at high levels with under-reporting

Higher-Order (H-O) Scales

EID *Emotional/Internalizing Dysfunction*—problems associated with mood and affect
THD *Thought Dysfunction*—problems associated with disordered thinking
BXD *Behavioral/Externalizing Dysfunction*—problems associated with undercontrolled behavior

Restructured Clinical (RC) Scales

RCd *Demoralization*—general unhappiness and dissatisfaction
RC1 *Somatic Complaints*—diffuse physical health complaints
RC2 *Low Positive Emotions*—lack of positive emotional responsiveness
RC3 *Cynicism*—non-self-referential beliefs expressing distrust and a generally low opinion of others
RC4 *Antisocial Behavior*—rule breaking and irresponsible behavior
RC6 *Ideas of Persecution*—self-referential beliefs that others pose a threat
RC7 *Dysfunctional Negative Emotions*—maladaptive anxiety, anger, irritability
RC8 *Aberrant Experiences*—unusual perceptions or thoughts
RC9 *Hypomanic Activation*—overactivation, aggression, impulsivity, and grandiosity

Specific Problems (SP) Scales
Somatic/Cognitive Scales

MLS *Malaise*—overall sense of physical debilitation, poor health
GIC *Gastrointestinal Complaints*—nausea, recurring upset stomach, and poor appetite
HPC *Head Pain Complaints*—head and neck pain
NUC *Neurological Complaints*—dizziness, weakness, paralysis, loss of balance, etc.
COG *Cognitive Complaints* —memory problems, difficulties concentrating

Internalizing Scales

SUI *Suicidal/Death Ideation*—direct reports of suicidal ideation and recent suicide attempts
HLP *Helplessness/Hopelessness*—belief that goals cannot be reached or problems solved
SFD *Self-Doubt*—lack of confidence, feelings of uselessness
NFC *Inefficacy*—belief that one is indecisive and inefficacious

STW *Stress/Worry*—preoccupation with disappointments, difficulty with time pressure
AXY *Anxiety*—pervasive anxiety, frights, frequent nightmares
ANP *Anger Proneness*—becoming easily angered, impatient with others
BRF *Behavior-Restricting Fears*—fears that significantly inhibit normal activities
MSF *Multiple Specific Fears*—fears of blood, fire, thunder, etc.

Externalizing Scales

JCP *Juvenile Conduct Problems*—difficulties at school and at home, stealing
SUB *Substance Abuse*—current and past misuse of alcohol and drugs
AGG *Aggression*—physically aggressive, violent behavior
ACT *Activation*—heightened excitation and energy level

Interpersonal Scales

FML *Family Problems*—conflictual family relationships
IPP *Interpersonal Passivity*—being unassertive and submissive
SAV *Social Avoidance*—avoiding or not enjoying social events
SHY *Shyness*—bashful, prone to feel inhibited and anxious around others
DSF *Disaffiliativeness*—disliking people and being around them

Interest Scales

AES *Aesthetic-Literary Interests*—literature, music, the theater
MEC *Mechanical-Physical Interests*—fixing and building things, the outdoors, sports

Personality Psychopathology Five (PSY-5) Scales

AGGR-r *Aggressiveness-Revised*—instrumental, goal-directed aggression
PSYC-r *Psychoticism-Revised*—disconnection from reality
DISC-r *Disconstraint-Revised*—undercontrolled behavior
NEGE-r *Negative Emotionality/Neuroticism-Revised*—anxiety, insecurity, worry, and fear
INTR-r *Introversion/Low Positive Emotionality*—Social disengagement and anhedonia

Ben-Porath (2012) provides a detailed review of the literature supporting their construct validity.

As a result of his illness, Wiggins, unfortunately, was unable to learn of or comment on the RC Scales. Nevertheless, it is possible to consider how he might have appraised this effort in light of his 2003 *Empirical Paradigm* chapter. Recall that Wiggins (2003) viewed his own development of the MMPI Content Scales (Wiggins, 1966) and the subsequent adoption of an "official" set of content scales for the MMPI-2 as implementing Loevinger's (1957) extended view of construct validity, which incorporated consideration of item content, structure, and external correlates. A primary difference between the two sets of content scales (one developed for the MMPI, the second for the MMPI-2) and the RC Scales is that item selection for the former was based on content, whereas development of the RC Scales (as just described) was guided by empirical analyses. Item content did, however, play an important role in conceptualizing the resulting measures and plays a standard role in test score interpretation, as illustrated later by Madeline's MMPI-2-RF. As also just reported, structural (factor) analyses and subsequent correlational analyses documenting convergent, discriminant, and, ultimately, construct validity link the RC Scales empirically to contemporary models of personality and psychopathology (Ben-Porath, 2012). Given his writings and these considerations, I believe Wiggins would have lauded the effort to finally "do something" about the Clinical Scales and would have viewed the RC Scales as a meaningful and successful step forward in the empirical paradigm.

Paradigm Shift #3b: The MMPI-2-RF

The nine RC Scales were carried over unchanged to the MMPI-2-RF and augmented by 33 substantive measures and 9 validity indicators intended to canvass the full range of constructs that can be reliably and validly assessed with the MMPI-2 item pool (Table 6.1). Ben-Porath and Tellegen (2008/2011) and Ben-Porath (2012) provide detailed descriptions of the development processes for these scales. Briefly, sets of Specific Problems and Interest Scales were developed using methods similar to those used in the construction of the RC Scales, with the aim of representing Clinical Scale components more narrowly focused than the RC Scales or not assessed by the Clinical and RC Scales. Higher-Order Scales were developed to represent three broad psychopathology domains identified in factor analyses of the RC Scales. The Personality Psychopathology Five (PSY-5) scales, which represented the first effort to introduce to the MMPI-2 measures linked to a dimensional model of personality psychopathology (Harkness & McNulty, 1994), were updated by Harkness and McNulty to provide revised measures of the five dimensions of personality disorder-related psychopathology represented by the MMPI-2 PSY-5 Scales (Harkness, Finn, McNulty, & Shields, 2012). As noted, central to the development of the MMPI-2-RF was linking the test to contemporary concepts and models of personality and psychopathology. Ben-Porath (2012) provides a detailed description of the constructs assessed by the 42 MMPI-2-RF Substantive Scales and the literature supporting the construct validity of these measures.

The MMPI-2-RF Validity Scales include seven revised versions of MMPI-2 validity indicators and two new measures. Revisions were intended primarily to eliminate item overlap, which reduced the distinctiveness of the MMPI-2 Validity Scales. The two new indicators were developed by identifying items with somatic content answered uncommonly in the keyed direction by medical patients (*Infrequent Somatic Responses*) and items correlated with scoring below established cutoffs on performance of a validity indicator in neuropsychological assessments (*Response Bias Scale*).

The 51 MMPI-2-RF Scales are listed and described briefly in Table 6.1. Ben-Porath (2012) provides detailed interpretive guidelines for the instrument. These guidelines reflect the hierarchical, three-tiered structure of the test, anchored by the Higher-Order Scales, derived by factor analyses of the RC Scales that identified three broad dimensions assessing emotional, thought, and behavioral dysfunction. Ben-Porath (2012) notes that the Higher-Order Scales can on the one hand be viewed as dimensional measures of the constructs assessed by the three most commonly occurring MMPI-2 Clinical Scale code types (the 27/72, 68/86, and 49/94 respectively), and, as noted earlier and discussed next, the MMPI-2-RF Substantive Scales can be linked conceptually and empirically to current models of personality and psychopathology.

Sellbom (2019) provides an up-to-date, comprehensive review of the literature linking the MMPI-2-RF Substantive Scales to contemporary models of personality and psychopathology. Titled *The MMPI-2-Restructured Form (MMPI-2-RF): Assessment of Personality and Psychopathology in the Twenty-First Century*, Sellbom's (2019) review focuses on two current psychopathology models, the Hierarchical Taxonomy of Psychopathology (HiTOP; Kotov et al., 2017) and the DSM-5 Alternative Model of Personality Disorders (AMPD; American Psychiatric Association, 2013). Regarding the former, Sellbom (2019) notes:

> To summarize, quantitative hierarchical research using the MMPI-2-RF scales indicates that the test's hierarchical organization conforms to the same structure as identified in the extant psychopathology epidemiology literature as represented by the HiTOP model. All six proposed spectra can be accounted for within the instrument, along with many subfactors and syndromal-level constructs as well. . . . Overall, this overlap bodes well not only for a research operationalization of HiTOP but also for clinical application and measurement, as the MMPI-2-RF allows for the translation of HiTOP research into clinical practice with a widely used instrument.
>
> (p. 159)

Regarding the Alternative Model of Personality Disorders, Sellbom (2019) observes:

> In summary, a substantial body of research supports MMPI-2-RF scales converging with the DSM-5 AMPD traits in a theoretically expected manner. To be clear, there is no one-to-one correspondence at the trait facet level; however, MMPI-2-RF scores can capture most of the relevant variance in the DSM-5 AMPD traits and can generate interpretations that reflect the presence of personality pathology from this perspective. Further research is needed with other

samples and using additional measures of AMPD traits and personality impairment (i.e., the Level of Personality Functioning Scale). It should also be noted that, at this point, the empirical evidence to support the clinical use of the MMPI-2-RF far exceeds that available for any HiTOP- or AMPD-specific operationalization.

(p. 161)

Sellbom's (2019) final point is worth further consideration. Although both the HiTOP and AMPD have received considerable attention in the research literature, their clinical utility in applied assessment has yet to be established. The availability of MMPI-2-RF-based links to these models can be mutually beneficial. Clinicians using the test can incorporate conceptual insights and empirical findings obtained through these models, and the clinical utility of doing so can serve to illustrate and support the applicability of these models in applied psychological assessments. As discussed earlier, Wiggins (2003) quoted Craik (1986) as noting that "the MMPI came to serve as the centerpiece of this period's [post-World War II] predominant or mainstream agenda" (p. 21). This quote reflected the central role played by MMPI research in the main debates pertaining to personality assessment through the 1970s. However, as Sellbom (2019) observes:

At the time of its publication, the MMPI was a trailblazer with respect to scale construction and psychometric measurement. In its early years, it was the most widely used measure of psychopathology in both basic and applied research. However, as chronicled in this review, the absence of further development and refinement of the original Clinical Scales led psychopathology and personality researchers to lose interest in the inventory, severing the mutually beneficial pipeline of clinically rich data and conceptually grounded test applications. Concerns about the Clinical Scales were left unaddressed by the MMPI-2.

(pp. 168–169)

Sellbom (2019) then goes on to note:

The development of the MMPI-2-RF in 2008 has allowed for modernization of the instrument, relinking it with contemporary psychopathology and personality research. In addition to making available scales constructed following contemporary psychometric standards, the test now measures dimensional transdiagnostic psychological constructs that are the focus of current work in this area.

(p. 169)

Conclusions

Sellbom's (2019) observations bring this historical overview of the MMPI as exemplar of the empirical paradigm full circle. Wiggins (2003) began his review of the paradigm by noting both its origins in Kraepelinian clinical syndromes and the inherent incompatibility of these categorical constructs with dimensional assessment of individual differences. He recognized that the failure of the Clinical Scales to meet their developers' objectives was likely a product of this incompatibility and observed, citing Widiger and Frances (1994), that the field of psychopathology was poised to move from a categorical medical model to a dimensional perspective. Wiggins (2003) then reviewed 60 years of developments with the MMPI and MMPI-2, which resulted in a psychometrically and conceptually disjointed instrument. Our subsequent efforts to modernize the MMPI, beginning with Tellegen's RC Scales and culminating with the MMPI-2-RF, have produced a revision consistent with Wiggins' (2003) vision of an instrument grounded firmly in the empirical paradigm but one adhering to Loevinger's (1957) extended definition of construct validity.

WWJT (What would Jerry think)? He may well have disagreed with some aspect of our efforts to modernize the MMPI or preferred that a different perspective (interpersonal?) at least be explored. However, I like to think that he would have approved wholeheartedly of the effort to finally "do something" and viewed it as a substantial advancement (but by no means the final stop) in the evolution of the empirical paradigm.

Madeline G.

In this section, I briefly revisit Madeline's earlier MMPI-2 findings and then turn to her current MMPI-2-RF protocol.

Madeline's 2000 MMPI-2

Figures 6.1 and 6.2 provide Madeline's MMPI-2 Validity, Clinical, and Content Scale scores from the first assessment.

The interested reader can find a detailed analysis of these results in my chapter in the original *Paradigms* book (Ben-Porath, 2003). As seen in Figure 6.1, Madeline produced a valid MMPI-2 protocol, with the only unusual finding being the considerably higher score on F than on Fb. The absence of involvement with the mental health system in her history, led me to conclude that her moderate elevation on F (T score = 82) indicated:

Madeline has openly reported a number of psychological problems or undesirable characteristics, and that in doing so she has probably

MMPI-2 Validity and Clinical Scales

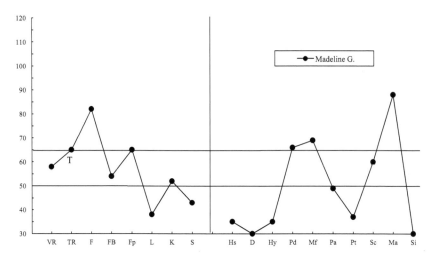

Figure 6.1 Madeline's 2000 MMPI-2 Validity and Clinical Scale Profile

Source: Madeline's 2000 MMPI-2 Validity and Clinical Scales Profile. Minnesota Multiphasic Personality Inventory-2 Profile. Copyright © by the Regents of the University of Minnesota. 1942, 1943 (renewed 1970), 1989. All rights reserved. Used by permission of the University of Minnesota Press. "MMPI®" and "Minnesota Multiphasic Personality®" are trademarks owned by the Regents of the University of Minnesota.

MMPI-2 Content Scales

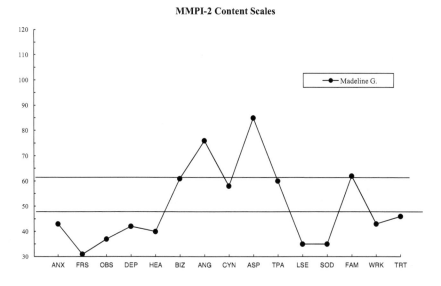

Figure 6.2 Madeline's 2000 Content Scale Profile

Source: Madeline's 2000 MMPI-2 Content Scales Profile. Minnesota Multiphasic Personality Inventory-2 Profile. Copyright © by the Regents of the University of Minnesota. 1942, 1943 (renewed 1970), 1989. All rights reserved. Used by permission of the University of Minnesota Press. "MMPI®" and "Minnesota Multiphasic Personality®" are trademarks owned by the Regents of the University of Minnesota.

embellished their extent and significance. This response pattern does not compromise the validity of the resulting test scores. It indicates that the respondent is quite willing to acknowledge problems and shortcomings, and in fact has acknowledged more of these shortcomings, but may be overly dramatic in describing some of these features. (Ben-Porath, 2003, p. 284)

When discussing Madeline's Clinical Scale findings, I observed that the most noteworthy aspect of these results was the considerable amount of scatter, with T scores ranging from 88 on Scale 9 to a 30, the lowest possible score, on Scales 2 and 0. The very high Scale 9 score was almost five standard deviations above the normative mean. In contrast, her highest Content Scale scores were on Antisocial Practices and Anger (see Figure 6.2). Following is the narrative interpretation I provided for these results:

Madeline produced a valid MMPI-2 profile. She was able to understand and respond relevantly to the test items and did so in a forthcoming manner. Her scores indicate that she openly acknowledged some psychological problems or undesirable personality characteristics, and that she may have exaggerated or embellished the significance of these features of her personality. She has little or no interest in being perceived as a person who conforms to societal norms or morals. Her scores on the substantive scales of the MMPI-2 will likely yield an accurate portrayal of Madeline's psychological functioning, though they may also reflect an attempt to amplify the significance of her self-identified negative characteristics.

Madeline feels rather positive about her current situation and denies presently experiencing any negative emotions. She likely presents as a socially outgoing, energetic, confident and poised individual. She gives the impression of having a very positive self-view. She is likely creative and enterprising and may be particularly effective at developing new projects and ideas, but less effective at seeing them through to completion. Madeline does not adhere to and may in fact reject traditional social moral values. She also rejects the stereotypically feminine gender role. She has very little tolerance for frustration or delay and may act out impulsively against perceived injustice. She may have difficulties with time management and planning. She may be preoccupied with activities designed to prevent herself from becoming bored, a situation she finds particularly aversive. Madeline is at risk for developing substance abuse problems and acknowledges past and possible current problems in this area.

Madeline reports a significant tendency toward past and present antisocial behavior. She has likely experienced difficulties with the law and does not report much remorse about these experiences. She views people as selfish, deceitful, and dishonest, and may be viewed similarly by others. She harbors anger and resentment and tends to act out impulsively when angry at others. She may occasionally resort to physical aggression in such instances. Madeline feels very alienated from members of her family and likely blames them for many of her difficulties.

In spite of her problems with anger, Madeline likely creates a favorable first impression and people may find her to be charming and engaging, although a bit domineering. She may have difficulty maintaining deeply rooted social relationships, and some may view her as being interpersonally manipulative. Madeline's outward presentation of social poise and confidence may mask long-standing doubts and fears about inadequacy. Finally, Madeline's MMPI-2 profile indicates the possibility that she is at risk for experiencing manic or hypomanic symptoms.

(Ben-Porath, 2003 pp. 293–294)

I then went on to discuss Madeline's MMPI-2 findings in the context of her life story, which was summarized in the chapter by McAdams (2003).

Madeline's MMPI-2 profile can assist in illuminating some of the issues identified in McAdams' analysis of her life story and vice versa. In light of her extraordinarily difficult childhood, Madeline's current alienation from family members is quite understandable. It may also help explain her difficulties in forming and maintaining warm interpersonal relationships. Madeline's turbulent years as a teenager and young adult likely account for the MMPI-2 findings of a significant history of antisocial behavior. Her substance abuse, beginning in childhood, is consistent with indications throughout her profile that Madeline is at significant risk for difficulties in this area. The story about brutally beating a female inmate who had harassed her is consistent with MMPI-2 indications that Madeline harbors a great deal of anger and aggression that, when triggered, may result in physically violent reactions.

McAdams' description of Madeline's current life view is consistent with MMPI-2 findings that she presents as poised, confident, self-assured, and currently free of significant emotional discomfort. However, it is possible that Madeline's self-view that she is a "spectacularly successful lawyer" who has "won 53 legal cases in a row," and her expectation that she will be "wildly successful" may reflect some of the excessive optimism and the tendency toward presenting in an unrealistically positive manner typical of individuals who produce highly elevated scores on Scale 9.

In describing Madeline's dispositional traits, McAdams notes that on the Big Five Inventory she scored very high on Extraversion,

Conscientiousness, and Openness, and moderately on Agreeableness. The MMPI-2 findings on scales 0 and 9 are consistent with Madeline's high scores on Extraversion and Openness respectively. However, the very high score on Conscientiousness is quite inconsistent with MMPI-2 findings. Not surprisingly, McAdams struggles somewhat when attempting to incorporate the high Conscientiousness score in Madeline's life story. Madeline's moderate score on the Big Five Inventory's Agreeableness scale is also contradicted by MMPI-2 findings that suggest that Madeline harbors significant anger and is likely to act out on these feelings in interpersonal contexts. Here too, there appears to be greater consistency between the MMPI-2 findings and Madeline's life story. It will be interesting to learn how Madeline scores on the NEO-PI-R version of these scales.

Finally, McAdams notes that Madeline suggests there might be a few "storm clouds" on her horizon. Will Madeline be able to fit in at her new law firm? Will the two father figures in her life live up to her expectations? Will she be able to avoid feelings of boredom and the trouble that in the past has followed such feelings? These concerns are consistent with MMPI-2 indications that Madeline's outward presentation of confidence and poise may mask some underlying insecurity. In light of her history, Madeline's concerns about these issues appear more realistic than the picture of bluster and assurance she projects. That she is aware of these issues and is able to articulate them toward the end of her interview, is an important step toward increasing the likelihood that she will be able to navigate successfully through the setbacks that she may experience.

(Ben-Porath, 2003, pp. 294–295)

Information about developments in Madeline's life after her assessment, provided by Trobst and Wiggins (2003) in the second to last chapter of the *Paradigms* book, indicated that the concerns just mentioned were justified.

Madeline's 2017 MMPI-2-RF

For her current assessment, Madeline was administered the MMPI-2-RF. This section begins with a review of the current MMPI-2-RF findings and concludes with MMPI-2-RF-based answers to the questions developed for Madeline's therapeutic assessment.

Madeline's MMPI-2-RF Interpretive Report

A full MMPI-2-RF Interpretive Report for Madeline's results is reproduced below.

Madeline's 2017 Interpretive Report

MMPI-2-RF Higher-Order (H-O) and Restructured Clinical (RC) Scales

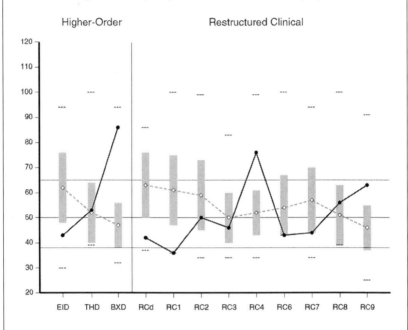

	EID	THD	BXD	RCd	RC1	RC2	RC3	RC4	RC6	RC7	RC8	RC9
Raw Score:	5	2	20	1	0	4	4	14	0	3	3	18
T Score:	43	53	86	42	36	50	46	76	43	44	56	63
Response %:	100	100	100	100	100	100	100	100	100	100	100	100

Comparison Group Data: Outpatient, Independent Practice (Women), N = 432

Mean Score (◊--◊):	62	52	47	63	61	59	50		52	54	57	51	46
Standard Dev (±1 SD):	14	12	9	13	14	14	10		9	13	13	12	9
Percent scoring at or below test taker:	10	67	100	11	6	35	41	99.3	46	19	75	97

The highest and lowest T scores possible on each scale are indicated by a "---"; MMPI-2-RF T scores are non-gendered.

EID	Emotional/Internalizing Dysfunction	RC3	Cynicism
THD	Thought Dysfunction	RC4	Antisocial Behavior
BXD	Behavioral/Externalizing Dysfunction	RC6	Ideas of Persecution
RCd	Demoralization	RC7	Dysfunctional Negative Emotions
RC1	Somatic Complaints	RC8	Aberrant Experiences
RC2	Low Positive Emotions	RC9	Hypomanic Activation

MMPI-2-RF Validity Scales

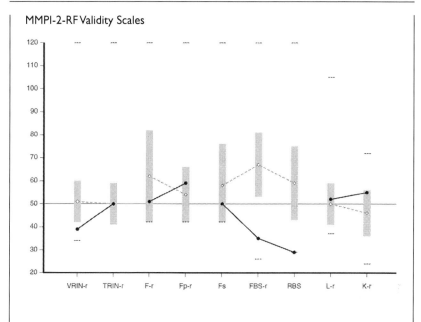

Raw Score:	1	11	2	2	1	3	0	3	9
T Score:	39	50	51	59	50	35	29	52	55
Response %:	100	100	100	100	100	100	100	100	100

Cannot Say (Raw):   0   Percent True (of items answered):   40%

Comparison Group Data: Outpatient, Independent Practice (Women), N = 432

Mean Score (◇--◇):	51	50	62	54	58	67	59	50	46
Standard Dev (±1 SD):	9	9	20	12	18	14	16	9	10
Percent scoring at or below test taker:	16	41	44	81	52	0.7	0.5	71	86

The highest and lowest T scores possible on each scale are indicated by a "---"; MMPI-2-RF T scores are non-gendered.

VRIN-r	Variable Response Inconsistency
TRIN-r	True Response Inconsistency
F-r	Infrequent Responses
Fp-r	Infrequent Psychopathology Responses
Fs	Infrequent Somatic Responses
FBS-r	Symptom Validity
RBS	Response Bias Scale
L-r	Uncommon Virtues
K-r	Adjustment Validity

MMPI-2-RF Somatic/Cognitive and Internalizing Scales

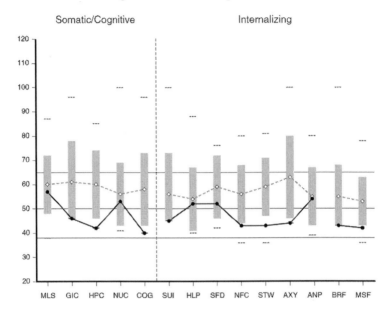

	MLS	GIC	HPC	NUC	COG	SUI	HLP	SFD	NFC	STW	AXY	ANP	BRF	MSF
Raw Score:	3	0	0	1	0	0	1	1	1	1	0	3	0	1
T Score:	57	46	42	53	40	45	52	52	43	43	44	54	43	42
Response %:	100	100	100	100	100	100	100	100	100	100	100	100	100	100

Comparison Group Data: Outpatient, Independent Practice (Women), N = 432

Mean Score (◇--◇):	60	61	60	56	58	56	54	59	56	59	63	55	55	53
Standard Dev (±1 SD):	12	17	14	13	15	17	13	13	12	12	17	12	13	10
Percent scoring at or below test taker:	52	50	24	51	21	68	63	39	20	12	33	61	42	13

The highest and lowest T scores possible on each scale are indicated by a "---"; MMPI-2-RF T scores are non-gendered.

MLS	Malaise
GIC	Gastrointestinal Complaints
HPC	Head Pain Complaints
NUC	Neurological Complaints
COG	Cognitive Complaints
SUI	Suicidal/Death Ideation
HLP	Helplessness/Hopelessness
SFD	Self-Doubt
NFC	Inefficacy
STW	Stress/Worry
AXY	Anxiety
ANP	Anger Proneness
BRF	Behavior-Restricting Fears
MSF	Multiple Specific Fears

MMPI-2-RF Externalizing, Interpersonal, and Interest Scales

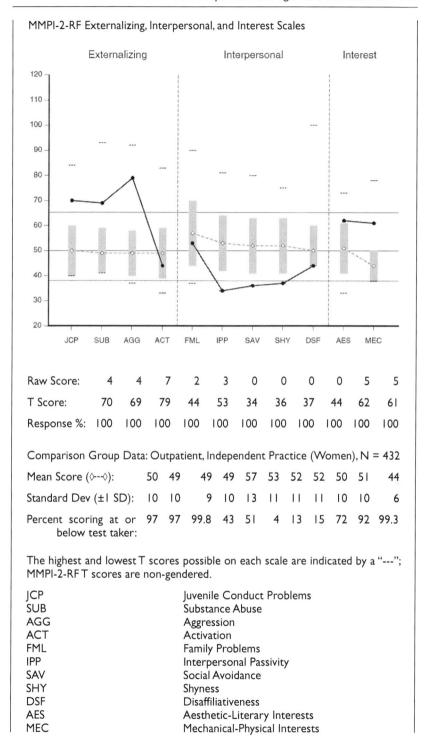

Raw Score:	4	4	7	2	3	0	0	0	0	5	5
T Score:	70	69	79	44	53	34	36	37	44	62	61
Response %:	100	100	100	100	100	100	100	100	100	100	100

Comparison Group Data: Outpatient, Independent Practice (Women), N = 432

Mean Score (◊--◊):	50	49		49	49	57	53	52	52	50	51	44
Standard Dev (±1 SD):	10	10		9	10	13	11	11	11	10	10	6
Percent scoring at or below test taker:	97	97		99.8	43	51	4	13	15	72	92	99.3

The highest and lowest T scores possible on each scale are indicated by a "---"; MMPI-2-RF T scores are non-gendered.

JCP	Juvenile Conduct Problems
SUB	Substance Abuse
AGG	Aggression
ACT	Activation
FML	Family Problems
IPP	Interpersonal Passivity
SAV	Social Avoidance
SHY	Shyness
DSF	Disaffiliativeness
AES	Aesthetic-Literary Interests
MEC	Mechanical-Physical Interests

MMPI-2-RF PSY-5 Scales

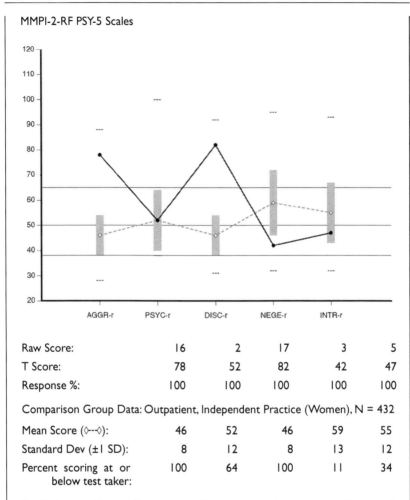

	AGGR-r	PSYC-r	DISC-r	NEGE-r	INTR-r
Raw Score:	16	2	17	3	5
T Score:	78	52	82	42	47
Response %:	100	100	100	100	100

Comparison Group Data: Outpatient, Independent Practice (Women), N = 432

Mean Score (◇--◇):	46	52	46	59	55
Standard Dev (±1 SD):	8	12	8	13	12
Percent scoring at or below test taker:	100	64	100	11	34

The highest and lowest T scores possible on each scale are indicated by a "---"; MMPI-2-RF T scores are non-gendered.

AGGR-r	Aggressiveness-Revised
PSYC-r	Psychoticism-Revised
DISC-r	Disconstraint-Revised
NEGE-r	Negative Emotionality/Neuroticism-Revised
INTR-r	Introversion/Low Positive Emotionality-Revised

MMPI-2-RF T SCORES (BY DOMAIN)

PROTOCOL VALIDITY

Content
Non-Responsiveness

0	39	50
CNS	VRIN-r	TRIN-r

Over-Reporting

51	59		50	35	29
F-r	Fp-r		Fs	FBS-r	RBS

Under-Reporting		52	55				
		L-r	K-r				

SUBSTANTIVE SCALES

Somatic/Cognitive Dysfunction		36	57	46	42	53	40
		RC1	MLS	GIC	HPC	NUC	COG

Emotional Dysfunction	43	42	45	52	52	43	
	EID	RCd	SUI	HLP	SFD	NFC	
		50	47				
		RC2	INTR-r				
		44	43	44	54	43	42	42
		RC7	STW	AXY	ANP	BRF	MSF	NEGE-r

Thought Dysfunction	53	43	
	THD	RC6	
		56	
		RC8	
		52	
		PSYC-r	

Behavioral Dysfunction	86	76	70	69		
	BXD	RC4	JCP	SUB		
		63	79	44	78	82
		RC9	AGG	ACT	AGGR-r	DISC-r

Interpersonal Functioning		53	46	34	36	37	44
		FML	RC3	IPP	SAV	SHY	DSF

Interests		62	61
		AES	MEC

Note: This information is provided to facilitate interpretation following the recommended structure for MMPI-2-RF interpretation in Chapter 5 of the MMPI-2-RF *Manual for Administration, Scoring, and Interpretation*, which provides details in the text and an outline in Table 5-1.

This interpretive report is intended for use by a professional qualified to interpret the MMPI-2-RF. The information it contains should be considered in the context of the test taker's background, the circumstances of the assessment, and other available information.

SYNOPSIS

This is a valid MMPI-2-RF protocol. Scores on the substantive scales indicate behavioral and interpersonal dysfunction. Behavioral-externalizing problems include antisocial behavior, juvenile conduct problems, substance abuse, and aggression. Interpersonal difficulties relate to over-assertiveness.

PROTOCOL VALIDITY

This is a valid MMPI-2-RF protocol. There are no problems with unscorable items. The test taker responded to the items relevantly on the basis of their content, and there are no indications of over- or under-reporting.

SUBSTANTIVE SCALE INTERPRETATION

Clinical symptoms, personality characteristics, and behavioral tendencies of the test taker are described in this section and organized according to an empirically guided framework. Statements containing the word "reports" are based on the item content of MMPI-2-RF scales, whereas statements that include the word "likely" are based on empirical correlates of scale scores. Specific sources for each statement can be accessed with the annotation features of this report.

Somatic/Cognitive Dysfunction

There are no indications of somatic or cognitive dysfunction in this protocol.

Emotional Dysfunction

There are no indications of emotional-internalizing dysfunction in this protocol.

Thought Dysfunction

There are no indications of disordered thinking in this protocol.

Behavioral Dysfunction

The test taker's responses indicate considerable externalizing, acting-out behavior that is very likely to result in marked dysfunction and to have gotten her into difficulties[1]. More specifically, she reports a significant history of antisocial behavior[2] and is likely to have poor impulse control[3], to have been involved with the criminal justice system[4], and to have difficulties with individuals in positions of authority[5]. She is also likely to act out when bored[7] and to have antisocial characteristics[8]. She also reports a history of problematic behavior at school[9]. She is likely to have a history of juvenile delinquency and criminal and antisocial behavior[10] and to experience conflictual interpersonal relationships[11]. In addition, she reports significant past and current substance abuse[12], and is indeed likely to have a history of problematic use of alcohol or drugs[13], to be sensation-seeking[14], and to have had legal problems as a result of substance abuse[15].

She reports engaging in physically aggressive, violent behavior and losing control[16], and is indeed likely to have a history of violent behavior toward others[17].

Interpersonal Functioning Scales

The test taker describes herself as having strong opinions, as standing up for herself, as assertive and direct, and able to lead others[18]. She is likely to believe she has leadership capabilities, but to be viewed by others as domineering, self-centered, and possibly grandiose[19]. She also reports enjoying social situations and events[20], and is likely to be perceived as outgoing and gregarious[21]. In addition, she reports little or no social anxiety[22].

Interest Scales

The test taker reports an average number of interests in activities or occupations of an aesthetic or literary nature (e.g., writing, music, the theater)[23]. She also reports an average number of interests in activities or occupations of a mechanical or physical nature (e.g., fixing and building things, the outdoors, sports)[24].

DIAGNOSTIC CONSIDERATIONS

This section provides recommendations for psychodiagnostic assessment based on the test taker's MMPI-2-RF results. It is recommended that she be evaluated for the following:

Behavioral-Externalizing Disorders

- Antisocial personality disorder, substance use disorders, and other externalizing disorders[25]
- Disorders associated with interpersonally aggressive behavior such as intermittent explosive disorder[26]

TREATMENT CONSIDERATIONS

This section provides inferential treatment-related recommendations based on the test taker's MMPI-2-RF scores.

Psychotherapy Process Issues

- Unlikely to be internally motivated for treatment[27].
- Acting-out tendencies can result in treatment non-compliance and interfere with the development of a therapeutic relationship[28].

Possible Targets for Treatment

- Inadequate self-control[29]
- Reduction or cessation of substance abuse[30]
- Reduction in interpersonally aggressive behavior[26]

ITEM-LEVEL INFORMATION

Unscorable Responses

The test taker produced scorable responses to all the MMPI-2-RF items.

Critical Responses

Seven MMPI-2-RF scales—Suicidal/Death Ideation (SUI), Helplessness/Hopelessness (HLP), Anxiety (AXY), Ideas of Persecution (RC6), Aberrant Experiences (RC8), Substance Abuse (SUB), and Aggression (AGG)—have been designated by the test authors as having critical item content that may require immediate attention and follow-up. Items answered by the individual in the keyed direction (True or False) on a critical scale are listed below if her T score on that scale is 65 or higher. The percentage of the MMPI-2-RF normative sample (NS) and of the Outpatient, Independent Practice (Women) comparison group (CG) that answered each item in the keyed direction are provided in parentheses following the item content.

Substance Abuse (SUB, T Score = 69)

49. REDACTED (True: NS 29.6%, NS (33.5%)
141. REDACTED (True; NS 34.2%, CG 28.7%)
192. REDACTED (True; NS 11.2%, CG 8.6%)
237. REDACTED (False; NS 27.4%, CG 28.2%)

Aggression (AGG, T Score = 79)

23. REDACTED (True; NS 39.0%, CG 45.8%)
84. REDACTED (True; NS 12.1%, CG 8.3%)

231. REDACTED (True; NS 6.3%, CG 2.5%)
312. REDACTED (True; NS 5.5%, CG 4.9)
316. REDACTED (True; NS 45.1%, CG 32.2%)
329. REDACTED (True; NS 12.7%, CG 8.1%)
337. REDACTED (True; NS 50.2%, CG 63.7%)

ENDNOTES

This section lists for each statement in the report the MMPI-2-RF score(s) that triggered it. In addition, each statement is identified as a Test Response, if based on item content, a Correlate, if based on empirical correlates, or an Inference, if based on the report authors' judgment. (This information can also be accessed on-screen by placing the cursor on a given statement.) For correlate-based statements, research references (Ref. No.) are provided, keyed to the consecutively numbered reference list following the endnotes.

[1] Correlate: BXD=86, Ref. 17, 36
[2] Test Response: RC4=76
[3] Correlate: RC4=76, Ref. 11, 12, 13, 22, 23, 24, 25, 27, 32, 36, 40; DISC-r=82, Ref. 36
[4] Correlate: RC4=76, Ref. 4, 14, 25, 29, 36
[5] Correlate: RC4=76, Ref. 36; JCP=70, Ref. 36
[6] Correlate: RC4=76, Ref. 36
[7] Correlate: RC4=76, Ref. 10, 36
[8] Correlate: RC4=76, Ref. 1, 2, 8, 9, 10, 14, 15, 16, 19, 22, 26, 27, 28, 29, 30, 31, 32, 33, 36, 37, 39
[9] Test Response: JCP=70
[10] Correlate: RC4=76, Ref. 6, 25, 29, 36; JCP=70, Ref. 36
[11] Correlate: RC4=76, Ref. 1, 36; JCP=70, Ref. 36
[12] Test Response: SUB=69
[13] Correlate: RC4=76, Ref. 4, 6, 7, 9, 11, 13, 14, 15, 25, 26, 29, 32, 34, 35, 36, 39, 40; SUB=69, Ref. 7, 9, 34, 36
[14] Correlate: SUB=69, Ref. 36; DISC-r=82, Ref. 36
[15] Correlate: SUB=69, Ref. 36
[16] Test Response: AGG=79
[17] Correlate: AGG=79, Ref. 36
[18] Test Response: IPP=34
[19] Correlate: IPP=34, Ref. 5, 16, 36; AGGR-r=78, Ref. 36
[20] Test Response: SAV=36
[21] Correlate: SAV=36, Ref. 5, 10, 36
[22] Test Response: SHY=37
[23] Test Response: AES=62
[24] Test Response: MEC=61
[25] Correlate: BXD=86, Ref. 36; RC4=76, Ref. 2, 15, 27, 32, 36, 38, 39; JCP=70, Ref. 38; SUB=69, Ref. 38
[26] Inference: AGG=79
[27] Inference: BXD=86
[28] Correlate: RC4=76, Ref. 3, 18, 20, 21
[29] Inference: BXD=86; RC4=76; DISC-r=82
[30] Inference: SUB=69

RESEARCH REFERENCE LIST

1. Anderson, J. L., Sellbom, M., Ayearst, L., Quilty, L. C., Chmielewski, M., & Bagby, R. M. (2015). Associations between DSM-5 Section III personality traits and the Minnesota Multiphasic Personality Inventory 2-Restructured Form (MMPI-2-RF) scales in a psychiatric patient sample. *Psychological Assessment, 27,* 801–815. doi: 10.1037/pas0000096

2. Anderson, J. L., Sellbom, M., Pymont, C., Smid, W., De Saeger, H. & Kamphuis, J. H. (2015). Measurement of DSM-5 Section II personality disorder constructs using the MMPI-2-RF in clinical and forensic samples. *Psychological Assessment, 27,* 786–800. doi: 10.1037/pas0000103

3. Anestis, J. C., Gottfried, E. D., & Joiner, T. E. (2015). The utility of MMPI-2-RF substantive scales in prediction of negative treatment outcomes in a community mental health center. *Assessment, 22,* 23–35. doi: 10.1177/1073191114536771

4. Arbisi, P. A., Sellbom, M., & Ben-Porath, Y. S. (2008). Empirical correlates of the MMPI-2 Restructured Clinical (RC) Scales in psychiatric inpatients. *Journal of Personality Assessment, 90,* 122–128. doi: 10.1080/00223890701845146

5. Ayearst, L. E., Sellbom, M., Trobst, K. K., & Bagby, R. M. (2013). Evaluating the interpersonal content of the MMPI-2-RF Interpersonal Scales. *Journal of Personality Assessment, 95,* 187–196. doi: 10.1080/00223891.2012.730085

6. Binford, A., & Liljequist, L. (2008). Behavioral correlates of selected MMPI-2 Clinical, Content, and Restructured Clinical scales. *Journal of Personality Assessment, 90,* 608–614. doi: 10.1080/0022389080 2388657

7. Block, A. R., Ben-Porath, Y. S., & Marek, R. J. (2013). Psychological risk factors for poor outcome of spine surgery and spinal cord stimulator implant: A review of the literature and their assessment with the MMPI-2-RF. *The Clinical Neuropsychologist, 27,* 81–107. doi: 10.1080/13854046.2012.721007

8. Bolinskey, P. K., Trumbetta, S. L., Hanson, D. R., & Gottesman, I. I. (2010). Predicting adult psychopathology from adolescent MMPIs: Some victories. *Personality and Individual Differences, 49,* 324–330. doi: 10.1016/j.paid.2010.01.026

9. Burchett, D. L., & Ben-Porath, Y. S. (2010). The impact of over-reporting on MMPI-2-RF substantive scale score validity. *Assessment, 17,* 497–516. doi: 10.1177/1073191110378972

10. Finn, J. A., Ben-Porath, Y. S., & Tellegen, A. (2015). Dichotomous versus polytomous response options in psychopathology assessment: Method or meaningful variance? *Psychological Assessment, 27,* 184–193. doi: 10.1037/pas0000044

11. Forbey, J. D., & Ben-Porath, Y. S. (2007). A comparison of the MMPI-2 Restructured Clinical (RC) and Clinical Scales in a substance abuse treatment sample. *Psychological Services, 4,* 46–58. doi: 10.1037/1541-1559.4.1.46

12. Forbey, J. D., & Ben-Porath, Y. S. (2008). Empirical correlates of the MMPI-2 Restructured Clinical (RC) Scales in a non-clinical setting. *Journal of Personality Assessment, 90,* 136–141. doi: 10.1080/00223 890701845161

13. Forbey, J. D., Ben-Porath, Y. S., & Gartland, D. (2009). Validation of the MMPI-2 Computerized Adaptive Version (MMPI-2-CA) in a correctional intake facility. *Psychological Services, 6,* 279–292. doi: 10.1037/a0016195

14. Handel, R. W., & Archer, R. P. (2008). An investigation of the psychometric properties of the MMPI-2 Restructured Clinical (RC) Scales with mental health inpatients. *Journal of Personality Assessment, 90,* 239–249. doi: 10.1080/00223890701884954

15. Kamphuis, J. H., Arbisi, P. A., Ben-Porath, Y. S., & McNulty, J. L. (2008). Detecting comorbid Axis-II status among inpatients using the MMPI-2 Restructured Clinical Scales. *European Journal of Psychological Assessment, 24,* 157–164. doi: 10.1027/1015-5759.24.3.157

16. Kastner, R. M., Sellbom, M., & Lilienfeld, S. O. (2012). A comparison of the psychometric properties of the Psychopathic Personality Inventory full-length and short-form versions. *Psychological Assessment, 24,* 261–267. doi: 10.1037/a0025832

17. Lanyon, R. I., & Thomas, M. L. (2013). Assessment of global psychiatric categories: The PSI/PSI-2 and the MMPI-2-RF. *Psychological Assessment, 25,* 227–232. doi: 10.1037/a0030313

18. Mattson, C. A., Powers, B. K., Halfaker, D., Akenson, S. T., & Ben-Porath, Y. S. (2012). Predicting drug court treatment completion with the MMPI-2-RF. *Psychological Assessment, 24,* 937–943. doi: 10.1037/ a0028267

19. Phillips, T. R., Sellbom, M., Ben-Porath, Y. S., & Patrick, C. J. (2014). Further development and construct validation of MMPI-2-RF indices of global psychopathy, fearless-dominance, and impulsive-antisociality in a sample of incarcerated women. *Law and Human Behavior, 38(1),* 34–46. doi: 10.1037/lhb0000040

20. Scholte, W., Tiemens, B. G., Verheul, R., Meerman, A., Egger, J., & Hutschemaekers, G. (2012a). The RC Scales predict psychotherapy outcomes: The predictive validity of the MMPI-2's restructured clinical scales for psychotherapeutic outcomes. *Personality and Mental Health, 6,* 292–302. doi: 10.1002/pmh.1190

21. Scholte, W., Tiemens, B. G., Verheul, R., Meerman, A., Egger, J., & Hutschemaekers, G. (2012b). Predictive validity of the MMPI-2 Clinical, PSY-5, and RC Scales for therapy disruptive behavior. *Journal of Psychiatric Practice, 18(6),* 420–429. doi: 10.1097/01. pra.0000422740.87495.91

22. Sellbom, M., Anderson, J. L., & Bagby, R. M. (2013). Assessing DSM-5 Section III Personality Traits and Disorders with the MMPI-2-RF. *Assessment, 20,* 709–722. doi: 10.1177/1073191113508808

23. Sellbom, M., & Ben-Porath, Y. S. (2005). Mapping the MMPI-2 Restructured Clinical (RC) Scales onto normal personality traits:

Evidence of construct validity. *Journal of Personality Assessment, 85,* 179–187. doi: 10.1207/s15327752jpa8502_10

24. Sellbom, M., Ben-Porath, Y. S., & Bagby, R. M. (2008). Personality and psychopathology: Mapping the MMPI-2 Restructured Clinical (RC) Scales onto the five factor model of personality. *Journal of Personality Disorders, 22,* 291–312. doi: 10.1521/pedi.2008.22.3.291

25. Sellbom, M., Ben-Porath, Y. S., Baum, L. J., Erez, E., & Gregory, C. (2008). Predictive validity of the MMPI-2 Restructured Clinical (RC) Scales in a batterers' intervention program. *Journal of Personality Assessment, 90,* 129–135. doi: 10.1080/00223890701845153

26. Sellbom, M., Ben-Porath, Y. S., & Graham, J. R. (2006). Correlates of the MMPI-2 Restructured Clinical (RC) Scales in a college counseling setting. *Journal of Personality Assessment, 86,* 89–99. doi: 10.1207/s15327752jpa8601_10

27. Sellbom, M., Ben-Porath, Y. S., Lilienfeld, S. O., Patrick, C. J., & Graham, J. R. (2005). Assessing psychopathic personality traits with the MMPI-2. *Journal of Personality Assessment, 85,* 334–343. doi: 10.1207/s15327752jpa8503_10

28. Sellbom, M., Ben-Porath, Y. S., Patrick, C. J., Wygant, D. B., Gartland, D. M., & Stafford, K. P. (2012). Development and Construct Validation of MMPI-2-RF Indices of Global Psychopathy, Fearless-Dominance, and Impulsive-Antisociality. *Personality Disorders: Theory, Research, and Treatment, 3(1),* 17–38. doi: 10.1037/a0023888

29. Sellbom, M., Ben-Porath, Y. S., & Stafford, K. P. (2007). A comparison of measures of psychopathic deviance in a forensic setting. *Psychological Assessment, 19,* 430–436. doi: 10.1037/1040-3590.19.4.430

30. Sellbom, M., Graham, J. R., & Schenk, P. (2006). Incremental validity of the MMPI-2 Restructured Clinical (RC) Scales in a private practice sample. *Journal of Personality Assessment, 86,* 196–205. doi: 10.1207/s15327752jpa8602_09

31. Shkalim, E. (2015). Psychometric evaluation of the MMPI-2/MMPI-2-RF Restructured Clinical Scales in an Israeli sample. *Assessment.* doi: 10.1177/1073191114555884

32. Simms, L. J., Casillas, A., Clark, L. A., Watson, D., & Doebbeling, B. I. (2005). Psychometric evaluation of the Restructured Clinical Scales of the MMPI-2. *Psychological Assessment, 17,* 345–358. doi: 10.1037/1040-3590.17.3.345

33. Sullivan, K. A., Elliott, C. D., Lange, R. T., & Anderson, D. S. (2013). A known groups evaluation of the Response Bias Scale in a neuropsychological setting. *Applied Neuropsychology: Adult, 20,* 20–32. doi: 10.1080/09084282.2012.670149

34. Tarescavage, A. M., Scheman, J., & Ben-Porath, Y. S. (2015). Reliability and validity of the Minnesota Multiphasic Personality Inventory-2-Restructured Form (MMPI-2-RF) in evaluations of chronic low back pain patients. *Psychological Assessment, 27,* 433–446. doi: 10.1037/pas0000056

35. Tarescavage, A. M., Windover, A. K., Ben-Porath, Y. S., Botuacoff, L. I., Marek, R. J., Ashton, K., Merrell, J., Lavery, M., & Heinberg, L. J. (2013). Use of the MMPI-2-RF Suicidal/Death Ideation and Substance Abuse Scales in screening bariatric surgery candidates. *Psychological Assessment, 25,* 1384–1389. doi: 10.1037/a0034045

36. Tellegen, A., & Ben-Porath, Y. S. (2008/2011). *The Minnesota Multiphasic Personality Inventory-2-Restructured Form (MMPI-2-RF): Technical manual.* Minneapolis: University of Minnesota Press.

37. Van der Heijden, P. T., Egger, J. I. M., Rossi, G., & Derksen, J. J. L. (2012). Integrating psychopathology and personality disorders conceptualized by the MMPI-2-RF and the MCMI-III: A structural validity study. *Journal of Personality Assessment, 4,* 345–357. doi: 10.1080/00223891.2012.656861

38. Van der Heijden, P. T., Egger, J. I. M., Rossi, G., Grundel, G., & Derksen, J. J. L. (2013). The MMPI-2 Restructured Form and the standard MMPI-2 Clinical Scales in relation to DSM-IV. *European Journal of Psychological Assessment, 29,* 182–188. doi: 10.1027/1015-5759/a000140

39. Wolf, E. J., Miller, M. W., Orazem, R. J., Weierich, M. R., Castillo, D. T., Milford, J., Kaloupek, D. G., & Keane, T. M. (2008). The MMPI-2 Restructured Clinical Scales in the assessment of posttraumatic stress disorder and comorbid disorders. *Psychological Assessment, 20,* 327–340. doi: 10.1037/a0012948

40. Wygant, D. B., Boutacoff, L. A., Arbisi, P. A., Ben-Porath, Y. S., Kelly, P. H., & Rupp, W. M. (2007). Examination of the MMPI-2 Restructured Clinical (RC) Scales in a sample of bariatric surgery candidates. *Journal of Clinical Psychology in Medical Settings, 14,* 197–205. doi: 10.1007/s10880-007-9073-8

End of Report

This and previous pages of this report contain trade secrets and are not to be released in response to requests under HIPAA (or any other data disclosure law that exempts trade secret information from release). Further, release in response to litigation discovery demands should be made only in accordance with your profession's ethical guidelines and under an appropriate protective order.

The report is included in its entirety to provide a comprehensive standard interpretation of the test findings and to illustrate how Wiggins' (2003) vision of the empirical paradigm, as represented by Loevinger's (1957) extended definition of construct validity is implemented in the MMPI-2-RF.

The report begins with 5 profiles that provide Madeline's scores on the 51 MMPI-2-RF scales. Page 2 depicts her Validity Scale findings. In addition to Madeline's raw scores, T scores, and percent of scorable responses for each scale (which in this case is 100 for all scales because she responded to all 338 MMPI-2-RF items), data are provided for a comparison group of women tested as outpatients assessed at an independent practice. This is one of numerous comparison groups available for the MMPI-2-RF. Comparison group data, although not required for MMPI-2-RF interpretation, are used to provide information about how a test-taker's scores compare with those of a sample of individuals tested in a similar context (see Ben-Porath and Tellegen [2011] for a full list of available MMPI-2-RF comparison groups). Given the therapeutic assessment approach taken in this project, the outpatient independent practice sample was deemed the most appropriate comparison group for Madeline's results. As seen on page 2 of the report, comparison group data include the sample mean and standard deviation on each scale and, in the final row, the percent of comparison group members who scored at or below the test taker. This final set of numbers is analogous to a set of percentiles and can be interpreted as such. In Madeline's Validity Scale profile, for example, these numbers illustrate the rarity of her very low scores on scales FBS-r and RBS among women tested at an outpatient independent practice. The most remarkable aspect of Madeline's MMPI-2-RF Validity Scale findings, when contrasted with her 2000 assessment, is the absence of any evidence of embellishment.

Page 3 of Madeline's interpretive report provides her scores on the Higher-Order and Restructured Clinical Scales. Her highly elevated Behavioral/Externalizing Dysfunction (BXD) score stands out both in reference to all of her other scores and the comparison group, where the figure 100 in the final row labeled "Percent scoring at or below test taker" indicates that none of the 432 women in the selected sample scored higher than Madeline on this scale. Her low scores on Demoralization (RCd) and Somatic Complaints (RC1) are also quite uncommon for this population. More detailed information about Madeline's externalizing behavioral proclivities can be found in her scores on the Externalizing Scales (page 5) and the PSY-5 Scales (page 6). Page 5 also includes noteworthy findings on Madeline's Interpersonal Scale scores.

Page 7 of Madeline's interpretive report provides a summary of her scores on the 51 MMPI-2-RF scales. As seen in the footnote on this page, this summary can facilitate MMPI-2-RF interpretation following a process described in detail in the test manual. Organization of scores on the

Substantive Scales on this page reflects a three-tiered hierarchical structure, which, as discussed earlier, links the MMPI-2-RF to current hierarchical-dimensional models of personality and psychopathology (Sellbom, 2019).

Implementation of the recommended approach to Madeline's test results is illustrated on pages 8–10 of her interpretive report. As noted in the italicized paragraph at the top of page 8, the statements included in the report need to be considered in the context of each test taker's unique background, the circumstances of the evaluation, and other available information. This is illustrated in the following section, in which answers to Madeline's assessment questions are discussed.

A unique feature of this and all other MMPI-2-RF interpretive reports is the annotation. Beginning with the first sentence under *Behavioral Dysfunction* on page 8 of the report, every interpretive statement is followed by a superscripted number, which is linked to endnotes that appear on page 11 of Madeline' report. Language at the top of page 11 indicates:

> *This section lists for each statement in the report the MMPI-2-RF score(s) that triggered it. In addition, each statement is identified as a Test Response, if based on item content, a Correlate, if based on empirical correlates, or an Inference, if based on the report authors' judgment. . . . For correlate-based statements, research references (Ref. No.) are provided, keyed to the consecutively numbered reference list following the endnotes.*

The endnotes and research references (on the subsequent pages of the standard report) provide transparency about the origins of each statement and implement Wiggins' (2003) vision of the extended empirical paradigm and Loevinger's (1957) extended definition of construct validity. Every statement is linked to a specific score or set of scores and designated as being content-based, empirically grounded, or a construct validity-based inference of the report authors. For example, the first two sentences under *Interpersonal Functioning Scales* on page 9 read:

> The test taker describes herself as having strong opinions, as standing up for herself, as assertive and direct, and able to lead others[18]. She is likely to believe she has leadership capabilities, but to be viewed by others as domineering, self-centered, and possibly grandiose.[19]

As indicated in endnote number 18 on page 11:

[18] Test Response: IPP=34

the first statement is content based, reflecting what Madeline reported about herself when producing a low T score of 34 on the Interpersonal Passivity (IPP) scale. The second statement is empirical correlate-based:

[19] Correlate: IPP=34, Ref. 5, 16, 36; AGGR-r=78, Ref. 36

and is generated by scores on two scales (the low IPP score and the elevated PSY-5 Aggressiveness [AGGR-r] scale score). Because this statement is based on empirical correlates, it is also linked to research references that appear on the subsequent pages of the report. For example, the first IPP reference (Ref. 5) is a study by Ayearst, Sellbom, Trobst, and Bagby (2013), mapping the MMPI-2-RF Interpersonal Scales onto Wiggins' (1979) elaboration of the Interpersonal Circumplex Model. Statements identified on page 11 as inferences are construct-validity based and listed primarily under *Diagnostic and Treatment Considerations*.

MMPI-2-RF-Based Responses to Madeline's Assessment Questions

As described earlier in this volume, Madeline's 2017 assessment included a first meeting designed to develop her assessment questions and administer the assessment instruments, followed by a second meeting in which she amended her questions and was provided answers to her new set of questions in a therapeutic assessment framework. Following are Madeline's questions and MMPI-2-RF-based.

Why Am I Not so Driven Right Now? Where Has That Gone?

Essentially, you are the same person you were some 20 years ago, though the MMPI results also point to some noteworthy changes. At the broadest level you remain someone who acts on impulse, takes risks, thinks unconventionally, and is comfortable interacting with others. The most significant change is a noteworthy reduction in your activation or energy level. Heightened energy, a very positive (perhaps even overly positive) self-view, and decreased need for sleep and rest are typically part of the experiences of individuals who scored as you did previously on the MMPI. However, a comparison of the two sets of MMPI scores shows that though you are not someone who lacks energy and drive, these have quite substantially diminished since you were last assessed. For someone accustomed to the "natural high" associated with elevated mood and energy levels, this can be quite a letdown, leaving you feeling disoriented. Recognizing that you have reached a new stage of life, one in which your energy level is just "normal," and that things you were able to do with no thought at all may now require more effort and planning, could assist you with getting oriented to the "new you," or, perhaps more accurately, your new way of interacting with the world. At your core, you are the same person. Your history hasn't changed. Your interests are likely the same. Your feelings about people, both good and bad, are likely the same.

Your proclivity toward assertiveness/aggressiveness is also unchanged. Your loss of energy, moving from very, very high to just normal, though disorienting, may also have positive consequences. Needing to build up toward action rather than acting immediately may help you avoid negative outcomes.

How Do I Get Judges I've Alienated Before to See the New Person I'm Becoming and Believe It's Authentic?

Your assertiveness and aggressiveness, coupled with a tendency to be impulsive, can create difficulties, particularly when interacting with authority figures such as judges. Being mindful of these features of your personality, particularly when acting in your professional role, may assist in reigning in your natural inclination to respond strongly to perceived wrongs or injustices. Developing a habit of thinking before you act (or speak), and actively thinking about how those with whom you're interacting are likely to perceive your words and actions, could help you avoid conflict. As you adopt and practice these new habits, they will require less conscious effort and increasingly be perceived by others as authentic.

What Tools Do I Need to Effectively Remain Inspired?

MMPI data alone are insufficient to answer this question. Most people lose some of their energy and drive as they reach middle age. People with particularly high levels of energy and drive, such as you were when last assessed, have more energy to lose and may be particularly cognizant of this loss. What were some of their defining features (e.g., high energy, little need for sleep) are reduced to levels that are average for most people, but represent a significant loss for them. And though you are likely to continue to have unconventional interests and would like to continue to act spontaneously on impulses you experience, the drive needed to do so seems to have diminished. Remaining engaged with causes you believe in and people you care about will be important as you adjust to this new reality.

How Do I Deal With the [Inner] Chatter and the Typical Rumor Mill? How Do I Address All That?

Assuming that by this question you mean that those with whom you interact now are aware of and may discuss (perhaps behind your back) unflattering aspects of your past, a potentially helpful strategy would be to make a concerted effort to behave consistently. As those with whom you're currently interacting perceive your behavior to be reasonable and predictable, the old chatter and rumors will become increasingly irrelevant. Toward this end, the transition mentioned in response to your first question, from "high" to "normal" energy, could indeed be a silver lining.

Summary and Future Directions

Wiggins (2003) observed that the history of personality assessment is interlocked with MMPI developments. This continues to be the case. As discussed earlier, Sellbom (2019) documents how recent shifts in the conceptualization of psychopathology, embodied in the Hierarchical Taxonomy of Psychopathology (HiTOP; Kotov et al. 2017) and the DSM-5 Alternative Model of Personality Disorders (AMPD; American Psychiatric Association, 2013), are reflected in the MMPI-2-RF, which now provides a hierarchical dimensional perspective to the most widely used self-report measure of personality and psychopathology. In Madeline's case, the test shows that her primary difficulties remain in the behavioral externalizing domain and that her level of dysfunction in this area remains very high, although some of its specific manifestations have changed dramatically. Madeline's MMPI-2-RF results also demonstrate the continued importance of interpersonal functioning in personality assessment.

In addition to its empirical roots and the continued centrality of empirical correlates to test score interpretation, another hallmark of the MMPI has been its ongoing evolution and amenability of its item pool to further empirical development and refinement. As of this chapter's writing, work on the next version of the instrument is ongoing. The MMPI-3 will pick up where the MMPI-2-RF left off. New normative samples, targeting demographic projections for the 2020 census and adding a separate set of norms for use with the Spanish translation of the test, have been collected. Approximately 20% of the MMPI-2-RF items have been replaced with new items written to expand the test's scope. Revisions have been designed to make some of the longer MMPI-2-RF scales more efficient and to broaden the range of constructs covered by the instrument. These refinements are intended to provide a modern instrument deeply rooted in the evolving empirical paradigm. As has been the case with the MMPI since the beginning, there is, however, no expectation that the MMPI-3 will be the final word on this paradigm.

Chapter 7

Communicating the Assessment Findings to Madeline G.

Stephen E. Finn

The test interpretations offered by the group of experts are the basis of the previous four chapters of this book. Greg Meyer and I did not have access to these complete analyses when we met with Madeline for the second parts of the Therapeutic Assessment (TA). But each expert (or team of experts) did an excellent job of addressing Madeline's AQs based on their test(s), and some went as far as to write direct answers that could be read or shared with Madeline if we wished. Greg and I were struck by the convergence between many of the tests but also by how the tests complemented each other. For the next steps of the TA, our job was to integrate all this information and use it to plan our subsequent contacts with Madeline. Let me explain how this task is typically handled in Therapeutic Assessment.

Case Conceptualization in TA

In TA, we place great emphasis on case conceptualization: the process of constructing a "big picture" after the standardized tests have been administered, the Extended Inquiries have been completed, and each test has been scored and interpreted. The case conceptualization informs how we interact with clients in the latter stages of the assessment, and a good case conceptualization provides containment, hope, and a sense of being seen and understood to clients. In essence, a case conceptualization is a theory that integrates history, observations, countertransference experiences, and psychological test data into an understanding of the client's current situation, past experiences, and trajectory at the time of the assessment. The case conceptualization may use concepts from many areas of psychology: neurobiology, attachment, cognitive psychology, social psychology, lifespan development, psychodynamic theory, learning theory, etc., and it continues to be refined in the Assessment Intervention Session and Summary/Discussion Session. The case conceptualization forms the basis of a new narrative about the client's current development and challenges in way that makes sense, reduces shame, brings compassion from others, and highlights viable next steps.

Initial Conceptualization Based on Madeline's Test Results

In preparing for our subsequent visits with Madeline, Greg and I focused on two aspects of Madeline's testing: comparing current and previous test results and comparing self-report to performance-based data.

Comparing Current With Previous Testing

There was a great deal of overlap in the test results reported by Wiggins (2003) and those from the current assessment, suggesting that, in many ways, Madeline was the same person she had been 17 years ago. However, there were also notable differences. Many of the experts noted signs that Madeline had somewhat less energy and drive, less hostility and impulsiveness, and a greater capacity for self-awareness and interpersonal relatedness than was evident in the previous assessment. Several experts commented that Madeline seemed more psychologically mature than she had been 17 years ago, with more ability to tolerate dysphoric feelings and inner conflict rather than avoiding psychological distress through action or aggression.

Comparing Self-Report to Performance-Based Testing

Another important aspect of Madeline's testing was present in both the 2000 and 2017 results. Her descriptions of herself on self-report tests like the MMPI-2-RF and the NEO-PI-R showed very little psychological distress and mainly reflected a sense of herself as assertive, extraverted, decisive, excitement-seeking, and fearing closeness but also conscientious and concerned about others. In contrast, scores on performance-based tests like the R-PAS and the SCORS-G suggested marked psychological distress (shame, depression, anxiety) consistent with complex PTSD and gave evidence of distorted thinking that was most prominent in emotionally arousing situations. These latter tests also suggested that Madeline had remarkable "ego strengths" and resilience.

There is an ample literature on this pattern of discrepant scores between self-report and performance-based tests and how such test-score divergences may be highly meaningful (Bornstein, 2002; Finn, 1996b, 2011; Smith & Finn, 2014); Greg and I relied on this literature to develop our working theory. We hypothesized that Madeline's life experiences had provided the crucial elements for her to develop complex PTSD: 1) an early disorganized attachment, combined with 2) extensive and severe trauma in later childhood (Brown & Elliott, 2016). The underlying painful affect states visible in Madeline's Rorschach, her struggles in intimate relationships, and the prominent characterological features in her presentation and self-report testing were all consistent with this conceptualization. What differentiated Madeline from many people with complex PTSD were her considerable psychological resources/ego strength: intelligence, reflective capacity, determination, and resiliency. Whatever the source of these resources, we hypothesized that they had protected Madeline from sequelae that would be typical of someone with her early history (i.e., a dissociative disorder, multiple addictions, an inability to work, and unremitting depression and anxiety) and allowed her to achieve the successes she had in life, despite her early history. Now, however, a variety of experiences since the previous testing (her previous intimate relationship and its ending, her father's death, the closer relationship with her uncle as he grew sick and died, the re-engagement with her brother, and the process of aging) seemed to have "softened" Madeline's character defenses, led to more self-reflection, and brought her more in contact with painful affect states she had previously been able to avoid/contain. Madeline's current dilemma of change centered on how to adapt to and make use of this new balance of affective awareness and coping mechanisms, and she was confused and off-balance because she had not yet worked out a new equilibrium. Although uncomfortable, this new way of being presented an opportunity for Madeline to achieve a more flexible, integrated way of being in the world—especially if she was willing to ask for and accept help from others in a vulnerable way. But her past trauma made relying on others quite frightening.

Our goals for the next part of the Therapeutic Assessment were to test out this case conceptualization, share it in a therapeutic way with Madeline, and see if we could identify viable next steps that would be useful to Madeline.

Madeline's Second Visit to Austin, February 3–4, 2017

Plan for Later TA Sessions

Greg and I planned that on the first day, we would check in with Madeline in the morning, review the AQs, and make modifications if need be. After lunch, we would conduct an Assessment Intervention Session. The second day would be devoted to processing the AIS and collaboratively discussing the test results and Madeline's AQs. We would end by discussing next steps, planning the Follow-Up Session, and saying good-bye.

Check-In on First Day

Madeline arrived on time for our meeting, nicely but comfortably dressed, and I felt an easy familiarity when we all greeted each other. One of the first things she said was that the butterfly postcard I had given her was hanging in her office and whenever she saw it, she had "lots of positive memories" from our previous time, including our discussions of Card V. We read back the response she had given of the people "trapped" in the butterfly wings who wanted to come out, but it would "require a totally new identification." We laughed again about the "brilliance of her unconscious." I asked how she had been after she left Austin, and Madeline said that she had left feeling "really good," had pursued the job she had told us about and gotten it, and now was being paid extremely well to help train legal advocates for Native Americans. Madeline said she was very busy and satisfied with this new position, and we all agreed that she was out of the "limbo" she had been in at our first meeting. She reflected on how debilitating her grief over her uncle had been and how much she had taken from the experience of being with him while he died and then losing him. She said she still missed her uncle but felt "less encumbered" and "less armored" than she had previously. She also reflected on the major impact on her of having loved and been loved by her partner—and by that relationship having ended. She acknowledged how important it had been to be "armored" earlier in her life but also, "I've missed opportunities because my armor was more important" and that now she wanted a "new reconciliation" of different aspects of herself. I was amazed at how closely this statement matched our sense—described earlier—of Madeline's dilemma of change.

At one point, Madeline brought up her discomfort that she had no memory of going to Chicago and being interviewed by Dan McAdams for the previous assessment. To my surprise, she was open this time to the idea she had previously rejected, that this might have been an emotionally significant event. As we talked, she suddenly said, "Wait. A bell is ringing!" After a pause, she said she had just realized that McAdams was the first person to whom she had "ever told the absolute truth" about her early life. Madeline said that even with her former partner, she had "always left big pieces out" or lied. She seemed to grasp how overwhelming the discussion with McAdams might have been, sat with this understanding for a moment, and then announced, "I have to go to the ladies' room," abruptly ending the conversation.

When Madeline returned, we reviewed her previous assessment questions and agreed that most were no longer relevant as she had a new job that felt meaningful to her. The new set of questions we developed were:

How Do I Get Judges I've Alienated Before to See the New Person I'm Becoming and Believe It's Authentic?

This was Madeline's main question at that point in time, and she saw it as a revision of her previous question, "Who the hell am I now?" In her new work position, she was required to work with many judges she was certain she had alienated before as an aggressive defensive attorney. And she didn't pin her past behavior solely on this role, saying: "I did create that situation. I resonated 'I don't respect you' . . . and a lot of it had to do with insecurity." She was aware she had shifted personally to be less aggressive and diplomatic and also that she would be different in her new role, but she worried that these judges would dismiss her or block her work because of past resentments. She said she very much wanted to "get people on board" with the "new me."

Why Am I Not so Driven Right Now? Where Has That Gone?

Madeline was ready to cut this question because she felt she had the answer: "I'm not driven because I don't want to be. I wanted to be inspired instead." However, she was willing to keep the question when I suggested we had more to tell her from the testing about this topic. I felt this AQ could be a valuable "door" into some of the more important Level 3 test findings.

What Tools Do I Need to Effectively Remain Inspired?

Madeline said she didn't want to go back to being "driven;" she wanted her motivation for work to come instead from a place of inspiration. She felt she was inspired at that point but that she would need tools to "get patience and sustain patience." When I asked what tools she already used, she told of "self-messaging" in the past by talking to herself in the mirror each morning. She was excited about the idea that we could give her more concrete tools that would help her.

How Do I Deal With the [Inner] Chatter and the Typical Rumor Mill? How Do I Address All That?

This question emerged in two stages. At first, Madeline was focused on how to deal with the gossip and intrusive questions that might come to her from people in the legal system. Her concern was heightened by the fact that when she had closed her practice to take care of her uncle, she had not told a single person why she was leaving and in fact had answered any questions with, "None of your business." After our lunch break, Madeline said she wanted to revise this AQ by inserting the word "inner" in brackets. I write more about this below.

Process Observation

I noticed a real difference formulating these AQs compared to the parallel discussion during the initial visit. I experienced Madeline as more open and willing to ask for help and less challenging of suggestions and statements Greg and I made. Also, although Greg and I still mirrored Madeline's strengths and competence, we did less of that than in the initial session, I think because we felt less need to do so. It seemed clear that we had more alliance with Madeline and had increased her epistemic trust. This enabled us to take more risks in the Assessment Intervention Session.

Assessment Intervention Session

As described earlier (Chapter 2), in Assessment Intervention Sessions assessors set up in vivo experiences that both test the initial case conceptualization and help clients become more aware of potential Level 3 information relevant to their AQs. Greg and I believed that the most important Level 3 findings from the assessment were: 1) Madeline was still managing a great deal of underlying negative affect states (shame, sadness, anxiety, anger) connected to her early traumas, 2) the coping mechanisms she typically used to avoid and counteract these emotions were costly in many ways, and 3) Madeline would greatly benefit from support and skilled professional help to heal from her trauma and disorganized attachment and reach a healthier resolution. We felt Madeline was on the verge of accepting all of these aspects of a new narrative.

Plan for AIS

Our plan was to tell Madeline we wanted to do another test to address two AQs: "How do I get judges I've alienated before to see the new person I'm becoming . . ." and "How do I deal with the [inner] chatter and the typical rumor mill?"[1] We would then ask Madeline to tell stories to picture story cards from various performance-based personality tests where the characters are typically perceived as scared, hurt, ashamed, sad, or lonely. Call Out Box 1 shows the cards that we chose. We anticipated that Madeline might respond in two ways: 1) She might tell stories where the characters felt vulnerable (if so, we would see if she could relate to the characters personally and then discuss how the vulnerable emotions were relevant to her AQS); and/or 2) Madeline might construct stories where the characters defended against vulnerable emotions by avoidance or aggression (if so, we would see if she could recognize the underlying vulnerability, the costs and benefits of the coping mechanisms used, and the relevance to her AQs and to her goal of being less aggressive and more relational in her current job).

PROCESS OF THE AIS

After lunch, we checked in with Madeline and reviewed the typed new assessment questions. As reported earlier, she revised her fourth question to become: *How do I deal with the [inner] chatter and the typical rumor mill? How do I address all that?* She explained to us that in challenging situations she can be beset by a host of self-doubting voices saying, "Can I do this?" "Should I do this?" "What was I thinking" and "Have I bitten off more than I can chew?" In response to our queries, she said these voices were loudest when she hits roadblocks and that in response she becomes "driven," takes a "pile drive approach" to a situation, and becomes a "bully." She repeated her determination to build "collaborative, healthy, collective relationships" with her colleagues. I was struck by her shift toward looking more at herself and by her growing insight that to succeed she would need to deal with an insecure part of her. This encouraged me that our plan for the AIS was a good one.

As planned, I then introduced the rationale for the AIS; Madeline was curious and agreeable. I gave the standard instructions for many picture story tests: *I will show you some cards with drawings of various situations. Please tell a story that fits with the scene on the card. In your story, please include what happened before, what the people in the scene are thinking and feeling, and what happens after.* Madeline's stories are presented in Call Out Box 1.

Call Out 1   Madeline's Responses to Assessment Intervention Session Stimuli

Stimulus 1. Thurston-Cradock Test of Shame (TCTS; Thurston & Cradock O'Leary, 2009) Card 2 (Classroom): Three children stand in front of a blackboard containing arithmetic problems in a classroom with a teacher. One boy looks downcast, another boy is pointing and possibly jeering; a third girl has her hand over her mouth.

Response: Oh poor kid. He doesn't have an answer. The young black kid doesn't have an answer above the head; the other two clearly do. This pisses me off. I'll be quite frank. Not surprisingly in a kind of gender specific the young girl hand over her mouth is, "Oh no!" And I feel like she's being apathetic towards him, whereas the boy's mocking. And I don't like the stance of the teacher. [SF: So tell me a story.] It's not a good one. I wish we could make good stories. (pause) You know what the first thing that pops into my head? This poor little kid's a foster kid. And it's not that he's not as smart as these other too. And it's not that he's not as capable as these other two. Even in looking at the clothes . . . the clothes don't quite fit him. They're not nearly as nice. Bounced around. Bounced around. Bounced around. Never had a chance to actually learn, not that he can't do it. Not had an opportunity to be taught, and it's because of people like this. (Points to teacher.) The skank with the hands on her hip and her knee pushed forward. Berating him. Not caring about all his external circumstances just the task that she's supposed to do is teach him how to do math. If he fails, she fails. [SF: So what happened right before this scene?] They got called upon. The first two on the far right put their hands up. He didn't, and she picked him. So it's like she's part of the problem. And probably not even consciously. *[OK, then what happened?]* The other two come up and put their answers on the board, and I really like that the answer above the smart-ass kid with the plaid . . . his answer's wrong. You donkey! So as much as he thinks he's a smarty pants and so much better, he's got the wrong answer. *[And what are the characters thinking and feeling?]* Well that is so plainly evident for me anyway. The teacher's is disappointment, but what I like is she's not even looking at him. She's more directed to the answer. She's gonna die of cancer (chuckles) . . . a slow painful death, the skag! *[How about the other people?]* Buckoo in the plaid shirt with the wrong answer who can't add to 21, he's the stereotypical, "Yeah it's recess time go outside bully someone and go play football." I think the young girl's gonna stay behind and she's gonna talk to him. She's gonna make him her friend. And she's gonna teach him what he needs to know so these bastards on either side of him don't have this impact any longer. She cares. She's gonna be the one in all of this that makes a difference in this whole paradigm. *[And what is the foster kid feeling and thinking?]* "Here we go again." Dejection, rejection, less than. And whoever did this, you don't even have to make a different racial indicator here—all Caucasian but for him. Like it just doesn't get any worse. *[Anything else?]* It turns out that he's not only good at math but he's a math genius and ends up being a professor at Harvard. And these two (points to black boy and girl) stay friends forever. This guy goes on to be a football player and then blows out a knee and then never leaves town and ends up being one of those dudes on Friday night and who's at the bar and tells stories about his high school glory days that's all there ever is.

Stimulus 2: TCTS Card 3 (Basketball): *A young person of ambiguous gender in an athletic uniform stands on the side of a basketball court in front of a suited adult man who is screaming in a threatening way and pointing away. Bystanders look on from the bleachers, including a younger man in a suit who looks uncomfortable.*

Response: Asshole! That's not even the coach. That's a parent. The coach is sitting down. Look at all the faces. Oh my God! Sad. Bewilderment. Stunned. Shocked. Disgusted. [OK, so tell me a story.] The parent there watching the game. That's the parent's child, but not so much a child, suggesting that that's probably high school? Come over screaming, "You didn't do this! You did that wrong!" The coach sitting down shouldn't be sitting down, should be standing up, but it's like nobody will stand up to the bully except the daughter. I like the way her 2 feet are planted. Her shoulders are back. She's only got one arm on the other arm, a little self protection but not backing up even though the father's advancing towards her. And she's making up her mind. If this is what it's like in public I can only imagine what it's like at home for her. And she's standing there going, "I'm done with your shit!" "It ends here" And this is a turning point in her life where she determines that no longer is what he has to say especially in this matter going to affect her. [**What happens next?**] She says, "I'm done." Finally the coach changes his facial expression, stands up, and he (she points to "father") gets evicted from the game. Instead of dad pointing for her to get out, she stays, the team goes on to win, dad gets kicked out, and she goes and stays with her best girlfriend that night. And she's never ashamed again because she never goes back. [**Doesn't go back home?**]No. What an asshole! If he's wearing a suit like that to a game, then he's probably a prominent member where no one in the community stands up to him. And this is the night she does, and it all changes. Go girl!

Stimulus 3. TCTS Card 8 (Baseball): A boy in a baseball uniform walks away from the field holding a bat and hanging his head. Other players in different uniforms are nearby cheering and jumping. Bystanders and other teammates watch from the background.

Response: Oh this is all guys. (pause) It's the reverse Casey at Bat. (pause) I think this is really emblematic of life, you know. You got 2 opposing sides. Only one can come out the winner. And when you play on a team, you either all win together or lose together. I don't see this as all bad at all. [So tell me the story.] I think the guy that is standing with his arms crossed next to the fence in the uniform . . . I think him and the younger guy are either twins or really closely related in some way. [**What happened before this scene?**] Oh it's probably one of those situations where it's like the bottom of the ninth and the other team was winning and a couple of guys on base and number 14 here—the boy with his back to us—if he can only get a run in then they'll tie it; if he can do the big hit then they can win, and he comes up short. And life is like that sometimes. I think that character comes with how you deal with those adversities, not that there are adversities. [**And how's he thinking or feeling?**] Oh absolute dejection. You can just . . . the body language. The body slumped. A little bit of a pigeon-toed stance. Dragging the bat on the ground. I'm surprised he's even still carrying the bat. (pause) And shame. But it's a game. It could be as simple as if he'd hit the ball and it had been a good shot. Then exactly the same except then these players (points to opposing team) suffer that sense of loss. [**What happens next?**] I hope . . . given the look on what I think is the brother . . . I hope what he does is step forward and put his arms around him and say, "It's okay. It's just a game. There will be other games." [**It's your story. You get to make it however you want.**] Well that's what he does then. Puts his arm around his shoulder. "We got this far. We wouldn't have got this far without you. It takes a team to win and a team to lose. Now let's go for pizza." So there's no big celebration but it's no big awful loss either. And I think it makes them closer that he has a support at the end. Instead of berating him or "You caused this . . . " or "It's your fault" or . . . It all works out. And I think after baseball is football season anyway so there's always another game to go to.

Stimulus 4. TCTS Card 7 (Water Cooler): A person of ambiguous gender walks through a door to a room where other people are gathered in a circle around a water cooler talking and laughing.

*Response: This is entitled "Office Gossip." (pause) Vest walks in and . . . funny water cooler and anything. These must be from like the 70's or something. So the man in the vest walks in. Everyone's standing around the water cooler. The one who you can't see if he's wearing a tie or not, he's clearly the center of attention. Then you've got the typical sidekick piping up with a little bit to add. The girls in rapt attention. Telling a story. And I like the vest guy walking in, everyone's having a laugh, and makes a correction. "Oh I heard so and so is doing such and such with another person." And it turns out they don't even actually know what they're talking about. They're spreading rumors. And vest guy walks in and says, "Actually, you know, you got that wrong. So and so is my . . . " Fill in the blank. Someone close like a roommate. "And I know that not to be the case because we were over here. So you probably shouldn't be spreading rumors that are false. And that is absolutely false." So he gets to correct something that started our wrong and could have hurt a number of people. But in doing so he doesn't make friends with the two guys who think they're so smart. Which is okay because he is smart and he stays on and the other two get laid off a week later. (Laugh) [**And what happens?**] Oh the girls get a crush on him because they think he's a man of good character but he doesn't like any one of them because they were all laughing and thinking the gossip was fun. So he doesn't think they have good characters and he has no interest in them. And he's smart enough to know you don't fish in the company pond. And the other two go on to become used car salesmen. (laugh) Which is a fitting end to their office attempt.*

Stimulus 5. Adolescent Apperception Cards (AAC; Silverton, 1993) Card 4F: A group of adolescent girls stands together. One girl has her arm on the shoulder of another. Another girl stands alone a short distance to the side, looking somber.

*Response: Girl band. I love it. Connected. Cohesive. They're out at a show . . . outdoor festival. They're not the headliners, but in a few years they're gonna be. And they stick together. And it's a 5-group band, and the gal who's got her arm around the shoulder of the other one, she's the manager. She's the driving force around keeping people happy, healthy, creative. And she got them this gig, and this is going to turn into their big break. There's all these other bands and all their other people. And managers and promoters are all there. And they see one of the best shows they're ever going to see. And this is the band that becomes as successful as like Sarah McLachlan's Love Affair. And it's all because this one in the bad suit keeps them together. [**And how's everybody thinking or feeling?**] Apprehensive right now because they don't know how good it's going to be. And that apprehension is part of what fuels the creative process and you get it up there and put it all out and leave it all out on the stage. They turn out . . . they're not the headliners, but they turn out to be the best act of the whole festival. Lots of fun. And obviously that's the drummer.*

(points to girl off on the side) [**Oh. Why?**] *Well you notice how everyone else is clothed? That's how a drummer would dress.* [**OK. Is she feeling the same?**] *Oh, absolutely. These two on both ends are funny, cause that's your rhythm section, right? Your drummer and your bass player. And you lay down that right beat, everything else follows that. And when that connects, that's amazing. So we got our little manager-friend connection here. Creative process all around. Rhythm section kind of like the bookends that makes it happen. Very cool. Finally a happy one. Are there more?* [**There are a few more.**] *Are we gonna get sad again?*

Stimulus 6. *Family Apperception Test (FAT; Julian, Sotile, Henry, & Sotile, 1985) Card 8: A woman walks on the street with her arm around a younger boy, while behind an older boy and girl follow. The older boy appears to be making fun of the younger boy.*

Response: (long pause) It's funny. When I first looked at this it was like this is kind of thing you always wanted when you're young. I was like, "They look like a family." And then the more I look at it it's like . . . This poor guy's adopted (laughing) and he just found out. [**How'd he find out?**] *They told him. But they told all the kids at the same time. And the other two are having a sense of, "Oh now we're better than him." And I think the mother figure is questioning herself about whether they should have told him. And maybe should have told him separately instead of all the kids together. Because obviously the impact has been different.* [**And what's he thinking or feeling?**] *I'm thinking that he's thinking and feeling protective of her. That he's young enough that his whole life has been that they've loved him and he's secure in that. And he's old enough to realize that it was hard for them to do that, to tell him. But he loves them for having loved him for as long as they have. He's very protective of her. As she is of him.* [**And is he affected by the other kids?**] *In his head not so much because in his head he's got a little dialogue going on that says, "They actually wanted me" (laugh). They're kind of stuck with him. (laughing) "They wanted me." I think it will have a bad impact on him and the brother in terms of their relationship because now the brother has this sense of superiority. And the sister adores her older brother so she's going along with that. Over time she's going to realize what a jackass he is and feel bad for alienating the younger brother. They'll work it out, but the older brother is always gonna end up—interestingly, even though he's a biological kid—he's gonna be the one who alienates himself from the rest of the family. And the adoption's not gonna mean a damn thing. But the truth came out, and that was necessary.*

Stimulus 7. *Roberts Apperception Test—2 (RAT-2; Roberts, 2005) Card 2 (Female): An adult woman and a girl kneel hugging each other and looking distressed.*

Response: Death. Sudden death. And I'd say probably the father and not a sibling. And this is the finding out. And they obviously cared about one another or they wouldn't be collapsed on their knees. The initial shock. [**So tell me the story.**] *It wasn't work related so I'm going to say like a car* *accident. The mom's worried that he was drinking and driving or the daughter just lost the dad.* [**And did they find out at the same time?**] *Yeah. This is one of those police-officer-knocks-on-the-door kind of thing. "There's no easy way of saying this . . . " And she's coming up the walk after the police. She sees the police car in the driveway, runs to the front of the house, runs to the door. Mom's just answering the door. He's just explaining to her that there's been an accident. She's behind the policeman. She hears it. Then the policeman says that he's dead and she pushes the police officer aside, runs to her mom, and they drop to their knees. Mom's lost a husband. She's lost her dad. And the mom's worried that he was drinking because it's not just after school. It's like after her after school sports. So it's like 5:30, 6:00 o'clock at night. So. It might have been dad left work and had a few drinks after work and drove and . . . There you go.* [**Anything else they're thinking or feeling in this moment?**] *That the wife feels relief to some degree. But the daughter just feels the anguish. And the police officer has questions and she's still standing at the door. And this is from the view of the police officer after just having told them he's dead in an accident.* [**And what happens after this scene?**] *It gets worse not better at first.* [**In what way?**] *There's other people involved.* (pause) *And I can't tell yet if it's because there's a woman in his car with him that she doesn't know. Suggesting an affair. Or if there's an innocent person in another vehicle who got killed. It gets worse before it gets . . . before these two get better.*

As you can see, Madeline told rich dramatic stories, including two where characters were feeling shame (TCTS 1, TCTS7) and one where a girl was shocked and sad after her father's sudden death (RAT 2). In all three stories, the characters received significant support from friends or family members. In two other scenarios (TCTS 3, FAM 8), the characters were protected from potential shame and embarrassment by their seemingly unshakeable self-confidence, and in one, a girl was also helped by her coach (TCTS 3). The level of connectedness in all these stories surprised me and led me to think that Madeline was truly becoming more open to supportive relationships. In one story (AAC 4F), Madeline did not even identify the character most people see as dysphoric as uncomfortable in any way, and she said her resulting story was "cool" and "happy." Similarly, in TCTS 8 (the man coming upon coworkers gossiping), Madeline's main character is never vulnerable himself.

Interestingly, none of Madeline's main characters coped with their vulnerable feelings by becoming aggressive. Instead, as the omniscient narrator, Madeline herself took revenge by inflicting dire outcomes on those figures who had believed they were better than others and/or treated others unfairly. One character dies a slow painful death from cancer, one "blows out a knee" playing football and "never leaves town," one is publicly humiliated and is left by his daughter, and two end up as "car salesmen." Madeline took great pleasure in doling out these "just desserts," and I believed this tactic might be useful to discuss with her.

As expected, it was easy to engage Madeline in reflecting on her stories. She almost immediately said she had identified with at least one character in each card and then went through and told us which. I explained that we had chosen these particular scenes because they pulled for characters struggling with "inner voices," which we thought could help us explore her AQ about "inner chatter." She understood immediately, and we collaborated in analyzing what had helped her various characters be successful. Before too long, with some scaffolding from us, Madeline recognized the other people helping in her stories and said, "I need to stay connected. This whole solo isolation thing is not working for me!" Again, I was pleased and surprised, and the three of us balanced Madeline's apparent openness with several caveats: I assured her she would never lose her ability to isolate if she needed to, and she explained, "I'm getting better at boundaries so I don't have to be so absolute." At one point, she grimaced and announced, "Yes! I'm going to let some people in. Look—it's hard to say and hard to do! But it's on my radar." I told her this was evident in her stories: "Some part of you told these stories to bring into focus what you need to stay inspired and not driven." She liked that idea, and there was a good feeling in the room.

I then led the way talking about Madeline's previous ways of coping: "I was also impressed because in the past I think one of the ways you've coped when you've been treated unjustly has been 'scorched-earth' solutions. But none of your characters took scorched-earth solutions." Madeline agreed and said that aspect of her stories reflected a big change in her. We imagined what "scorched-earth solutions" would look like in several of the cards (e.g., the girl on the basketball court would have quit the team and run away from home) and underlined once more that Madeline's characters had not needed to go there because they had interpersonal connectedness and support. She again said it was important that she maintain her "Fuck You Solution;" we agreed, and this led to a poignant moment of self-revelation.

Pointing to the character in TCTS 1 she had labeled as a foster child, Madeline told of having used the Freedom from Information Act in the 1980s to obtain records from her years in foster care, saying, "I wanted to know why I got treated the way I did." She discovered that she had been considered a "hard-to-place" foster child for being Native American and "a retard." Madeline then told of how she had been labeled mentally deficient because she didn't understand her school lessons. But, she said, it all boiled down to her not being able to read the blackboard from the back of the classroom where the "retards" were forced to sit. She only got corrective glasses when she was 13 or 14 years old because she wanted to drive. She also told of the severe racial prejudice she had faced from social service agencies that restricted her education ("There's no reason to put her in school because she's going to end up in jail") and how that cultural projection became a self-fulfilling prophecy ("And I did go to jail!"). I was amazed at her level of insight and decided to try to take things another step.

Reminding Madeline of her AQ about dealing with judges who might be prejudiced by her past behavior, I asked, "How, when someone is projecting on you, can you resist becoming who they think you are?" Madeline said she thought that was an important question: "I get my back up right away. I can feel it physiologically. I can feel the armor thicken!" I suggested we "thank the armor for having saved her life" and then think about how to approach it. We came up with several steps of a new strategy: 1) Recognize the armor is thickening because you feel a threat; 2) Ask yourself: "How much is there a real threat, or is my armor just being set off by old events that are triggered?" Madeline said she liked those ideas. I then asked her to collaborate with me in telling more stories.

She agreed, and I began a story to TCTS 7 (people at watercooler) where a man discovers his coworkers laughing about him and goes back to his desk full of "inner voices" of self-doubt. I asked Madeline to finish the story, and she immediately said the character called his "strong girlfriend," who told him that his co-workers "were wrong." After some discussion, Madeline emphasized, "You can't do this alone!" She somewhat joking said she was grieving losing her "Mistress of Power" persona, and I reframed the shift, "It's a new kind of strength to reach out to others for help when you are vulnerable." Madeline seemed delighted and quipped, "Can you imagine if I was here for 2 weeks!?" She then took a short break to get some more water. When she returned, she said, "I definitely need to try something new to stay inspired; it's not as desperate. . . . I'm not a sole lone soldier. I don't want to be that anymore. And I don't feel less-than as a result of that. I thought I would feel I lost something; instead I am gaining new ground." She then brought in a movie title she loved that was running through her head, *The Unbearable Lightness of Being*. Remembering the story, she and I agreed that the movie was not very inspiring, but that the title had a lovely sound.[2] Again, there was a very good feeling in the room.

We then slowly got into a discussion that was quite delicate for Madeline. She had been talking about needing help "slowing down" engaging her "automatic armor." Greg asked, "You recognize that the armor is tied to feeling vulnerable, don't you?" And Madeline half-jokingly said, "I don't admit that—even to myself." She said, "Two or three years ago, the word 'vulnerable' would have been like vinegar in my mouth!" She explained that the relationship with her previous partner had been her testing ground for "vulnerability," again not acknowledging that she might have felt burned by the way the relationship ended. I ventured,

"There is a vulnerable part of you that is not up to date. It's an old, very traumatized little Madeline that has not yet been healed. . . . You had to lock her in a closet, and put on armor in order to survive, you did it well, and thank God."

At that point, Madeline signaled her great discomfort: "Even you talking like that . . . if I don't shut down now, I'll cry. So it only exemplifies, amplifies what you're saying. I know that. And no way in my life am I going to sit here and cry! . . . As you soon as you go 'little girl,' it [the armor] just goes bang on!" She then began to target herself, saying, "It's funny, because it's so gone, it's so done, it's so old. This is where I have very little patience with myself. 'Get over that!!'" Greg and I made shame interventions at that point, with me giving words to her dilemma of change: "You can't get over it. It's been zippered up and you can't just unzip it because it's too humiliating. There's a dilemma there. To heal it you need to open it but you can't open it because it feels scary."

Greg then began a question with the phrase, "Getting back to the little girl . . ." and Madeline cut him off: "That's the shit I hate. Do we have to do that?" I jumped in and said, "No, you don't!" I then reinforced the need for her to collaborate with us in pacing our exploration of difficult material, saying we only wanted to go into topics she wanted to explore and that would be useful to her and that it was very important that she help decide when and how to "unzip." Madeline admitted she was feeling very uncomfortable but said she would allow Greg to finish his question because she didn't want to walk away with regrets. We supported her setting limits again, and she explained that she didn't want to tell stories of her traumatic past because, "It's just fucking awful and why would I want to go over that again?!" We assured her we never intended her to do that and that we didn't believe it would be advisable. Greg said, "Where I come from, we all have parts that are associated with times we'd rather just forget, and embracing those parts is a developmental challenge. I'm thinking about parts of yourself that want an arm put on their shoulder."

This then led to a very productive discussion, where after assuring Madeline that she didn't need to expose her "little girl" to anyone else, I told her, "It will help for *you* to get in touch with that part of yourself you had to lock up and protect, and to learn how to take care of her yourself." Madeline breathed a huge sigh of relief and said that sounded much better to her than letting anyone else deal with that aspect of her. In a moment of joining with Madeline's discomfort, I joked to Greg that if Madeline let us see that part of her fully, "She'd have to kill us." For a second I worried I had gone too far, but uproarious, spontaneous laughter immediately filled the room, and I felt the built-up tension ease. Then Madeline said, "You had me scared there for a minute!" apparently meaning that she feared we would ask her to expose her vulnerability directly.

We spent the rest of the session making a repair with Madeline. Greg said he felt she had let us in and he appreciated that. I said I didn't think it was the time to do the kind of work we were discussing since she was moving in fast forward on so many fronts. I also shared that I had a traumatic past myself and had had to use my own pacing in dealing with that. Madeline confessed, "I feel a little bit beat up today. You hit my soft spot." I apologized and said that perhaps we had been overzealous in trying to do too much. Madeline said she appreciated knowing what "other doors" she could open in the future to pursue her goal of being a better person. At one point, she said, "I'm not feeling vulnerable!" and we all laughed heartily and infectiously again and riffed off that for up to five minutes. Greg said, "I was never thinking that!" I quipped, "Maybe I was for a moment but not now!" Greg continued, "If I was thinking that, I was thinking it warmly." Madeline said, "God, you're funny!" and wiped tears of laughter away from her eyes: "God, I haven't had this much fun since pigs ate my little brother!" After we calmed down, Madeline signaled she still felt some discomfort, and I asked her to talk about "something joyous you're looking forward to." She told about the upcoming mock court she was setting up in her new job, and Greg and I asked detailed questions to distract her and help regulate her emotions. I told her I felt "inspired" listening to the mock court plans, and then we agreed to stop and meet the next day. Madeline said she was better and was going to go driving around.

AFTERTHOUGHTS

After Madeline left, Greg and I talked. Both of us felt good about the session, which had accomplished more than we had ever anticipated in terms of Madeline's becoming aware of Level 3 information. We reminded ourselves not to underestimate her. However, we were both somewhat concerned about Madeline's saying she felt "somewhat beat up." We reassured each other that we had not been overly aggressive with Madeline, that we had challenged her because it could help her, and that she had protected herself when she needed to with our full encouragement. As the day before, we were both very tired and also aware that we needed to prepare for the Summary/Discussion Session the next day, so we shifted to doing that.

Plan for Summary/Discussion Session

As mentioned earlier, the Summary/Discussion Session in TA is a collaborative discussion of test results presented by the assessor along with tentative "answers to the client's questions" and suggestions for next steps. I have written elsewhere about strategies for organizing and preparing such sessions (Finn, 1996a, 1996b, 2007; Tharinger et al., 2008). As is my usual practice, Greg and I put together a detailed outline before the session that we used to guide our discussion. We also made copious notes on the printout about Madeline's comments and examples.

Our overall plan was to begin with mirroring Madeline's strengths and giving a big picture summary that laid out her dilemma of change. We would review the self-report tests, which contained more Level 1 information, and highlight some of the positive changes we saw over the two assessments. We would then move to an in-depth discussion of the Rorschach scoring, which had more Level 2 and 3 information. Finally, if there was time, we would engage Madeline in a collaborative discussion of her AQs. Throughout, we frequently referenced metaphors, turns of phrase we had developed together, and Madeline's own words, seeking to build upon the good work we had done in previous sessions. We brought copies of test profiles and a graph from an article I had co-authored on the Rorschach Trauma Content Index as visual aids. Also, because Madeline had specifically requested concrete "tools" in her third AQ, we carefully thought about therapeutic activities, worksheets, and a book we could recommend that might be useful to her.

There were two sets of findings we had not yet broached with Madeline that we carefully thought through. Madeline was quite curious about the ratings done of her on the NEO-PI-R and circumplex measures by her close friend Tom. We did not yet have a lot of information about Tom's ratings but were aware that he had rated Madeline somewhat more negatively on the interpersonal measures than she had herself. We decided to be matter of fact about this. Also, we had not previously discussed the significant thought disorder shown in Madeline's R-PAS. We decided to put this element on our outline and to share our hypothesis that Madeline's thinking fell apart when she was full of emotion she could not regulate. We even considered the strong possibility that this finding was Level 1 information for her.

Check-In on the Second Day

Madeline arrived on time the next morning, looking slightly rumpled and uncharacteristically eating an energy bar. She said that after she left the previous afternoon, she had vacillated between being "choked" (angry) and not. When we inquired, she said she had realized, "There is a lot of work still to go" and thought, "Why do I have to be responsible for cleaning this up when it's not something I created?" She summarized her own dilemma of change: "You spend a whole lifetime saying, 'Shut this off,' which enabled me to get a whole lot of things done. But there's leftovers that obviously leak out like hazardous material. The container won't keep it there forever." Apparently, she had reached a resolution to her anger after much thought, concluding, "If you clean it up, you'll be a better person" and "If I can put that kind of work into other people, how ridiculous not to do it for myself. It only makes everything else even better." Madeline said she had also been comforted knowing she didn't need to work on her past trauma right away and could do so little by little in her own time.

Madeline also shared a very touching story of the night before. She had not gone driving around as she first thought she might but had returned to the hotel, washed her face, and lay down to read her book. To her surprise, she woke up three hours later. ("I don't even sleep three hours in a row!") Hungry, Madeline had gone to the hotel restaurant, but nothing on the menu looked appetizing to her. She finally asked the waiter, "Can you make me a bowl of tomato soup and a grilled cheese sandwich? I need some comfort food." To deliver this request, she had battled a critical inner voice, "What are you, nine?", eventually deciding, "Who gives a shit?! That's what I want!" After eating, Madeline had returned to her room, watched a bit of TV, and then "slept hard" the entire night—a "once in a decade sleep." We all agreed that she had worked very hard the day previously in our sessions and also had thought hard about our work after she left. Greg and I expressed our appreciation for the way she had reflected on the previous day's events.

Summary/Discussion Session

Madeline was highly engaged and found the process of reviewing the self-report tests fascinating, especially when we compared her previous and current scores on the NEO-PI-R profile. She resonated with all the findings and seemed to feel very understood. She liked that the tests showed less hostility and impulsivity and more Agreeableness than 17 years previously ("I am WAY calmer than I used to be!"). She seemed thrilled that her highest scores were on Openness ("Do not live an uneventful life!"), Extraversion, and Conscientiousness. She identified a great deal with being Tenderminded, both in the past and currently ("I feel for the underdog") and low on Compliance ("I think that [defiance] is a positive trait!"). Also, she was delighted and relieved that the validity scales of the MMPI-2-RF showed that she had been "open and honest," mentioning several times how good it felt to her to have this recognized. When we discussed the interpersonal measures, and in particular her friend Tom's ratings, Madeline found a way to explain his having rated her as having more interpersonal struggles than she saw herself as having: "I was thinking about myself in professional situations with clients. . . . He sees me in a lot of social situations. He has a huge variety of different circumstances to make those observations." That reasoning didn't all add up in our minds, but we saw no reason to challenge it and said we understood.

After a short lunch break, we returned and began talking about Madeline's Rorschach, at first emphasizing her impressive psychological resources and her complexity. She asked many questions about the R-PAS profile pages, which we addressed in part by referring back to specific responses as metaphors of who she was. When she saw the extremely high scores on Stress and Distress ("all those black dots!"), she readily acknowledged that she carries a great deal of emotional pain within her. She was intrigued by our suggestion that if she could address that pain, her considerable psychological resources would be even more available for creativity and happiness. Interestingly, Madeline strongly expressed her disappointment and irritation that her emotional pain had shown through in the test results, saying, "For Christ's sake, I thought I was better at hiding that. . . . These damn tests!" As we thought might happen, Madeline readily accepted our hypothesis that her judgment and thought clarity can get impaired when she is flooded by emotions or hit by trauma triggers: "It's like my head is spinning . . . like those car rims that keep spinning when the car stops . . . anything I create in that space is fucked."

Building on the work of the AIS, we were able to discuss the many trauma markers in Madeline's Rorschach protocol, and I showed her a graph from a study of the Rorschach Trauma Content Index (Kamphuis, Kugeares, & Finn, 2000) that drove home how extreme her score was ("I told you it [the abuse] was brutal!"). In response to one of her questions, we all agreed that Madeline kept people at a distance in part not to reactivate her trauma and that working more on her inner pain would make it safer for her to love. We also validated how important it had been in the past for Madeline to "just shut down" her past trauma but that now she had other options.

At that point, Madeline said that she needed to know more about how to heal from trauma and what tools she could use, so we jumped ahead on our feedback outline to talk about next steps. I had made copies of worksheets from the DBT client skills training worksheets (Linehan, 2014) on emotional regulation, and Madeline was delighted with these ("I can do this!"). We began to talk about strategies that might work for her, and she decided that mindful walking for 30 minutes each morning would be the best for her. As Greg and I talked about current psychotherapy methods for trauma, we emphasized the need to "develop a pause button" and have tools to help "close the zipper" before starting to "open it up." I also emphasized that modern trauma therapies do not focus on "digging up all one's traumatic memories," and Madeline expressed great relief. We said she should do this work "in her own time" and that professional help was available. She asked if I would speak with her current psychotherapist about the assessment results, and I agreed.

Touchingly, after all her insistence that she didn't want to "dig up" her past trauma, at that point in the session, Madeline dropped into telling an explicit trauma memory from her early childhood. It was told as a flashback, in present tense: Madeline is flat on the ground, five years old, her father is drunk and looming over her ("He was over six feet tall!"), striking her repeatedly in the face. ("Smack, smack, smack"—mimicking her head rolling from side to side.) She sees the anger, the sweat, feels the spittle. She grows numb. At one point he pauses, and she asks, "Are you done?" He screams, "No!" and starts again.

"And that was your daily existence," she concluded. I felt a mixture of horror and concern for Madeline at that point, but she seemed almost relieved to have shared the memory with us. She went on to explain how her uncle who had died recently had visited the family when she was young, seen her father's violence, and had physically fought him. After that, when the uncle visited, there would be a break from the father's beatings while he was there. The violence would resume and be worse after the uncle left, but "it was worth it for two magic days of freedom."

I felt that Madeline's recounting all this at that point in the assessment was a sign of how safe and connected she felt to Greg and to me and that she was indeed ready to start facing her past trauma.

We next discussed brief answers to Madeline's AQs, with her taking the lead. She poignantly talked about her anxiety about dealing with judges she had "pissed off" in the past, and we spent some time envisioning how to manage the situation. At this point, Madeline began to thank us and say good-bye, which I saw as a sign that she had had enough and was ready to wrap up. We discussed the next steps in the assessment (I would talk to her therapist if she had him contact me, we would send the feedback letter, we would do a follow-up session by phone.) Madeline lamented that she had not brought something material to give Greg and me at the end. As we stood, I reached to shake her hand, and to my surprise she gestured and offered both me and Greg hugs, literally sweating from the effort. We openly acknowledged the rarity and preciousness of the gift, and after Madeline left, we sat speechless for a few moments, reveling in what had just happened. Needless to say, I was touched, moved, proud . . . and exhausted.

Written Feedback, Follow-Up Session, and Feedback From Madeline

This is the feedback letter Greg and I sent to Madeline:

May 25, 2017
Madeline G

Address

Dear Madeline,

This is the letter we promised you, summarizing the results of the psychological assessment we did together in January and February this year. Although some time has passed, we hope what you read here is familiar and mainly reminds you of our discussions, especially those on February 4, 2017 when we reviewed the test results and addressed your questions for the assessment.

Before getting to the results, we want to thank you again for taking part in the assessment. We know you volunteered largely to benefit science and carry on Jerry Wiggins' work; but we hope and trust you also found it useful personally. We both certainly learned a lot from working with you and are still processing the intense experience. As we said that last day we met, you're so smart, full of life, thoughtful, and intolerant of bullshit that we were challenged to be at the top of our games, and that was exciting. You are a remarkable and memorable person, Madeline, and we're really glad we got to work with you.

Opportunities for Assessment

To review, we met for a total of 23 hours on the weekends of January 6–7 and February 3–4, 2017 at Steve's office in Austin, Texas. The first weekend we discussed your experience being assessed in 1999–2000 for the Wiggins case study, caught up on developments in your life since that time, and developed questions we hoped to address through the assessment this time. You then completed a series of psychological tests:

Minnesota Multiphasic Personality Inventory—2-Restructured Form (MMPI-2-RF)
Interpersonal Adjective Scale (IAS)
Inventory of Interpersonal Problems—Short Circumplex (IIP-SC)
Interpersonal Sensitivities Circumplex (ISC)
Circumplex Scales of Interpersonal Experiences (CSIE)
Circumplex Scales of Interpersonal Values (CSIV)
Washington University Sentence Completion Test, female version (WUSCT-F)
Rorschach Performance Assessment System (R-PAS)
Thematic Apperception Test (selected cards)

After you returned home, you kindly completed several more measures and mailed them back to Steve:

NEO Personality Inventory—Revised (NEO-PI-R), Form S (self-report)
Object Relations Inventory (ORI)

You took many of these tests (or earlier versions) during the 1999 assessment, and we had access to those earlier results also.

Last, you gave your friend, Tom, several inventories to fill out about his observations and experiences of you. He mailed his ratings directly to Steve:

IAS Informant
IIP-SC Informant
NEO-PI-R, Form R (observer report)

Once we had your current test responses, we shared them with our team of experts as follows:

    MMPI-2-RF: Dr. Yossef Ben-Porath, Kent State University
    NEO-PI-R (Forms S and R): Dr. Thomas Widiger and Cristina Crego, University of Kentucky, Lexington
    IAS, IIP-SC, ISC, CISE, CISV: Dr. Chris Hopwood, University of California, Davis, and Dr. Aaron Pincus and Sindes Dawood, Pennsylvania State University
    R-PAS, WUSCT, TAT, and ORI: Dr. Joni Mihura, University of Toledo, and Dr. Mark Waugh, Oak Ridge, Tennessee

Each expert was given only the particular test(s) they were responsible for, as well as your assessment questions and some general information about the sessions we had together. None of them knows your real name. They then provided expert analyses of the tests, which they sent to us (Greg and Steve) to review and integrate for our second meeting with you.

Next you and we met again in February. On the first morning we discussed developments in your life since January and revised your questions for the assessment. In the afternoon we discussed your reactions to cards from various "picture-story" tests: Thurston-Cradock Test of Shame (TCTS), Adolescent Apperception Cards (AAC), Family Apperception Test (FAT), and Roberts Apperception Test (RAT). The second day we shared with you the results of many of the tests you took, comparing some to the results of the 1999 assessment. You gave us your thoughts about the test results, and the three of us discussed your questions for the assessment. We closed by talking about your next steps and by saying good-bye.

The contents of this letter are based on all these sources of information, and importantly, on your thoughts, comments, and reactions as we discussed the test results. Now let us turn to the assessment findings.

The Big Picture

Madeline, we thought it could be helpful, as we did in our final meeting, to first share our sense of the "big picture" that emerges from the assessment results.

    *Basically, the testing suggests you are a **psychologically rich and complex** person with **incredible psychological resources** that literally are "off the charts!" These include your intelligence, perceptiveness, ability to interact with people, big heart, boldness, analytic skills, and creativity.*

Psychologists consider these qualities to be aspects of "ego strength," and you have them in spades. People with lots of ego strength can handle stress and painful events that would put other people under the table, and not only survive, but function well. We experienced your resiliency each time we met, and one way it was evident was in your ability to engage and "play" with new ideas we brought up from the testing.

*Second, no surprise to you, your test scores suggest that you came through **severe trauma** and **emotional neglect** that might have destroyed another person with less fortitude. No testing can say for sure what happened to you in the past, but you told us some, and you have many scores in common with people who have been exposed to severe abuse—with little or no support or protection—and who had to learn to deal with these events on their own. As we just wrote, you not only survived your early challenges, but you have excelled in your life and gone on to help many other people. In addition, from looking at the previous testing, we believe you have continued to change and grow since the time of the first assessment, and this has accelerated recently because of the recent experiences you had with your uncle as he was sick and dying.*

In particular, it seems one of the major ways you coped with your early trauma was by growing impervious "armor" and finding exciting and creative ways to avoid painful feelings. Your armor shifted during the relationship you had with your partner, and this shifting of armor has accelerated recently. Now you've created a life where you no longer need this armor in the same way, and therefore you are more aware of some of the downsides of wearing it all the time. As we discussed, you're now getting to a place where you can use the armor if you need it, but also sometimes put it aside, and even envision opening the "zipper" both from the top and the bottom on your own terms. This presents an opportunity to face some of the painful feelings you had to put aside to survive, and to integrate them in a new way into your personality.

Specific Test Findings

Self-Report Tests

A number of the tests you completed fall under the rubric of "self-report tests" of personality, and involved your responding to True-False questions or rating yourself on various adjectives and items; these include the MMPI-2-RF, NEO-PI-R, IAS, IIP-SC, ISC, CISE, and CSV. These tests are important in showing how you think about yourself and present yourself to the world. They are also valuable in that there are many research studies linking scores on self-report tests to various behaviors and characteristics that are not immediately obvious from the test items.

Your scores on all these tests were generally very consistent with each other, and so, as we did in our last meeting, we will summarize your scores on the NEO-PI-R, the MMPI-2-RF, and the interpersonal circumplex measures (IAS, IIP-SC, ISC, CISE, and CSIV). With all these tests, we can also compare your current scores to those you took in 1999.

NEO-PI-R. This is the "Big 5" personality test developed by Paul Costa and Robert (Jeff) McCrae that you are familiar with from the research you helped with. We are attaching two profile sheets that show your test scores graphically. Let's start with the one marked "Profile 1." The solid dark line shows your current scores on each of the Big 5 scales and the "facet scales" that make them up. We reviewed these findings in our last meeting. Let's first summarize your Total Scores on the main scales. You scored:

- *Low on **Neuroticism**, suggesting you are an emotionally stable, well functioning woman.*
- *Very High on **Extraversion**, suggesting that you are assertive, talkative, upbeat, energetic, optimistic, forceful, able to take a leader role, and able to experience a wide range of positive emotions such as joy, excitement, and laughter.*
- *Very High on **Openness to Experience**, implying you are curious about both your inner and outer worlds, your life is experientially rich, you have an active fantasy life and vivid imagination, are intrigued by music, moved by art, and like novelty. As we discussed, openness to experience appears to be one of the defining features of who you are. For example, you told us about one of your fundamental maxims: Do not lead an uneventful life!*
- *Low to Average on **Agreeableness**—but the total score is not that useful, because you have one very high and two low facet scores. Specifically, you scored:*

  > *High on **Tendermindedness**, meaning you have empathy for the underdog, feel protective, and want to help people you see as hurt and unfairly treated.*
  > *Very Low on **Modesty**. You're not a shrinking violet, can be bold and audacious, are able to take the lead and put yourself in the front where people will see you if you need to—maybe especially to help others. You might be perceived at times by others as blunt, bossy, overly confident, or aggressive*
  > *Low on **Compliance**. You don't like rules imposed on you; when someone tries to do this, you have a tendency to do the opposite automatically, even if it might not be in your best interests. We developed the metaphor that rules are a "red cape" that gets your bull to charge!*

- *You also are generally high on **Conscientiousness**, suggesting you are hard-working, organized, reliable, and carry through tasks to completion. One facet score is very low: **Deliberation**, suggesting that at times you might act hastily without considering the consequences.*

You generally agreed with all these interpretations when we discussed them.

What was really fascinating, and is also shown in Profile 1, are the changes in your scores since the 1999 assessment:

- ***Neuroticism**: there are big drops in your self-reported **Angry Hostility** and **Impulsiveness**. You said these fit with your sense of yourself as being much calmer these days. There were also healthy increases in your recognition of **Anxiety** and **Depression**. Your previous scores suggested these were disavowed states for you; now you can accept them more as part of your experience, while not being overwhelmed by them.*
- ***Extraversion**: you went from being off the charts to being still high, but not as extreme. Particularly, **Gregariousness** and **Excitement Seeking** show the biggest changes; both have dropped some, suggesting you are more able to enjoy being alone, don't have to engage others all the time, and are able to tolerate and enjoy being quiet. You confirmed this change, telling us you used to enjoy "being over the top," but that this is less true of you nowadays.*
- ***Openness to Experience**: there are no major changes at all, suggesting this is a very stable, defining feature of your personality.*
- ***Agreeableness**: this is the area where you see yourself as having changed the most since 1999. You are more **Straightforward** now and less **Defiant** (i.e., more Compliant). You are less likely to "charge at the red cape" if someone waves a rule at you. You are still able to be bold and assertive, but in a more balanced way.*
- ***Conscientiousness**: this area too is very much the same, suggesting that being highly conscientious is another core aspect of who you are. You are slightly more **Dutiful** now than in 1999 and more likely to **Deliberate** before acting.*

MMPI-2-RF. As we discussed, the MMPI-2-RF is a problem-screening instrument, but it can also give information on your personality, and your scores were remarkably consistent with the NEO-PI-R in showing that you are a well-functioning woman with no major mental illness, and that you are tough-minded, daring, active, adventurous, like excitement, and can push limits at times. Your extraversion is also very apparent; your scores suggest you are not at all shy, have a great desire to be around people, and are not at all passive in your relationships.

Because the MMPI-2-RF is a problem-focused test, there were a few areas that showed up that are not measured by the NEO-PI-R:

- *A tendency towards substance abuse. You can and have used substances for fun and to cope with difficult things. This can lead to all kinds of problems, and it's great that you are using your counselor, Michael Jones, to help keep an eye on your drinking.*
- *Interpersonal struggles. Your scores suggest that people who don't know you well may think you are cold, uncaring, and don't need anything from others. As we'll write about below, we think this presentation is part of the 'armor" you had to develop to survive both your early life and the prejudices you've faced as a native person and woman.*

There was one highly significant change since 1999 in your MMPI scores—in your activity level. Dr. Ben-Porath, our MMPI expert, wrote to you about this. To quote:

". . . a comparison of the two sets of MMPI scores shows that though you are not someone who lacks energy and drive, these have become quite substantially diminished since you were last assessed. For someone accustomed to the "natural high" associated with elevated mood and energy levels, this can be quite a letdown, leaving you feeling disoriented. . . . Most people lose some of their energy and drive as they reach middle age. People with particularly high levels of energy and drive, such as you were when last assessed, have more energy to lose and may be particularly cognizant of this loss. What were some of their defining features (e.g., high energy, little need for sleep) are reduced to levels that are average for most people, but represent a significant loss for them . . . Your loss of energy, moving from very, very high to just normal, though disorienting, may also have positive consequences. Needing to build up toward action rather than acting immediately may help you avoid negative outcomes. Embracing this new part of you could be a meaningful part of your redirection."

Interpersonal circumplex measures. As we discussed in our last meeting, the information from these tests was largely consistent with the NEO-PI-R. In general you rated yourself as a person who can be both kind or compliant and assertive, and who has less interpersonal problems than the average person. You did recognize that at times you can appear too bossy or controlling. There is one area measured by these tests that is not covered well by the other measures—comfort with emotional closeness. Your scores suggest that you are put off by people who try to get close and generally prefer it when people keep their distance. When we discussed this, you told us that in general you are not a "hugger." Your scores also suggest that you are less bothered than the average person when people are cold to you.

Informant Ratings

Your friend, Tom, filled out ratings of you on the NEO-PI-R and on the interpersonal circumplex measures. We now have more information about these ratings than when we last talked, and we are enclosing another NEO profile sheet (Profile 2) that compares Tom's ratings to yours from the current assessment.

Before getting into these, we should say that it is common for there to be substantial differences between self-report and informant ratings, and it is not always clear why this is so. However, it is typical to have at least some characteristics where we see our self differently from how others we are close to see us.

As you can see, you and Tom were in close agreement on your very high level of **Conscientiousness** *and your high* **Extraversion,** *although on the facet scales for the latter he rated you as less* **Warm** *and* **Gregarious** *than you rated yourself. Tom also rated you as high on* **Openness to Experience,** *although not as high as you rated yourself. Openness to experience is primarily subjective, so it is fairly common for self-ratings and information ratings to disagree. This same kind of reasoning may help explain the differences in your and his ratings on several of the facet scales of Agreeableness; you rated yourself as average on* **Trust** *these days and also as very high in* **Tendermindedness,** *whereas Tom rated you as very low on* **Trust** *and as average to low on* **Tendermindedness.**

The area where you and Tom differed the most was on **Neuroticism.** *In general, you rated yourself average to low, whereas Tom rated you as average but with high scores on* **Anxiety** *and very high scores on* **Angry Hostility** *and* **Depression.** *We discussed these differences in our last session and you were pretty sure you knew why the ratings were different; you had been thinking about how you are at work and with clients, while Tom was probably rating you more as you come off socially. It's also possible that because Tom is a close friend that you disclose more of your uncomfortable emotions to him than you show to other people.*

Similarly, on the interpersonal circumplex forms, Tom rated you as having an average level of interpersonal problems—in contrast to your low ratings—and specifically that you can be too cold and dominant at times.

Rorschach

The Rorschach is a very different type of test than the self-reports, and it "lifts the hood" and gets below the top layer of personality. Because the Rorschach taps areas of the brain that are less connected to conscious thought, it sometimes shows things that people may not be as aware of, or things people are on the verge of putting into words about themselves. This was apparent when we discussed some of your actual responses to the inkblots and explored their metaphorical meaning together. But let us first review the information that comes from your test scores:

1) *You are a complex person! Madeline, your Rorschach protocol was rich, complex, and highly creative. In part this shows what a remarkably complex person you are psychologically and how difficult it is to "summarize you" in any brief account. We experienced this very challenge in writing this letter! Your being so complex has advantages in terms of keeping life interesting, but it could also lead others to find you confusing at times.*

   As we discussed, there was also an increase in how complex your Rorschach was compared to the one you took with Rebecca Behrends in 1999; the three of us considered various possibilities as to why. Your sense was that this time you felt freer to say what you saw because we were genuinely interested and open to your responses, whereas you perceived Rebecca as challenging, distant, and skeptical.

2) *You have amazing psychological strengths. You'll remember our earlier statement that you have incredible "ego strength." Well the Rorschach is one of the major tests that show this clearly. Your scores are associated with people who are resilient, hard working, thoughtful, creative, skilled with people, empathic, and good at analyzing situations. Basically, as we wrote earlier, this all means that you have an incredible capacity to deal with psychological stress and do well in situations that others would not be able to survive. Your Rorschach scores also validated the boldness, assertiveness, and take-charge attitude shown by the other tests, and we agreed that a good metaphor for this aspect of you was the powerful ship you saw pushing forward on Card I of the Rorschach.*

3) *Underlying pain and vulnerability related to past trauma. As we discussed, your Rorschach scores suggested that underneath your excellent coping skills, there is a lot of emotional discomfort, in part left over from your difficult childhood. This was powerfully captured in your image of the opera singer on Card II of the Rorschach, who was singing a powerful lament full of emptiness and sadness while her eyes dripped with tears.*

   We also looked at a graph of the Rorschach Trauma Index, where your score was much higher than that found in groups of women who were highly traumatized. Your score here suggests you are still recovering from your past traumas, but this is not likely visible to others. You agreed with this finding, but were surprised—and a bit disappointed—that the Rorschach was able to reveal this aspect of your experience. It's possible that this underlying pain is closer to the surface right now because of your recent experiences with your uncle, as well as more visible because of the openness and spontaneity you brought to the assessment.

4) *You can get caught up in your emotions. Although your incredible psychological strengths have allowed you to do well in the face of your traumatic early life, the Rorschach shows a few areas where you didn't get off scot-free. Your scores suggest you experience very strong and sometimes opposite emotions; these shape your experience greatly and can lead to rapid intense changes in the way the world looks to you. (Remember your image of the strong peaceful caribou that transformed into the KKK guys with guns blazing? Or the party in Paris that morphed into the London policemen who were being tortured?) Your scores also suggest you have a tendency to get caught up in your emotions, have trouble applying the breaks, and can act impulsively. Last, when you are emotionally flooded, your judgment and thinking can get disorganized and you're not likely to make good decisions. You agreed and told us that when you get "spinning" emotionally, anything you create from that space is "fucked up!"*

5) *Underlying insecurity covered by disdain. Like anybody who's been abused as a child, your scores suggest there are some deep inner feelings of insecurity (not at all matching your real competence) that can get triggered at times, and that you might not always be aware of how they affect you. The Rorschach says one way you might react is by putting up your "armor"—where you can look dominant, powerful, cold, disdainful, and intimidating. This stance helps address the insecure inner voice that isn't able to hold onto the reality of how special you are, and it creates a different sense of being special based on being "better than" other people. Last, this presentation also deals with any outward challenge or trigger, by inviting or helping the other person to feel the underlying shame you don't want to experience.*

6) *You are in the middle of an important transformation. One of the strongest senses we came away with from your Rorschach is that you are in the middle of an important shift in your personality in which you are integrating aspects of yourself you had to put aside or deny earlier in your life in order to survive. This transformation appears to have begun much earlier in your life—when you decided to make something of yourself. It continued through your relationship with Sugarman, where you learned that being kind is not the same as being weak. And we think your recent experiences of being close to your uncle as he was sick and dying, and then letting yourself grieve his loss, have impacted you greatly and pushed you even further in your personal growth. As we discussed at length, one of your Rorschach*

responses seemed to capture this aspect of your journey clearly—your response to Card V that Greg gave you a copy of:

. . . within this, unfortunately you got considerable sadness on either outer side. Like being trapped in here. Like people; bodies being trapped in here. But if you look at it as a whole, a blossoming cocoon. But if you look at it closer, not so nice. And more trapped on the inner area of the wings at the bottom. More profiles trapped on the top. But if you look at the dark line down the center, you can unzip that and they can all just be free and not trapped . . . But the worst is this little bugger is carrying all that weight. Can't fly, can't move. Cause all of this is inside. Like grounded—and not in a good way. Like if an eagle was grounded. Not good. . . . The neat thing about this is see how it's all pushing from the inside out? If they can get their hands and unzip this seam and peel this off, then maybe they can come out of this. But they're not going to be a butterfly. So, possible for a transformation, but it will require a totally new identification

As this response captures, part of your current transformation appears to involve your recognizing sad and pained parts of you that you had to put aside in order to survive, but that are now "weighing you down" and interfering with new ways of "flying." One part of this change seems to be a new desire to relax your fierce independence and to work together in a team with other people. This need for affiliation was certainly there in your Rorschach from 1999, but it appears more intense and closer to the surface now.

Other Tests

The remaining tests you took (TAT, SCT, and ORI) were largely congruent with all that we have written above, but we wanted to comment on the change in your TAT results since 1999. As you may remember, you also took this test with Rebecca Behrends. Again, let us quote from the interpretation sent to us by one of our experts, Dr. Mark Waugh:

> "[Madeline's] current TAT responses include a greater sense of awareness of emotional conflict as opposed to [her 1999 stories] . . . her current stories revealed dark and disturbing emotions as opposed to the [earlier] responses in which she seemed to distance and cover over such content with "fun" and ribald narrative . . . Coping through blanket disavowal of vulnerable feelings likely has been strategically valuable for Madeline over her life . . . Madeline nonetheless risked self-revelation on the TAT. This probably occurred because she is (1) more mature psychologically now than in [1999] . . . and (2) she had achieved a degree of trust and comfort with her Examiners (SF and GM) at this point in the TA process. This observation further implies increased potential for improved personal and social relationships . . . ."

So as you see, many of the tests converge in presenting a picture of where you are now that is highly relevant to addressing your assessment questions.

Answers to Your Assessment Questions

Why Am I Not so Driven Right Now? Where Has That Gone?

First, as you told us clearly, you don't want to be so driven anymore. Something important in you shifted through your experiences with your uncle, and you want to be inspired, rather than driven. As you eloquently said, being driven feels "selfish" to you now, while being inspired feels like a movement towards something and towards other people.

Second, your test scores suggest that this shift is part of the mellowing that has taken place in your personality, in part through the experiences you've had of grief and connecting with others (like your uncle and your brother), and in part through a natural process of maturation based on your ability to reflect on life and yourself, and to learn and grow. Not everyone grows and becomes wiser as they age, but you have, and this is a reflection of your openness to the world around you and your capacity to think deeply and learn from your experiences.

Third, this transformation process you are in takes enormous amounts of psychic energy, and this is affecting your overall energy level. We used the metaphor of living in a house that is being remodeled; it's tiring and frustrating at times. It makes sense that you would approach life now in a less driven way, and this will help consolidate the changes you are making internally.

Last, your driven-ness was in part an old coping mechanism you used to cope with the difficult aspects of your life—a suit of armor you used to keep going and to stay above troubling feelings. Now this suit of armor isn't needed as much—the troubling feelings aren't as dangerous—and it no longer fits as well as it did in the past.

Having said all this this, we want to assure you, Madeline, that the testing says you're still a Ferrari! And we predict you will be better than ever as soon as the new updated "software" is finished being installed.

How Do I Get Judges I've Alienated Before to See the New Person I'm Becoming and Believe It's Authentic?

We're very interested in how this situation is developing! When we last met we all agreed there are some real parts of the current situation that could help: 1) you and the judges are in new roles, and in your new role you don't have to be the same kind of warrior you once were; 2) you also have equal footing and the situation doesn't give the judges a structural advantage for power, and 3) as we wrote above, you are a different person than you used to be, and the testing says this is likely to influence the way you handle all kinds of interpersonal situations.

Another idea we discussed: if you want the judges to give you a second chance, perhaps you also need to be willing to do the same. The testing says you faced traumatic events in the past, and one trauma survival mechanism is to sort people into friend and foe quickly, instinctively, and without too much pondering. Perhaps some of your "foes" can be reclassified while keeping your "sentinels" active. Your increasing ability to be more deliberative will help with this reclassification. The testing says you're also more able to see people as complex mixtures of positive and negative qualities than you were in the past. This was evident to us when you discussed all kinds of important people in your life, and it should apply to these judges also.

Last, we all agreed you should try not to get all ruffled and take it personally or absolutely if they at first treat you as if you're the old Madeline. They need time and exposure to the genuine changes you have made and are making. There may be some rigid assholes who can't shift, but we hope they won't be the majority.

What Tools Do I Need to Effectively Remain Inspired?

Let us start by reminding you of what you told us: you need community, a team, and supportive relationships to stay inspired. The work situation you were setting up when we last met seemed to fit this bill exactly, and we look forward to hearing more about how it is going.

Also, as you noted when we looked at the Big 5 measure together, there are some places you can work on yourself that will make you a better person and help you do your job better. In particular the testing says you should continue decreasing your tendency to charge the red cape of unjust authority, and you will benefit from more ability to deliberate and choose your course of action. All of this will involve getting more skills in emotional regulation, which will also help your thinking stay organized, realistic, and clear in tough situations.

We talked about various ways to work on emotional regulation:

1) *Referring to and practicing the skill sheets we gave you from Dialectical Behavior Therapy, which listed ways of using distractions and self-soothing to manage strong emotions.*
2) *"Mindfulness" techniques, like meditation, Tai Chi, and martial arts. Here you came up with a great idea that would work for you: walking in nature as often as you can. Activities like this not only influence daily mood and make it easier to manage emotions, but they also change the brain over time and make it easier to stay in a wise mind when we are in emotionally arousing situations.*
3) *New trauma recovery therapies—such as EMDR, Somatic Therapy, and Sensory Experiencing—which involve combinations of imagery*

work, body work, and breathing. We recommended a recent book by Bessel Van der Kolk, The Body Keeps the Score that mentions some of these, and you emailed Steve that you were reading it. We look forward to hearing your reactions.

Another way to stay inspired is to recognize and understand how your "armor" works.

- *What does it feel like as it is "thickening?" This step involves increasing awareness of the actual body sensations that can cue you that are going into trauma survival mode, like seeing the hair rise on the back of your dog.*
- *What triggers your armor? This step is more preemptive, as you recognize when conditions are ripe, which could include attitudes, nonverbal signals, body language, words, internal thoughts, fears, beliefs, and perceptions.*

Gaining these cues will allow you more and more to consciously decide earlier in the process whether you need your armor: "How much is there a real threat, vs. am I reacting to something that reminds me of old threats that are no longer as dangerous?" As you said when we discussed this, first you'll realize the next day that you went into defense mode, then 2 hours later, then 1 hour later, then right after it happens, then while it is happening, then just as it's about to happen. Your capacity to reflect on yourself and analyze will help this process unfold, as long as you can stay compassionate with yourself. This leads to your last question.

How Do I Deal With the [Inner] Chatter and the Typical Rumor Mill? How Do I Address All That?

We all agreed that the outer chatter can be dealt with using the techniques we described for handling the judges. You said the bigger deal is the inner chatter.

The testing suggests you're vulnerable to the inner chatter because of several things:

1) *Like all people who have been traumatized there is a part of you that came to feel worthless, defective, and undeserving because of the way your attachment figures treated you. (These are the people who were supposed to provide you with safety, nourishment, and protection as you developed.) You are so strong that these shame feelings went deep underground and were protected by the confident, strong warrior part of you who could go into "scorched earth mode" if needed to keep you safe. But, the underlying shame is still there to some extent and it can get you to set unreasonably high*

standards for yourself and other people, or keep you from giving yourself a break.

2) *You haven't yet been in the psychological place and had the support you needed to deal with the shamed and hurt parts of yourself. This hasn't been that necessary up till now for you to get what you want out of life. But your goals are shifting, and some part of you is recognizing the benefits of "unzipping" and letting these parts of yourself out into the light of day. When you're ready, learning how to speak to and comfort these parts YOURSELF, will bring you more stability, sturdiness, and less vulnerability to both inner and outer chatter. The goal here is not the absence of inner chatter (we both find we still have some) but being more able to manage it effectively. Michael, or another therapist, can help you with this process.*

In closing, Madeline, thank you again for participating in this Therapeutic Assessment and for your openness through the whole process. If you have any questions or comments about this letter feel free to email us. Otherwise, we propose to have a 60-minute follow-up session, either by phone or web conference, to discuss your reactions to the letter and the assessment. We are both very interested in how you are doing since we last saw you. Assuming you're open to talking, our next step is identify some possible dates. One or both of us is from away May 31-June 25, July 10-23, and August 3-16. So if there are days that work for you in between those days, email us what works for you, and we can suggest some possible specific times you can choose from.

One last thing: we're enclosing two forms Steve developed to get feedback from clients on their Therapeutic Assessments. We're hoping you will fill them out and mail them back in the enclosed envelope. (If you want to wait until after the follow-up session, that is fine with us.) Your honest reactions will help us learn more about how to help people in the future.

Warmly,

Stephen E. Finn

Licensed Psychologist
(TX # 23064)
sefinn@mail.utexas.edu

Gregory J. Meyer

Licensed Psychologist
(OH # 6076)
gregory.meyer@UToledo.edu

Encl: NEO Profiles (2)
Feedback Questionnaire
Assessment Questionnaire
SAE

As you can see from the date (May 25), I did not complete the final draft of this letter until several months after our final meeting with Madeline. While a delay like this is not unheard of given my busy life, I did take more time and care than usual writing Madeline's letter because I wanted to do justice to the intense process we had engaged in and I did not want to write anything that would damage the work we had done with Madeline. (I am aware it is different to read things in black and white than to hear them.) During the interval, I exchanged a number of emails with her regarding travel reimbursements owed her and other administrative matters. I let Madeline know that the feedback letter was in process, and she never signaled any distress or impatience about the wait. When I sent the letter by U.S. postal mail, I also sent an electronic version via email (in a password protected file). Madeline wrote back immediately to say she was away for several weeks and would read the letter when she got back. Three weeks later, she sent another email saying she had just returned, had a deadline to meet, and would get back to us after she had read the letter. Two weeks later, when we hadn't heard from her, I emailed again suggesting dates for the follow-up session—some closer in time and others a month away (because Greg and I would be traveling). Madeline responded immediately saying a month later would be better. I contacted her after a month, and Madeline responded immediately asking to wait more time. She said she still hadn't read the feedback letter because she wanted to give it "the time and thought it deserves." Of course we agreed, and I offered her specific times for a phone meeting several weeks later. Madeline didn't reply immediately, and ten days later I contacted her again about an email we had from her therapist, Michael Jones, asking to speak with Greg and me. Madeline again gave us permission to talk to Michael and proposed that we schedule our follow-up meeting a month later. We finally agreed to meet on September 15, 2017.

Telephone Follow-Up Session

Greg and I had initially proposed meeting by video conference so we could see each other's faces, but Madeline said she didn't want to "learn the technology" so we met by phone. She opened the call saying it had been "a wild ride" since she last saw us and telling about a number of work successes she had had. She said she was embracing her role as a teacher and had been presented with other exciting employment opportunities beyond her current job. When we asked how she was personally,

Madeline told us she had put an online profile on a dating website ("I took it seriously. Honest!"), had met a man she had become "enamored with," and had eventually broken off the relationship when she realized she was more serious than the man was. Her overall take on the experience was quite positive ("Exhilarating!"), and she was proud of herself both for having been open to trying a relationship and ending it when it didn't seem right. She summarized: "I got hurt a little, but so what!?" She also told of a new screen saver she had put on her computer that read, "I've been strong because I've been weak. I am wise because I've been foolish." She said she thought her willingness to date again definitely was connected to the assessment experience.

When we asked for other thoughts about the assessment, Madeline said it was a very positive experience, although sometimes she felt "overexposed" by what had been revealed. She repeated that the experience with us was very different and much more positive than with the first assessment and said, "You were interested in me as a person!" She said she was still troubled by the fact that she didn't remember her interview in Chicago with Dan McAdams but openly acknowledged, "I think this is because we talked about my trauma." She told us she had recently spent two weeks with her brother, talking about the past and "filling in the story."

When we inquired about the assessment feedback letter, Madeline said it had been very meaningful, there was nothing she disagreed with, and that she had reread it carefully a number of times. She also was reading the book we had recommended about healing from trauma (Van der Kolk's *The Body Keeps the Score*, 2014) and she said it was very helpful. Interestingly, Madeline had misplaced the DBT skills sheets I had given her and asked me to send them again. She reported she was walking some in nature but said she was still having trouble "turning her mind off." Greg said he would consult with a colleague about something for Madeline could read about mindfulness. He emailed Madeline later with a book recommendation. Madeline said the butterfly card I had given her was mounted on her wall, and she expressed appreciation for the ongoing contact with Greg and me ("Our engagement over a number of months is incredible. It helps you recognize who you are!") We all marveled in the changes that had occurred in her over the course of the assessment. ("I was a car that ran out of gas. I felt really empty. Now I feel full.")

Verbal and Written Feedback From Madeline

Several weeks after the follow-up meeting, Madeline mailed me the completed assessment feedback forms that I had sent with her letter: 1) a questionnaire with open-response questions and 2) the Assessment Questionnaire (AQ), a 48-item, standardized rating form used at the Center for Therapeutic Assessment to assess client's reactions to a psychological assessment (Finn et al., 1994).[3] The Assessment Questionnaire has four internally consistent subscales and a general score indicating a client's overall level of satisfaction with the assessment. Madeline's scores on each scale, where 5 equals "Strongly Agree" and 1 equals "Strongly Disagree" were: 1) New Self-awareness/ Understanding = 3.92 (T=51); 2) Positive-Accurate Mirroring = 3.5 (T=50); 3) Positive Relationship with the Assessor = 4.17 (T=53), 4) Negative Feelings about the Assessment = 2 (T=52), and 5) Overall Satisfaction = 3.85 (T=52).[4] All of these scores showed that Madeline felt very positively about the TA, especially about her connection to me and Greg. In Madeline's open-ended responses, she indicated that the assessment:

> [W]ent well beyond what I had anticipated . . . I was not prepared for the *intensity* that is associated with the assessment process. At the end of each day, I was surprised how exhausted and drained I *felt*. Though deeply rewarding, the process is also very revealing and this required work (self work) well after the assessment process was complete.

Phone Meeting With Madeline's Psychotherapist

Almost exactly one month later, Greg and I spoke by phone with Madeline's psychotherapist, Michael. He said that Madeline had given him a copy of the assessment feedback letter and he had found it very interesting. He said there had been no surprises for him, as he had an extensive background in treating traumatized clients and had known Madeline for some time, but he believed the assessment had helped Madeline become more self-aware. He told of changes he had seen in her since the assessment:

> "She has taken more personal responsibility . . . It has started to help calm her . . . It's actually been therapeutic for her . . . She is taking the drinking thing seriously and seeing the benefits of not drinking."

Michael explained that in his position with Legal Aid he was not able to see Madeline more than from time to time, so she would need another therapist if she wanted to do more intense work on her past trauma. We all agreed she would need an experienced psychotherapist if she wanted to do that work, because as Michael said, Madeline was "challenging . . . but also inspiring."

Reflections

As I have sat with the rich experience of working with Greg on this Therapeutic Assessment of Madeline, I have come to think of it as TA "pushed to its limits." Here we had an extraordinarily resourceful individual—Madeline—who was in a new "spurt" of what clearly had been a lifelong process of growth and development. She was recovering from "brutal" (to use her word) early childhood trauma and a disorganized attachment, as well as significant cultural prejudice against her as a woman and a Native American. Her life experiences and her inner strength and determination had made her who she was, a highly complex, competent woman who was committed to helping the underdog and who longed for and valued affiliation. But, the character armor (cf. Reich, 1945/1972) she had needed to survive throughout her life was catching up with her and had also been pierced in recent years by several important losses that had left her uncomfortably in touch with painful feelings she had successfully kept out of awareness for years.

Is it possible to use our psychological assessment tools as part of a collaborative interpersonal process to help someone like this, even if they themselves don't come seeking such assistance? To be sure, at the beginning of this project I had my doubts. But given the changes Greg and I witnessed in Madeline during our sessions, Madeline's feedback that the assessment had been very helpful, and her psychotherapist's report that the TA had been therapeutic, I must conclude, "Yes, TA can even be effective under these circumstances."

It is interesting to reflect on what "worked" about the model in this specific case. Clearly, we helped Madeline construct a more coherent narrative of how her personality, early history, and recent events came together to make sense of her behavior and her recent experiences. There was a considerable advantage to having assessment materials that spanned almost 20 years for this process of meaning making. Also, I believe we helped address Madeline's underlying shame, an inevitable result of her insecure attachment and early trauma but also of the various ways she had had to survive over the years at great cost to her and others. In particular, in a piece of the assessment that was both risky and very delicate, our collaborative use of performance-based personality tests (in the Extended Inquiry of the WUSCT and Rorschach, and the Assessment Intervention Session) allowed us to find a language for the pained and trapped aspects of Madeline that had been largely banished from her awareness and to bring them into the light where they could begin to be reintegrated. Although she was openly ambivalent about our having "seen" these parts of her, in the end it was Madeline who both gave us the needed information and acknowledged that we were "right." From a Control Mastery perspective (Cf. Finn, 2005; Weiss, 1993), we might say Madeline tested Greg and me to see if we believed she was strong enough to face her past trauma and whether we would be courageous enough to give full answers to her Assessment Questions. I now believe it was essential that we did and that the TA would not have been as effective if we had been too cautious. By inviting Madeline to confront her wounded side, we were able to send the message that this part of herself was not shameful and deserved her attention and care. Finally, the TA framework gave us the permission and the structure to provide Madeline with an experience of respect, authenticity, and professional caring that would not have been possible within an assessment model that focused too narrowly on information gathering at the expense of co-creating a healing interpersonal experience.

There is an additional healing element to TA that I have not yet written about but that was highlighted for me with in this case: the power of play. In reviewing the session videos in preparing for this chapter, I was struck by the playful quality of the rapid back and forth of ideas and emotions that spontaneously and creatively flowed between Madeline, Greg, and me in many of our meetings. We "played" at aggression, sexuality, tragedy, and healing—particularly in our Extended Inquiries and the Assessment Intervention Session—and so rendered these themes more comprehensible, less frightening, and more manageable. I was powerfully reminded of Handler's (1999) appeal that we all make more room for playfulness in our psychological assessments and his frequent references to Winicott's (1971) statement that "play facilitates growth and therefore health" (p. 144).

I wrote earlier about TA and the restoration of epistemic trust in individuals with personality disorders (Chapter 2), and I was well aware of this process during our work with Madeline. Early in our meetings, she was openly challenging whenever Greg or I made an interpretation or voiced a hypothesis about her or her life; in later sessions, she accepted and even sought out such input. Clearly one thing that helped reduce her hypervigilance was the personal meaning we all found in some of her Rorschach responses (for example, the "coyote sentinels" on Card I), which delighted her and promoted mentalization (Fonagy, 1998). Also, during the Summary/Discussion Session, Madeline frequently mentioned how impressed she was with the accuracy of the test interpretations we offered, and she said the same thing after reading the feedback letter. Assuming we did help restore some degree of epistemic trust in Madeline, this has import beyond helping her update her narrative via the assessment. Fonagy and colleagues (Fonagy et al., 2017) have written about a "virtuous cycle" in effective psychotherapy, where renewed epistemic trust allows clients to *continue* to take in input from the interpersonal environment long after therapy ends so they continue to adapt to changing circumstances. Only time will tell if this proves true for Madeline, but the fact that she was exploring romantic relationships again at the time of the follow-up session after ten years of having closed that door suggests to me that she is continuing to change and grow in new ways.

To guard against the danger of becoming too self-satisfied about the success of Madeline's TA, I find it important to remember that this assessment involved a coming together of many special circumstances. First, Madeline felt great loyalty to the assessment project she had taken part in

17 years ago and was willing to be assessed again, and although she would never have self-referred for a TA, she was in a period of great personal turmoil that rendered her open to and interested in professional help and personal exploration. Second, the clinical team comprised of two highly experienced assessors with a long relationship of respect and caring for each other, which proved essential for tolerating the intensity of the countertransference reactions to Madeline. Third, the consultants who reviewed and interpreted the tests were all experts at the top of the field, and they easily adopted a practical, experience-near language in analyzing their respective instruments. Fourth, Krista K. Trobst, whom Madeline had known for many years, was able to travel to Austin to support Madeline around the intense TA sessions. Fifth, the cost of Madeline's travel and of the professional time put into the assessment was donated by the members of the assessment team. This is especially relevant given that the TA involved 23 hours of face-to-face time with two Ph.D. psychologists. There are probably few people who could afford to pay for such an assessment, and it is unlikely that most health insurance companies would be willing to reimburse for it.

In fact, as successful as the TA of Madeline was, I also see it as a cautionary tale. I think it is crucial that we as psychologists understand the power of our psychological tests and procedures and hold this in mind when we engage our clients. I was struck by the fact that Madeline mentioned feeling "overexposed" after the assessment, even with all the attention Greg and I put to addressing and countering her shame. I was reminded of Schafer's (1954) warning that that clients may see the assessor as a "voyeur" and Ward's (2008) finding that clients may feel uncomfortable with the "perspicacity of the assessor." It seems important to note that this discomfort can occur also in TA, with its major emphasis on fostering a secure alliance and reducing shame.

Like Madeline, Greg and I were also struck by her apparently "blocking out" her interview with Dan McAdams from the previous assessment. It seems quite possible that Madeline's telling her true story for the first time in her life was overwhelming and perhaps retraumatizing and that she did this in part because of her desire to be a "good research subject" and because of McAdam's warm demeanor and skilled interviewing. Perhaps it should give us pause that no one on the well-meaning assessment team anticipated how difficult this might be for Madeline.

I believe the current assessment also sheds new light on the events of the subsequent leg of Madeline's assessment journey, when she went to Yale to be tested by Rebecca Behrends. We now know that Madeline met people as she traveled to New Haven and decided to go out drinking with them that night. Was this a way to cope with the emotional arousal of what had happened in Chicago? As recounted in the Wiggins (2003) book, when Madeline spoke with Dr. Behrends that night, she tried to negotiate a later starting time the next morning as she "had made other plans" but was told that was not possible. When Madeline was 45 minutes late the next morning, Rebecca called her and eventually reached her. Madeline showered and came right over to the clinic, where she was tested all day—we now know—with a severe hangover. Was Madeline's sense that Rebecca was "cold and judgmental" toward her a projection of her own guilt, a transference projection stemming from the cold dominant authority figures in her childhood, or simply a reflection of the typical boundaries of a traditional assessment relationship? We may never know, but it is worth considering whether any of the personological interpretations of Madeline's test data from that time could have been influenced by this series of events. And I believe all us must remember as assessment psychologists that when we ask clients to be tested, even as part of a research project, it is our responsibility to be cognizant of the intra- and interpersonal processes we may set in motion.

Of course, in the end, the data that Greg and I collected are also inevitably influenced by the relational context that we and Madeline built together; this fact is a fundamental aspect of the existential/phenomenological perspective that led Constance Fischer (1985/1994) to her pioneering work on collaborative assessment. I am left profoundly grateful for the experience of this assessment, proud of the amazing "empathy magnifiers" we call psychological tests, and humbled and rewarded to have been able to use Therapeutic Assessment with such an extraordinary person. I don't know if Madeline will ever read this chapter or this book (we discussed the possibility and she was not sure she wanted to) but in case she does, I close by addressing her directly.

Madeline, thank you so much for letting me and us get to know you and for telling your story. We are left inspired and enlarged from having known you and full of respect for all of who you are. I have no doubt that you will continue to grow and heal, and please know I will always be interested in how your life is unfolding.

Notes

1. TA assessors are trained to reference one or more of the client's AQs at the beginning of an AIS as a way to enlist curiosity and cooperation and lower epistemic hypervigilance (Finn, 2007; Kamphuis & Finn, 2018).
2. In retrospect, I am intrigued that Madeline associated to this film at this moment. Although she meant it as a positive reference, the message of this movie and the novel on which it is based (Kundera, 1984) is that we can escape repeating history by acting "freely" and recklessly, a theme that seems prominent in Madeline's approach to life.
3. A copy of the Assessment Questionnaire is available from the author.
4. The T-scores for the AQ are derived from a sample (N = 300) of clients from the Center for Therapeutic Assessment in Austin, TX. Because the clients were so highly satisfied, the range of scores was very restricted, and it is very difficult to get T-scores above 50.

Chapter 8

Past, Present, and Future in Personality Assessment

Christopher J. Hopwood and Mark H. Waugh

This project began with the landmark *Paradigms of Personality Assessment*, in which Wiggins (2003) provided a comprehensive and concise review of five major paradigms of personality assessment and then brought these paradigms to life through the collaborative evaluation of Madeline G. This book details the results of a follow-up assessment of Madeline 17 years later.

Wiggins summarized her as follows:

> On the whole, it is likely that Madeline is at most average in her communal tendencies, and that her less agreeable characteristics interfere with her being seen as particularly warm and nurturing by others, whatever her sympathetic thoughts and altruistic motives may be. It is likely that when Madeline expresses caring she does so through highly agentic actions; however welcome those actions may be, they probably leave intimates feeling more *assisted* than *nurtured*.
>
> (p. 307)

Wiggins also noted that people who knew her well experienced Madeline as a "highly complex and highly intelligent individual, who loves and lives life more fully than most" (p. 317). He concluded that the different assessment paradigms largely agreed in their depiction of Madeline's personality, although there were certain important differences in emphasis.

The general conclusion from our re-evaluation of Madeline 17 years later was largely consonant with Wiggins' (2003) description. Modest changes were in the direction of growth—she was perhaps a little less prone to anger and dysregulated behavior and a little more able to be emotionally vulnerable. As in the first evaluation, the reader will we see that each assessment paradigm converged on a rather similar portrait of Madeline despite differences in their historical traditions, theoretical frameworks, and methodological technicalities—as well as the personal differences between the chapter assessors/authors. At the same time, there were notable differences in emphasis across the paradigms and even some seemingly discrepant findings (e.g., the FFM data suggested Madeline was not particularly impulsive, whereas this feature stood out in MMPI-2-RF data). In this concluding chapter, we summarize key themes from the preceding chapters, acknowledge some of the limitations of our approach, and reflect on what we have learned from this project.

Therapeutic Assessment

What came across most clearly in Chapters 2 and 7 was the value of *trust* for reducing shame and allowing a vulnerable person to open up a bit more. Steve Finn's compassionate approach to personality assessment both validated Madeline's need to pace the process and also helped her see herself differently. Trust is not something that is easily established with Madeline, for reasons that anyone familiar with her history would readily understand. Thus, the remarkable changes observed between their initial meeting and the collaborative summary and discussion sessions speak to her willingness to engage in the process, Finn and Greg Meyer's clinical skills, and the power of Therapeutic Assessment (TA). We presume that the reader, like us, will feel hopeful that a close alliance can be developed even with a person who has had a lifetime of practice protecting herself from letting people in and avoiding feeling vulnerable.

Psychodynamic Assessment

In Chapter 3, Greg Meyer, Joni Mihura, and Mark Waugh demonstrated how to use psychodynamic theory to synthesize multimethod test data toward a clinically useful formulation. The theme of their chapter was *nuance*. Through their careful analysis of test scores, specific responses, and response sequences, they uncovered the conflicts underlying Madeline's complex personality and provided psychological explanations for her seemingly chaotic and inconsistent presentation. They protected against the danger of getting too far into the potentially unreliable weeds of individual responses by concatenating indicator scores and behaviors into a coherent narrative and trimming interpretations based on their fit with lived experience and the established psychometric characteristics of the tests. The reader comes to see Madeline from a more empathic point of view; rather than focusing on her self-defeating defenses and at times brash or antagonistic outward presentation, we begin to understand her as a courageous person persistently and creatively struggling to overcome her past by accepting disavowed or split-off aspects of herself. Perhaps the most touching feature of this project is that Madeline begins to see herself that way a little more, too.

Interpersonal Assessment

The other three chapters might seem a bit more distant because the authors did not have direct interactions with Madeline. Aaron Pincus, Sindes Dawood, and Chris Hopwood challenged clinicians to consider and employ more sophisticated data collection strategies to help identify the core interpersonal conflict underlying their patients' difficulties. They described how interpersonal theory has welcomed new interpretive approaches and technologies that provide data about interpersonal *dynamics*. The authors used multi-informant, multisurface assessment to show how Madeline's tendencies manifest across different levels of her personality and observational data to show how they manifested, and changed, in real interactions with the assessors. The synthesis of interpersonal theory and measurement in Chapter 4 painted the portrait of Madeline as a person who, for self-protective reasons, organizes her life around agentic strivings and denies her need for communion. Pincus, Dawood, and Hopwood predicted that, as she continues to be more vulnerable and open to her inner world, these motives will come into greater balance, and Madeline will achieve a greater capacity to accept all of herself and her past and thus experience deeper and more enduring relationships.

Multivariate Assessment

The theme of Tom Widiger and Cristina Crego's chapter was *evidence*. They summarized the massive body of literature documenting the Five-Factor Model's (FFM) ability to economically integrate other approaches to individual differences in personality and psychopathology. This literature leads naturally to the conclusion that the FFM is the most promising alternative to the medical model of the DSM for organizing mental disorders. Critically, the increasing prominence of the multivariate model in mainstream psychiatry provides an "in" for personality assessment within the mental health disciplines in general. Self-reported FFM data and informant-reported FFM data from Chapter 5 showed how Madeline, at her core, continues to be essentially the same person she always has been, while also maturing in certain key ways, such as being somewhat less angry and impulsive. An area of emphasis—enabled by the FFM's focus on normal range behavior that includes adaptive strengths—was the elucidation of Madeline's assets in the domains of extraversion and conscientiousness.

Empirical Assessment

Although the MMPI was described by Wiggins (2003) as the "empirical" approach, the underlying theme of Chapter 6 was *tradition*. Yossef Ben-Porath argued convincingly for the essential role of the MMPI in the history of personality assessment while also predicting the ongoing centrality of the MMPI family of instruments in the future. Ben-Porath documented the various ways in which the MMPI continues to meet the challenges of personality assessment and how recent innovations have brought it up to date with cutting-edge models of personality and psychopathology (Sellbom, 2019). The main differences in method and emphasis between the chapters focusing on the MMPI and the FFM are the use of validity scales, rather than informants, to frame Madeline's responses and the relatively greater focus on psychiatric problems, as opposed to normal-range personality dimensions. MMPI-2-RF data suggested that Madeline continues to be at risk for externalizing behavior, in part because she possesses relatively little access to more vulnerable aspects of herself. Ben-Porath suggested that developing the habit of reflecting prior to action and working toward more sustained and mutual relationships will be key for her ongoing well-being and personal growth.

What Could We Have Done Better?

A dominant refrain in Madeline's history involves having had to overcome societal obstacles related to her gender and ethnicity. We were thus sensitive to diversity issues at the outset of the project. We invited Krista Trobst to accompany Madeline on her visits to Austin, and lead authors asked ethnically diverse women to contribute to the project as co-authors on Chapters 3, 4, and 5. Nevertheless, in retrospect it is regrettable that, in the big picture, two white men evaluated a Native American woman and five white men led the chapters that presented the results. This arrangement does not reflect the demographics of contemporary clinical practice and may have been substantively influential in some ways. For example, it is clear that Madeline had a strikingly negative reaction to Rebecca Behrends, who assessed her in person in 2000. By all accounts, Rebecca was a lovely person about whom nobody other than Madeline ever had a negative thing to say. Thus, Madeline's impression raises interesting hypotheses about Madeline's interaction patterns with women that could have perhaps been tested had a woman been more directly involved in the present assessment.

A second limitation has to do with what we assessed. This was obviously a richer assessment of personality and psychopathology than would be realistic in many assessment-intensive settings. Nevertheless, there was no mental status exam, substance abuse evaluation, or measure of cognition. Other prominent personality assessment instruments such as the *Personality Assessment Inventory* (Morey, 1991), the Millon instruments (Millon, 1994), or various maladaptive trait approaches were not covered. There were no DSM-based structured psychiatric interviews, nor were there any psychophysiological or neuropsychiatric data or detailed medical history. These choices were made for reasons of efficiency, expedience, and fidelity to Wiggins (2003). They do not reflect an editorial statement on the relative value of such different assessment approaches.

Finally, although authors of different paradigms clearly distinguished between theory and instrumentation, we would like to put a fine point on this issue. As Meyer and colleagues argue in Chapter 3, performance-based measures are not intrinsically psychodynamic. Psychodynamic theory can be brought to bear on any set of psychological assessment data, and the R-PAS, WUSCT, ORI, or TAT could be used effectively by clinicians operating from other theoretical perspectives. The interpersonal tradition has never been strongly identified with any particular test, and there is substantial variability among multivariate psychologists regarding specific instrumentation. The evolving history of the MMPI shows the many ways its items can be combined based on research and theory to generate new and clinically useful configurations. Our point is that while there is a critical connection between theories that underlie personality assessment and the specific instrumentation that those theories use to operationalize constructs (Loevinger, 1957), theory and technology can be parsed and should not be conflated with one another in practice.

What Have We Learned?

In the conclusion to the 2003 volume and the preface of this book, Krista Trobst described how Jerry Wiggins chose to write *Paradigms of Personality Assessment*, which sadly turned out to be his last major contribution to the field of personality assessment, out of his devotion to students. Likewise, our ultimate hope is that students and clinicians learning personality assessment find this text useful. We offer summary conclusions from this project in this section, with these readers in mind.

Personality Assessment Works

An enormous body of evidence supports the reliability and validity of psychological assessment in general (Meyer et al., 2001) and the personality assessment tools from each of the paradigms covered in this book in particular. This project supplements that literature by providing compelling evidence that personality assessment works at the level of an individual life. Assessment results were remarkably reliable across 17 years and largely convergent across assessment paradigms. Most of the predictions from the first assessment were accurate and test findings from the current study corresponded closely to the specific features of Madeline's life. There can be little doubt about the value of personality assessment for generating deep and helpful insights about what people are like and what they may do to improve their lives.

Evidence-Based Assessment Is Multimethod

Despite their general convergence, this project also showed how different paradigms focus on unique aspects of personality and thus add incremental information or perspective relative to the others. The different assessment paradigms act like lenses, each offering a filter which permits slightly different angles of vision on the person. The psychodynamic approach uncovers complex nuances that underlie Madeline's behavior, with a focus on cognitive and narrative dynamics. The interpersonal perspective hones in on the core conflicts and representations that connect Madeline's inner world with her external behavior. The multivariate paradigm considers the entire range of stable individual differences in personality traits and, importantly, focuses to a greater degree than other paradigms on strengths. The empirical model couples a relatively thorough portrait of her adaptive difficulties with a large body of research that can be used to generate relatively precise, evidence-based interpretations. TA offers a systematic and experience-near suite of techniques for making the assessment process and results useful for the person.

Taken together, these chapters highlight the fact that multimethod assessment data is an essential feature of an evidenced-based psychological assessment (Bornstein, 2017). A battery of brief, symptom-focused questionnaires or an informal diagnostic interview provides only a narrow view of the person and exposes clinicians to a heightened risk for misunderstanding and interpretive error. In contrast, multimethod assessment provides a means for confirming and testing hypotheses generated by any single data source. Multimethod test score interpretation means making sense of test score convergences and divergences, and doing so invariably enriches our understanding of the person being assessed and avoids the pitfalls of relying too much on any particular approach.

Expertise Matters

However impressed the reader may be with the interpretations of test data in the preceding chapters, readers may wonder—as we did—whether they could use these personality assessment instruments to the same effect. Indeed, the assessors in this project were selected for their expertise, and clinicians who have not dedicated their lives to personality assessment might not be expected to get as much out of the data as the authors of the preceding chapters did. This fact highlights the importance of developing proficiency in personality assessment through training. A different and related point is that there was a confound between the authors and their paradigms. This might be most evident to people with the privilege of knowing the authors personally, who could see elements of both the paradigm and the author—as distinct from the paradigm—in Chapters

2–7. This distinction reinforced, for us, that the person of the clinician is important. Clinicians are not robots. They are, like their patients, human beings with their own personal styles, goals, perspectives, sensitivities, and blind spots. Although this insight is not new (Schafer, 1954; Sullivan, 1953), clinical psychology has been remarkably shy about studying the person of the clinician in a sustained and up-front way. We predict that such research would reveal the substantial clinical benefits for the clinician of leaning in to the person they are. In the meantime, we continue to bet on the value of being ourselves in our own practice, training, and supervision.

Communication Is Key

The goals of a personality assessment are not limited to the evaluation and enumeration of a person's problems. In fact, in applied settings, the value of precise description is lost if the data are not used in some meaningful way. A key use in most assessments is helping the person being assessed understand and make use of the results. This occurs both in the way the results are written in the report and how they are communicated verbally between clinician and client. This process developed slowly with Madeline, but by the end of Chapter 7, it becomes clear that headway had been made in this regard. One of the most important things Madeline learned about herself was that she would benefit from communicating more directly with herself and more sincerely and vulnerably with others. In a departure from the early days of clinical psychology, contemporary graduate assessment training seems to prioritize proper administration and interpretation of tests and the technical accuracy of reports over the communication of results, which is perhaps left to therapy courses. But critical clinical skills such as active listening, empathy, patience, and carefully chosen wording apply to both assessment and psychotherapy. Effective communication is a central preoccupation of TA, which blends therapy and assessment, and Chapter 7 of this book showcases how to communicate assessment results.

Personality Is Both Stable and Dynamic

We mentioned in the introductory chapter that, as a general rule, if you are more neurotic than your sister at age 20, you still will be at 50. Such was the case with Madeline, whose results showed impressive consistency across time. However, this does not mean that people do not also change. Indeed, there are strong normative trends in favor of maturity across the lifespan that provide a straightforward explanation for declining rates of mental health problems as people age. We can all plan to be less neurotic and more agreeable at 50 than we were at 20. This trend was also present in Madeline's data and life story. Thus, Madeline's life provides a revealing window on both the stable and the dynamic nature of personality and demonstrates how the idea of personality becomes a context for understanding the person as she navigates life. Conceptualizing people in terms of their personality—as opposed to just their illnesses or their current contexts—is critical for generating a coherent and contextualized understanding of who they are. This perspective waned over the last few decades in clinical psychology but is being rediscovered with new evidence regarding the ability of personality models to account for psychopathology and emerging evidence on personally tailored interventions. These are most certainly positive and welcome trends.

Conclusion

To paraphrase the poet T.S. Elliot, home is where we start from. Madeline's life had a rough start. Assessment data have consistently highlighted the role of Madeline's past in her present, and all of the experts involved in this project have consistently agreed that ongoing growth will depend on her ability to reconcile where she started with who she is. We are optimistic: all the individuals involved with this project were also impressed by Madeline's resilience, courage, life-spirit, and charisma. We were especially pleased to observe how she became more open, vulnerable, and close during the process and to learn that she found genuine value from her participation in this project.

Our own beginnings include our constitutional heritage, the life events we have experienced, and the specifics of our academic training. Wherever the reader of this book began, we hope that this book opens up new possibilities for them in the area of personality assessment and thus both provides inspiration and practical benefit to personality assessors but also contributes in some way to a re-emergence of personality assessment as the most central and unique proficiency in clinical psychology.

This project began with Jerry Wiggins' landmark case study of Madeline G., and this reassessment can be most profitably appreciated by rereading the original book. Shepherding this project has been one of the great honors of our careers. It gave us the opportunity to pay tribute to the work of one of our heroes, Jerry Wiggins, to work with some of our most talented and admired colleagues, and to revisit Madeline—one of the most remarkable people in the history of personality assessment case studies. We hope that it reflects Jerry Wiggins' generative, ecumenical legacy by promoting the value of different approaches to personality assessment for understanding human lives.

References

Alden, L. E., Wiggins, J. S., & Pincus, A. L. (1990). Construction of circumplex scales for the Inventory of Interpersonal Problems. *Journal of Personality Assessment, 55,* 521–536.

Allik, J., & Realo, A. (2017). Universal and specific in the five factor model. In T. A. Widiger (Ed.), *The Oxford handbook of the five factor model* (pp. 173–190). New York: Oxford University Press.

Allison, J., Blatt, S., & Zimet, C. N. (1968). *The interpretation of psychological tests.* New York, NY: Harper & Row Publishers.

Altenstein, D., Krieger, T., & Grosse Holtforth, M. (2013). Interpersonal microprocesses predict cognitive-emotional processing and the therapeutic alliance in psychotherapy for depression. *Journal of Counselling Psychology, 60,* 445–452.

American Psychiatric Association (APA). (1994). *Diagnostic and statistical manual of mental disorders* (4th ed.). Washington, DC: Author.

American Psychiatric Association (APA). (2013). *Diagnostic and statistical manual of mental disorders* (5th ed.). Washington, DC: Author.

Ando', A., Pineda, J. A., Giromini, L., Soghoyan, G., QunYang, Bohm, M., . . . Zennaro, A. (2018). Effects of repetitive transcranial magnetic stimulation (rTMS) on attribution of movement to ambiguous stimuli and EEG mu suppression. *Brain Research, 1680,* 69–76.

Asari, T., Konishi, S., Jimura, K., Chikazoe, J., Nakamura, N., & Miyashita, Y. (2010a). Amygdalar enlargement associated with unique perception. *Cortex, 46,* 94–99.

Asari, T., Konishi, S., Jimura, K., Chikazoe, J., Nakamura, N., & Miyashita, Y. (2010b). Amygdalar modulation of frontotemporal connectivity during the inkblot test. *Psychiatry Research: Neuroimaging, 182,* 103–110.

Aschieri, F. (2016). Shame as a cultural artifact: A call for reflexivity and self-awareness in personality assessment. *Journal of Personality Assessment, 98,* 567–575.

Aschieri, F., de Saeger, H., & Durosini, I. (2015). L'evaluation therapeutique et collaborative: preuves empiriques [Therapeutic/Collaborative Assessment: Empirical studies]. *Pratiques Psychologiques, 21,* 307–317.

Aschieri, F., Fantini, F., & Smith, J. D. (2016). Collaborative/Therapeutic Assessment: Procedures to enhance client outcomes. In S. Maltzmann (Ed.), *Oxford handbook of treatment processes and outcomes in counseling psychology* (pp. 241–269). New York: Oxford University Press.

Ayearst, L. E., Sellbom, M., Trobst, K. K., & Bagby, R. M. (2013). Evaluating the interpersonal content of the MMPI-2-RF Interpersonal Scales. *Journal of Personality Assessment, 95*, 187–196.

Bagby, R. M., Uliaszek, A. A., Gralnick, T. M., & Al-Dajani, N. (2017). Axis I disorders. In T. A. Widiger (Ed.), *The Oxford handbook of the five factor model* (pp. 479–506). New York: Oxford University Press.

Bakan, D. (1966). *The duality of human existence: Isolation and communion in Western man.* Boston, MA: Beacon Press.

Behrends, R. J., & Blatt, S. J. (2003). Psychodynamic assessment. In J. S. Wiggins (Ed.), *Paradigms of personality assessment* (pp. 226–245). New York, NY: Guilford Press.

Bender, D. S., Morey, L. C., & Skodol, A. E. (2011). Toward a model for assessing level of personality functioning in DSM-5, part I: A review of theory and methods. *Journal of Personality Assessment, 93*, 332–346.

Ben-Porath, Y. S. (1994). The MMPI and MMPI-2: Fifty years of differentiating normal and abnormal personality. In S. Strack & M. Lorr (Eds.), *Differentiating normal and abnormal personality* (pp. 361–401). New York, NY: Springer Publishing Company.

Ben-Porath, Y. S. (2012). *Interpreting the MMPI-2-RF.* Minneapolis, MN: University of Minnesota Press.

Ben-Porath, Y. S., & Tellegen, A. (2008/2011). *MMPI-2-RF (Minnesota Multiphasic Personality Inventory-2-Restructured Form): Manual for administration, scoring, and interpretation.* Minneapolis, MN: University of Minnesota Press.

Ben-Porath, Y. S., & Tellegen, A. (2011). *The Minnesota Multiphasic Personality Inventory-2 Restructured Form: User's guide for reports* (2nd ed.). Minneapolis, MN: University of Minnesota Press.

Benton, A. L. (1949). Review of the Minnesota Multiphasic Personality Inventory. In O. K. Buros (Ed.), *The third mental measurements yearbook* (pp. 104–107). Highland Park, NJ: Gryphon Press.

Berlin, I. (1953/2013). *The hedgehog and the fox.* Princeton, NJ: Princeton University Press.

Berry, L. L., & Dunham, J. (2013, September 20). Redefining the patient experience with collaborative care. *Harvard Business Review.*

Blashfield, R. K. (1984). *The classification of psychopathology: Neo-Kraepelinian and quantitative approaches.* New York: Plenum Press.

Blatt, S. J. (1981). *Assessment of qualitative and structural dimensions of object representations.* Unpublished manuscript. Yale University.

Blatt, S. J., Wein, S. J., Chevron, E. S., & Quinlan, D. M. (1979). Parental representations and depression in normal young adults. *Journal of Abnormal Psychology, 88*, 388–397.

Bollas, C. (1987). *The shadow of the object: Psychoanalysis of the unthought known.* New York, NY: Columbia University Press.

Bornstein, R. F. (1996). Construct validity of the Rorschach Oral Dependency Scale: 1967–1995. *Psychological Assessment, 8*, 200–505.

Bornstein, R. F. (1999). Criterion validity of objective and projective dependency tests: A meta-analytic assessment of behavioral prediction. *Psychological Assessment, 11*, 48–57.

Bornstein, R. F. (2002). A process dissociation approach to objective-projective test score relationships. *Journal of Personality Assessment, 78*, 47–68.

Bornstein, R. F. (2017). Evidence-based psychological assessment. *Journal of Personality Assessment, 99*, 435–445.

Bornstein, R. F., Maracic, C. E., & Natoli, A. P. (2018). The psychodynamic perspective. In V. Zeigler-Hill & T. K. Shackelford (Eds.), *The Sage handbook of personality and individual differences* (pp. 52–83). Thousand Oaks, CA: Sage Publications.

Bram, A. D., & Peebles, M. J. (2014). *Psychological testing that matters: Creating a road map for effective treatment.* Washington, DC: American Psychological Association.

Brown, D. P., & Elliott, D. S. (2016). *Attachment disturbances in adults: Treatment for comprehensive repair.* New York: Norton.

Bucheim, A., Erk, S., George, C., Kächele, H., Ruchsow, M, Spitzer, M., . . . Walter, H. (2005). Measuring attachment representation in an fMRI environment: A pilot study. *Psychopathology, 589*, 1–9.

Butcher, J. N. (1972). *Objective personality assessment: Changing perspectives.* Oxford, England: Academic Press.

Caspi, A., Roberts, B. W., & Shiner, R. L. (2005). Personality development: Stability and change. *Annual Review of Psychology, 56*, 453–484.

Clark, L. A. (2007). Assessment and diagnosis of personality disorder: Perennial issues and an emerging reconceptualization. *Annual Review of Psychology, 57*, 277–257.

Cloninger, C. R. (2000). A practical way to diagnose personality disorder: A proposal. *Journal of Personality Disorders, 14*, 98–108.

Cohn, L. D., & Westenberg, P. M. (2004). Intelligence and maturity: Meta-analytic evidence for the incremental and discriminant validity of Loevinger's measure of ego development. *Journal of Personality and Social Psychology, 86*, 760–772.

Cooper, S. H., & Arnow, D. (1986). *The Rorschach defense scales.* Unpublished manual. Department of Psychiatry, Cambridge Hospital, Cambridge, MA.

Costa, P. T., & McCrae, R. R. (1980). Still stable after all these years: Personality as a key to some issues in adulthood and old age. In P. B. Baltes & O. G. Brim (Eds.), *Life span development and behavior* (Vol. 3). New York: Academic Press.

Costa, P. T., & McCrae, R. R. (1992). *Revised NEO Personality Inventory (NEO PI-R) and NEO Five-Factor Inventory (NEO-FFI) professional manual.* Odessa, FL: Psychological Assessment Resources.

Costa, P. T., & McCrae, R. R. (2017). The NEO inventories as instruments of psychological theory. In T. A. Widiger (Ed.), *The Oxford handbook of the five factor model* (pp. 11–37). New York: Oxford University Press.

Costa, P. T., & Piedmont, R. L. (2003). Multivariate assessment: NEO PI-R profiles of Madeline G. In J. S. Wiggins (Ed.), *Paradigms of personality assessment* (pp. 262–280). New York: Guilford Press.

Craik, K. H. (1986). Personality research methods: An historical perspective. *Journal of Personality, 54*, 18–51.

Cramer, P. (2015). Defense mechanisms: 40 years of empirical research. *Journal of Personality Assessment, 97*, 114–123.

Cronbach, L. J., & Meehl, P. E. (1955). Construct validity in psychological tests. *Psychological Bulletin, 52*, 281.

Dawood, S., Dowgwillo, E. A., Wu, L. Z., & Pincus, A. L. (2018). Contemporary integrative interpersonal theory of personality. In V. Zeigler-Hill & T. Shackleford (Eds.), *The SAGE handbook of personality and individual differences, vol. 1: The science of personality and individual differences* (pp. 171–202). Los Angeles, CA: Sage Publications.

Dawood, S., & Pincus, A. L. (2016). Multi-surface interpersonal assessment in a cognitive-behavioral therapy context. *Journal of Personality Assessment, 98*, 449–460.

De Raad, B., & Mlačić, B. (2017). The lexical foundation of the Big Five factor model. In T. A. Widiger (Ed.), *The Oxford handbook of the five factor model* (pp. 191–216). New York: Oxford University Press.

Dermody, S. S., Thomas, K. M., Hopwood, C. J., Durbin, C. E., & Wright, A. G. C. (2017). Modeling the complexity of dynamic, momentary interpersonal behavior: Applying the time-varying effect model to test predictions from interpersonal theory. *Journal of Research in Personality, 68*, 54–62.

De Saeger, H., Bartak, A., Eder, E. E., & Kamphuis, J. H. (2016). Memorable experiences in Therapeutic Assessment: Inviting the patient's perspective following a pretreatment randomized controlled trial. *Journal of Personality Assessment, 98*, 472–479.

De Saeger, H., Kamphuis, J. H., Finn, S. E., Verheul, R., Smith, J. D., van Busschbach, J. J. V., . . . Horn, E. (2014). Therapeutic Assessment promotes treatment readiness but does not affect symptom change in patients with personality disorders: Findings from a randomized clinical trial. *Psychological Assessment, 26*, 474–483.

Diamond, D., Kaslow, N., Coonerty, S., & Blatt, S. J. (1990). Changes in separation-individuation and intersubjectivity in long-term treatment. *Psychoanalytic Psychology, 7*, 363–397.

Diener, M. J., Hilsenroth, M. J., Shaffer, S. A., & Sexton, J. E. (2011). A meta-analysis of the relationship between the Rorschach Ego Impairment Index (EII) and psychiatric severity. *Clinical Psychology & Psychotherapy, 18*, 464–485.

Engelman, D. H., Allyn, J. B., Crisi, A., Finn, S. E., Fischer, C. T., & Nakamura, N. (2016). "Why am I so stuck?": A collaborative/Therapeutic Assessment case discussion. *Journal of Personality Assessment, 98*, 360–373.

Exner, J. E. (1996). Critical bits and the Rorschach response process. *Journal of Personality Assessment, 67*, 464–477.

Exner, J. E. (2003). *The Rorschach: A comprehensive system, vol. 1: Basic foundations* (4th ed.). Hoboken, NJ: Wiley.

Eysenck, H. J., & Eysenck, S. B. G. (1993). *The Eysenck Personality Questionnaire-Revised.* London: Hodder & Stoughton.

Finn, S. E. (1996a). *A manual for using the MMPI-2 as a therapeutic intervention.* Minneapolis, MN: University of Minnesota Press.

Finn, S. E. (1996b). Assessment feedback integrating MMPI-2 and Rorschach findings. *Journal of Personality Assessment, 67*, 543–557.

Finn, S. E. (2005, March). *Please tell me that I'm not who I fear I am: Control Mastery Theory and Therapeutic Assessment.* Paper presented at the annual meeting of the Society for Personality Assessment, Chicago. Reprinted as

Chapter 16 of Finn, S. E. (2007). *In our clients' shoes: Theory and techniques of Therapeutic Assessment* (pp. 231–242). Mawah, NJ: Erlbaum & Associates.

Finn, S. E. (2007). *In our clients' shoes: Theory and techniques of Therapeutic Assessment*. Mawah, NJ: Lawrence Erlbaum Associates, Inc.

Finn, S. E. (2009). *Core values of Therapeutic Assessment*. Retrieved from www. therapeuticassessment.com

Finn, S. E. (2011). Journeys through the Valley of Death: Multimethod psychological assessment and personality transformation in long-term psychotherapy. *Journal of Personality Assessment, 93*, 123–141.

Finn, S. E. (2012). Implications of recent research in neurobiology for psychological assessment. *Journal of Personality Assessment, 94*, 440–449.

Finn, S. E., Fischer, C. T., & Handler, L. (Eds.). (2012). *Collaborative/Therapeutic Assessment: A casebook and guide*. Hoboken, NJ: Wiley.

Finn, S. E., & Martin, H. (2013). Therapeutic Assessment: Using psychological testing as brief therapy. In K. F. Geisinger (Editor-in-Chief.), *APA handbook of testing and assessment in psychology* (Vol. 2, pp. 453–465). Washington, DC: American Psychological Association.

Finn, S. E., Schroeder, D. G., & Tonsager, M. E. (1994). *The Assessment Questionnaire (AQ): A measure of client's experiences with psychological assessment*. Austin, TX: Therapeutic Assessment Institute.

Finn, S. E., & Tonsager, M. E. (1992). Therapeutic effects of providing MMPI-2 test feedback to college students awaiting therapy. *Psychological Assessment, 4*, 278–287.

Finn, S. E., & Tonsager, M. E. (1997). Information-gathering and therapeutic models of assessment: Complementary paradigms. *Psychological Assessment, 9*, 374–385.

Fischer, C. T. (1985/1994). *Individualizing psychological assessment*. Mahwah, NJ: Routledge.

Fonagy, P. (1998). An attachment theory approach to treatment of the difficult patient. *Bulletin of the Menninger Clinic, 62*, 147–169.

Fonagy, P., & Allison, E. (2014). The role of mentalizing and epistemic trust in the psychotherapeutic relationship. *Psychotherapy, 51*, 372–380.

Fonagy, P., Luyten, P., & Allison, E. (2015). Epistemic petrification and the restoration of epistemic trust: A new conceptualization of borderline personality disorder and its psychosocial treatment. *Journal of Personality Disorders, 29*, 575–609.

Fonagy, P., Luyten, P., Allison, E., & Campbell, C. (2017). What we have changed our minds about: Part 2. Borderline personality, epistemic trust, and the developmental significance of social communication. *Borderline Personality and Emotional Dysregulation, 4*(9).

Garb, H. N. (1999). Call for a moratorium on the use of the Rorschach Inkblot Test in clinical and forensic settings. *Assessment, 6*, 313–317.

George, C., & West, M. (2012). *The adult attachment projective picture system: Attachment theory and assessment in adults*. New York, NY: Guilford.

Ghaed, S. G., & Gallo, L. C. (2006). Distinctions among agency, communion, and unmitigated agency and communion according to the interpersonal circumplex, five-factor model, and social-emotional correlates. *Journal of Personality Assessment, 86,* 77–88.

Girard, J. M., & Wright, A. G. C. (2017). DARMA: Dual axis rating and media annotation. *Behavioral Research Methods.* Advanced online publication: doi. org/10.3758/s13428-017-0915-5

Giromini, L., Ando', A., Morese, R., Salatino, A., Di Girolamo, M., Viglione, D. J., & Zennaro, A. (2016). Rorschach Performance Assessment System (R-PAS) and vulnerability to stress: A preliminary study on electrodermal activity during stress. *Psychiatry Research, 246,* 166–172.

Giromini, L., Viglione, D. J., Pineda, J. A., Porcelli, P., Hubbard, D., Zennaro, A., & Cauda, F. (2019). Human movement responses to the Rorschach and mirroring activity: An fMRI study. *Assessment, 26,* 56–69.

Glover, N., Miller, J. D., Lynam, D. R., Crego, C., & Widiger, T. A. (2012). The Five-Factor Narcissism Inventory: A five-factor measure of narcissistic personality traits. *Journal of Personality Assessment, 94,* 500–512.

Goldberg, L. R. (1982). From Axe to Zombie: Some explorations in the language of personality. In C. D. Spielberg & J. N. Butcher (Eds.), *Advances in personality assessment* (Vol. 1, pp. 203–234). Hillsdale, NJ: Lawrence Erlbaum Associates, Inc.

Goldberg, L. R. (1993). The structure of phenotypic personality traits. *American Psychologist, 48,* 26–34.

Gough, H. G. (1946). Diagnostic patterns on the Minnesota multiphasic personality inventory. *Journal of Clinical Psychology, 2,* 23–37.

Graceffo, R. A., Mihura, J. L., & Meyer, G. J. (2014). A meta-analysis of an implicit measure of personality functioning: The Mutuality of Autonomy Scale. *Journal of Personality Assessment, 96,* 581–595.

Gritti, E. S., Marino, D. P., Lang, M., & Meyer, G. J. (2018). Assessing narcissism using Rorschach-based imagery and behavior validated by clinician-reports: Studies with clinical and nonclinical adults. *Assessment, 25,* 898–916.

Gurtman, M. B., & Balakrishnan, J. D. (1998). Circular measurement redux: The analysis and interpretation of interpersonal circle profiles. *Clinical Psychology: Science and Practice, 5,* 344–360.

Handler, L. (1999). The assessment of playfulness: Hermann Rorschach meets D. W. Winnicott. *Journal of Personality Assessment, 72,* 208–217.

Handler, L. (2006). The use of therapeutic assessment with children and adolescents. In S. Smith & L. Handler (Eds.), *Clinical assessment of children and adolescents: A practitioner's guide* (pp. 53–72). Mahwah, NJ: Erlbaum & Associates.

Harkness, A. R., Finn, J. A., McNulty, J. L., & Shields, S. M. (2012). The Personality Psychopathology Five (PSY-5): Recent constructive replication and assessment literature review. *Psychological Assessment, 24,* 432–443.

Harkness, A. R., & McNulty, J. L. (1994). The Personality Psychopathology Five (PSY-5): Issues from the pages of a diagnostic manual instead of a dictionary. In S. Strack & M. Lorr (Eds.), *Differentiating normal and abnormal personality* (pp. 291–315). New York, NY: Springer Publishing Company.

Harkness, A. R., Reynolds, S. M., & Lilienfeld, S. O. (2014). A review of systems for psychology and psychiatry: Adaptive systems, personality psychopathology five (PSY–5), and the DSM–5. *Journal of Personality Assessment, 96*(2), 121–139.

Hatcher, R. L., & Rogers, D. T. (2009). Development and validation of a measure of interpersonal strengths: The inventory of interpersonal strengths. *Psychological Assessment, 21*, 554–569.

Hathaway, S. R., & McKinley, C. J. (1972). Where have we gone wrong? The mystery of the missing progress. In *Objective personality assessment: Changing perspectives* (pp. 21–43). New York: Academic Press.

Hathaway, S. R., & McKinley, J. C. (1940). A multiphasic personality schedule (Minnesota): I. Construction of the schedule. *The Journal of Psychology, 10*, 249–254.

Helgeson, V. S., & Fritz, H. L. (2000). The implications of unmitigated agency and unmitigated communion for domains of problem behavior. *Journal of Personality, 68*, 1031–1057.

Hopwood, C. J., Ansell, E. B., Pincus, A. L., Wright, A. G. C., Lukowitsky, M. R., & Roche, M. J. (2011). The circumplex structure of interpersonal sensitivities. *Journal of Personality, 79*, 707–740.

Hopwood, C. J., Pincus, A. L., & Wright, A. G. C. (2019). The interpersonal situation: Integrating personality assessment, case formulation, and intervention. In D. Samuel & D. Lynam (Eds.), *Using basic personality research to inform personality disorders* (pp. 94–121). New York: Oxford University Press.

Hopwood, C. J., Thomas, K. M., Luo, X., Bernard, N., Lin, Y., & Levendosky, A. A. (2016). Implementing dynamic assessments in psychotherapy. *Assessment, 23*, 507–517.

Hopwood, C. J., & Vazire, S. (in press). Reproducibility in clinical psychology. In A. G. C. Wright & M. N. Hallquist (Eds.), *Cambridge handbook of research methods in clinical psychology*. Cambridge, UK: Cambridge University Press.

Horowitz, L. M. (2004). *Interpersonal foundations of psychopathology*. Washington, DC: American Psychological Association.

Hosseininasab, A., Meyer, G. J., Viglione, D. J., Mihura, J. L., Berant, E., Resende, A. C., . . . Mohammadi, M. R. (2019). The effect of CS administration or an R-Optimized alternative on R-PAS Variables: A meta-analysis of findings from six studies. *Journal of Personality Assessment, 101*, 199–212.

Huprich, S. K., Auerbach, J. S., Porcerelli, J. H., & Bupp, L. L. (2016). Sidney Blatt's Object Relations Inventory: Contributions and future directions. *Journal of Personality Assessment, 98*, 30–43.

Hy, L. X., & Loevinger, J. (1996). *Measuring ego development* (2nd ed.). Hillsdale, NJ: Lawrence Erlbaum Associates, Inc.

Jackson, D. N. (1984). *Personality Research Form manual* (3rd ed.). Port Huron, MI: Sigma Assessment Systems.

Jarnecke, A. M., & South, S. C. (2017). Behavior and molecular genetics of the five-factor model. In T. A. Widiger (Ed.), *The Oxford handbook of the five factor model* (pp. 301–318). New York: Oxford University Press.

Jenkins, S. R. (Ed.). (2008). *A handbook of clinical scoring systems for thematic apperceptive techniques*. Mahwah, NJ: Lawrence Erlbaum Associates, Inc.

John, O. P., Naumann, L. P., & Soto, C. J. (2008). Paradigm shift to the integrative Big Five trait taxonomy: History, measurement, and conceptual issues. In O. P. John, R. R. Robins, & L. A. Pervin (Eds.), *Handbook of personality: Theory and research* (3rd ed., pp. 114–158). New York: Guilford Press.

Johnson, D. P., Rhee, S. H., Friedman, N. P., Corley, R. P., Munn-Chernoff, M. A., Hewitt, J. K., & Whisman, M. A. (2016). A twin study examining rumination as a transdiagnostic correlate of psychopathology. *Clinical Psychological Science*, *4*, 971–987.

Johnson, J. H., Null, C., Butcher, J. N., & Johnson, K. N. (1984). Replicated item level factor analysis of the full MMPI. *Journal of Personality and Social Psychology*, *47*, 105.

Julian III, A. E., Sotile, W. M., Henry, S. E., & Sotile, M. O. (1985). *Family Apperception Test*. Los Angeles, CA: Western Psychological Services.

Kamphuis, J. H., Kugeares, S. L., & Finn, S. E. (2000). Rorschach correlates of sexual abuse: Trauma content and aggression indices. *Journal of Personality Assessment*, *75*, 212–224.

Kiesler, D. J., Schmidt, J. A., & Wagner, C. C. (1997). A circumplex inventory of impact messages: An operational bridge between emotion and interpersonal behavior. In R. Plutchik & H. Contes (Eds.), *Circumplex models of personality and emotions* (pp. 221–244). Washington, DC: American Psychological Association.

Klahr, A. M., Thomas, K. M., Hopwood, C. J., Klump, K. L., & Burt, S. A. (2013). Evocative gene-environment correlation in the mother-child relationship: A twin study of interpersonal processes. *Developmental Psychopathology*, *25*, 105–118.

Kleiger, J. H. (2017). *Rorschach assessment of psychotic phenomena: Clinical, conceptual, and empirical developments*. New York, NY: Routledge.

Kleiger, J. H., & Peebles-Kleiger, M. J. (1993). Toward a conceptual understanding of the deviant response in the Comprehensive Rorschach System. *Journal of Personality Assessment*, *60*, 74–90.

Kohut, H. (1984). *How does analysis cure?* Chicago: University of Chicago Press.

Köllner, M. G., & Schultheiss, O. C. (2014). Meta-analytic evidence of low convergence between implicit and explicit measures of the needs for achievement, affiliation, and power. *Frontiers in Psychology*, *5*, Article ID 826.

Kotov, R., Krueger, R. F., Watson, D., Achenbach, T. M., Althoff, R. R., et al. 2017. The Hierarchical Taxonomy of Psychopathology (HiTOP): A dimensional alternative to traditional nosologies. *Journal of Abnormal Psychology*, *126*, 454–477.

Kraepelin, E. (1896). *Clinical psychiatry: A text-book for students and physicians* (6th ed., A. R. Diefendorf, Trans.). London: Macmillan.

Krueger, R. F., & Eaton, N. R. (2010). Personality traits and the classification of mental disorders: Toward a complete integration in DSM-V and an empirical model of psychopathology. *Personality Disorders: Theory, Research, and Treatment*, *1*, 97–118.

Kuhn, T. S. (1962/2012). *The structure of scientific revolutions*. Chicago: University of Chicago press.

Kundera, M. (1984). *The unbearable lightness of being*. New York: Harper & Row Publishers.

Lance, B. R., & Krishnamurthy, R. (2003, March). *A comparison of three modes of MMPI-2 test feedback*. Paper presented at the Midwinter Meeting of the Society for Personality Assessment, San Francisco, CA.

Leary, T. (1957). *Interpersonal diagnosis of personality*. New York, NY: Ronald Press.

Lee, S. W. S., & Schwarz, N. (2014). Metaphor in judgment and decision making. In M. Landau, M. D. Robinson, & B. P. Meier (Eds.), *The power of metaphor: Examining its influence on social life* (pp. 85–108). Washington, DC: American Psychological Association.

Lilienfeld, S. O., Wood, J. M., & Garb, H. N. (2000). The scientific status of projective techniques. *Psychological Science in the Public Interest, 1*, 27–66.

Linehan, M. M. (2014). *DBT® skills training handouts and worksheets*. New York: Guilford Press.

Lizdek, I., Sadler, P., Woody, E., Ethier, N., & Malet, G. (2012). Capturing the stream of behavior: A computer-joystick method for coding interpersonal behavior continuously over time. *Social Science Computer Review, 30*, 513–521.

Lizdek, I., Woody, E., Sadler, P., & Rehman, U. S. (2016). How do depressive symptoms in husbands and wives relate to the interpersonal dynamics of marital interactions? *Journal of Counseling Psychology, 63*, 721–735.

Locke, K. D. (2000). Circumplex scales of interpersonal values: Reliability, validity, and applicability to interpersonal problems and personality disorders. *Journal of Personality Assessment, 75*, 249–267.

Locke, K. D., & Sadler, P. (2007). Self-efficacy, values, and complementarity in dyadic interactions: Integrating interpersonal and social-cognitive theory. *Personality and Social Psychology Bulletin, 33*, 94–109.

Loevinger, J. (1957). Objective tests as instruments of psychological theory. *Psychological Reports, 3*, 635–694.

Loevinger, J. (2002). Confessions of an iconoclast: At home on the fringe. *Journal of Personality Assessment, 78*, 195–208.

Luyten, P., & Blatt, S. J. (2013). Interpersonal relatedness and self-definition in normal and disrupted personality development: Retrospect and prospect. *American Psychologist, 68*, 172–183.

Luyten, P., Mayes, L. C., Blatt, S. J., Target, M., & Fonagy, P. (2015). Theoretical and empirical foundations of contemporary psychodynamic approaches. In P. Luyten, L. C. Mayes, P. Fonagy, M. Target, & S. J. Blatt (Eds.), *Handbook of psychodynamic approaches to psychopathology* (pp. 3–26). New York, NY: Guilford Press.

Lynam, D. R., & Widiger, T. A. (2001). Using the five factor model to represent the DSM-IV personality disorders: An expert consensus approach. *Journal of Abnormal Psychology, 110*, 401–412.

Markey, P. M., Lowmaster, S., & Eichler, W. (2010). A real-time assessment of interpersonal complementarity. *Personal Relationships, 17*, 13–25.

Markey, P. M., & Markey, C. N. (2009). A brief assessment of the interpersonal circumplex: The IPIP—IPC. *Assessment, 16*, 352–361.

McAdams, D. P. (1988). *Power, intimacy, and the life story: Personological inquiries into identity*. New York, NY: Guilford Press.

McAdams, D. P. (2003). Personological assessment. In J. S. Wiggins (Ed.), *Paradigms of personality assessment* (pp. 213–225). New York, NY: Guilford Press.

McClelland, D. C., Koestner, R., & Weinberger, J. (1989). How do self-attributed and implicit motives differ? *Psychological Review, 96*, 690–702.

McCrae, R. R., & Costa, P. T. (1983). Joint factors in self-reports and ratings: Neuroticism, Extraversion, and Openness to Experience. *Personality and Individual Differences, 4*, 245–255.

McCrae, R. R., & Costa, P. T. (1990). *Personality in adulthood: A five-factor theory perspective.* New York: Guilford Press.

McCullough, L., Kuhn, N., Andrews, S., Kaplan, A., Wolf, J., & Hurley, C. (2003). *Treating affect phobia: A manual for Short-Term Dynamic Psychotherapy.* New York, NY: Guilford Press.

Meehl, P. E. (1945). The dynamics of "structured" personality tests. *Journal of Clinical Psychology, 1*, 296–303.

Meehl, P. E. (1950). Configural scoring. *Journal of Consulting Psychology, 14*, 165–171.

Meehl, P. E. (1956). Wanted: A good cook-book. *American Psychologist, 11*, 263–272.

Meehl, P. E. (1978). Theoretical risks and tabular asterisks: Sir Karl, Sir Ronald, and the slow progress of soft psychology. *Journal of Consulting and Clinical Psychology, 46*, 806–834.

Meehl, P. E. (1992). Factors and taxa, traits and types, differences of degree and differences in kind. *Journal of Personality, 60*, 117–174.

Meehl, P. E., & Hathaway, S. R. (1946). The K factor as a suppressor variable in the Minnesota Multiphasic Personality Inventory. *Journal of Applied Psychology, 30*, 525–564.

Mervielde, I., & De Fruyt, F. (2002). Assessing children's traits with the Hierarchical Personality I Inventory for children. In B. de Raad & M. Perugini (Eds.), *Big five assessment* (pp. 129–146). Bern, Switzerland: Hogrefe & Huber.

Meyer, G. J., & Archer, R. P. (2001). The hard science of Rorschach research: What do we know and where do we go? *Psychological Assessment, 13*, 486–502.

Meyer, G. J., Erdberg, P., & Shaffer, T. W. (2007). Towards international normative reference data for the comprehensive system. *Journal of Personality Assessment, 89*, S201–S216.

Meyer, G. J., Finn, S. E., Eyde, L. D., Kay, G. G., Moreland, K. L., Dies, R. R., Eisman, E. J., Kubiszyn, T. W., & Reed, G. M. (2001). Psychological testing and psychological assessment: A review of evidence and issues. *American psychologist, 56*, 128–165.

Meyer, G. J., Gritti, E. S., Marino, D. P., & Sholander, L. E. (2019). *Coding criteria for potential Rorschach grandiosity and narcissism variables.* Unpublished manual, Department of Psychology, University of Toledo, Toledo, OH.

Meyer, G. J., Hsiao, W., Viglione, D. J., Mihura, J. L., & Abraham, L. M. (2013). Rorschach scores in applied clinical practice: A survey of perceived validity by experienced clinicians. *Journal of Personality Assessment, 95*, 351–365.

Meyer, G. J., Shaffer, T. W., Erdberg, P., & Horn, S. L. (2015). Addressing issues in the development and use of the Composite International Reference Values as Rorschach norms for adults. *Journal of Personality Assessment, 97*, 330–347.

Meyer, G. J., Viglione, D. J., Mihura, J. L., Erard, R. E., & Erdberg, P. (2011). *Rorschach Performance Assessment System: Administration, coding, interpretation, and technical manual.* Toledo, OH: Rorschach Performance Assessment System, LLC.

Mihura, J. L. (2006). Rorschach Assessment of Borderline Personality Disorder. In S. K. Huprich (Ed.), *The LEA series in personality and clinical psychology: Rorschach assessment to the personality disorders* (pp. 171–203). Mahwah, NJ: Lawrence Erlbaum Associates, Inc.

Mihura, J. L., Dumitrascu, N., Roy, M., & Meyer, G. J. (2018). The centrality of the response process in construct validity: An illustration via the Rorschach Space response. *Journal of Personality Assessment, 100*, 233–249.

Mihura, J. L., & Meyer, G. J. (2018). *Using the Rorschach Performance Assessment System (R-PAS)*. New York, NY: Guilford Press.

Mihura, J. L., Meyer, G. J., Bombel, G., & Dumitrascu, N. (2015). Standards, accuracy, and questions of bias in Rorschach meta-analyses: Reply to Wood, Garb, Nezworski, Lilienfeld, and Duke (2015). *Psychological Bulletin, 141*, 250–260.

Mihura, J. L., Meyer, G. J., Dumitrascu, N., & Bombel, G. (2013). The validity of individual Rorschach variables: Systematic reviews and meta-analyses of the comprehensive system. *Psychological Bulletin, 139*, 548–605.

Miller, J. D., Bagby, R. M., Pilkonis, P. A., Reynolds, S. K., & Lynam, D. R. (2005). A simplified technique for scoring the DSM-IV personality disorders with the five-factor model. *Assessment, 12*, 404–415.

Miller, J. D., Pilkonis, P. A., & Clifton, A. (2005). Self- and other-reports of traits from the five-factor model: Relations to personality disorder. *Journal of Personality Disorders, 19*, 400–419.

Millon, T. (1994). *Manual for the MCMI-III*. Minneapolis, MN: National Computer Systems.

Monroe, J. M., Diener, M. J., Fowler, J. C., Sexton, J. E., & Hilsenroth, M. J. (2013). Criterion validity of the Rorschach Mutuality of Autonomy (MOA) scale: A meta-analytic review. *Psychoanalytic Psychology, 30*, 535–566.

Morey, L. C. (1991). *Professional manual for the Personality Assessment Inventory*. Lutz, FL: Psychological Assessment Resources.

Morey, L. C., Waugh, M. H., & Blashfield, R. K. (1985). MMPI scales for DSM-III personality disorders: Their derivation and correlates. *Journal of Personality Assessment, 49*, 245–251.

Morgan, W. (2002). Origin and history of the Earliest Thematic Apperception Test. *Journal of Personality Assessment*, 422–445.

Morris, W. W. (1947). A preliminary evaluation of the Minnesota Multiphasic Personality Inventory. *Journal of Clinical Psychology, 3*, 370–374.

Murray, H. A. (1943). *Thematic Apperception Test manual*. Cambridge, MA: Harvard University Press.

Nilsen, E. S., Lizdek, I., & Ethier, N. (2015). Mother-child interpersonal dynamics: The influence of maternal and child ADHD symptoms. *Journal of Clinical and Experimental Psychopathology, 6*, 313–329.

O'Connor, B. P. (2002). A quantitative review of the comprehensiveness of the five-factor model in relation to popular personality inventories. *Assessment, 9*, 188–203.

O'Connor, B. P. (2005). A search for consensus on the dimensional structure of personality disorders. *Journal of Clinical Psychology, 61*, 323–345.

O'Connor, B. P. (2017). Robustness. In T. A. Widiger (Ed.), *The Oxford handbook of the five factor model* (pp. 151–172). New York: Oxford University Press.

Oltmanns, T. F., & Turkheimer, E. (2006). Perceptions of self and others regarding pathological personality traits. In R. F. Krueger and J. L. Tackett (Eds.), *Personality and psychopathology* (pp. 71–111). New York: Guilford Press.

Ozer, D. J., & Benet-Martinez, V. (2006). Personality and the prediction of consequential outcomes. *Annual Review of Psychology, 57,* 401–421.

Payne, F. D., & Wiggins, J. S. (1972). MMPI profile types and the self-report of psychiatric patients. *Journal of Abnormal Psychology, 79,* 1–8.

Piedmont, R. L. (1998). *The revised NEO Personality Inventory: Clinical and research applications.* New York, NY: Plenum Press.

Piedmont, R. L., & Rodgerson, T. E. (2017). Cross-over analysis: Using the FFM and NEO PI-3 for assessing compatibility and conflict in couples. In T. A. Widiger (Ed.), *The Oxford handbook of the five factor model* (pp. 423–448). New York: Oxford University Press.

Pincus, A. L. (2010). Introduction to the special series on integrating personality, psychopathology, and psychotherapy using interpersonal assessment. *Journal of Personality Assessment, 92,* 467–470.

Pincus, A. L., & Ansell, E. B. (2013). Interpersonal theory of personality. In H. Tennen, J. Suls, & I. B. Weiner (Eds.), *Handbook of psychology: Personality and social psychology* (Vol. 5, pp. 141–159). Hoboken, NJ: John Wiley & Sons.

Pincus, A. L., & Gurtman, M. B. (2003). Interpersonal assessment. In J. S. Wiggins (Eds.), *Paradigms of personality assessment* (pp. 246–261). New York: Guilford Press.

Pincus, A. L., Hopwood, C. J., & Wright, A. G. C. (in press). The interpersonal situation: An integrative framework for the study of personality, psychopathology, and psychotherapy. In D. Funder, J. F. Rauthmann, & R. Sherman (Eds.), *Oxford handbook of psychological situations.* New York: Oxford University Press.

Pincus, A. L., Sadler, P., Woody, E., Roche, M. J., Thomas, K. M., & Wright, A. G. C. (2014). Multimethod assessment of interpersonal dynamics. In C. J. Hopwood & R. F. Bornstein (Eds.), *Multimethod clinical assessment* (pp. 51–91). New York: Guilford Press.

Pincus, A. L., & Wright, A. G. C. (2011). Interpersonal diagnosis of psychopathology. In L. M. Horowitz & S. Strack (Eds.), *Handbook of interpersonal psychology: Theory, research, assessment, and therapeutic interventions* (pp. 359–381). Hoboken, NJ: Wiley.

Poston, J. M. & Hanson, W. M. (2010). Meta-analysis of psychological assessment as a therapeutic intervention. *Psychological Assessment, 22,* 203–212.

Rapaport, D., Gill, M., & Schafer, R. (1968). *Diagnostic psychological testing* (rev. ed.; R. Holt, Ed.). New York, NY: International Universities Press.

Reich, W. (1945/1972). *Character analysis* (3rd ed.). New York: Farrar, Straus, and Giroux.

Ritzler, B., & Nalesnik, D. (1990). The effect of inquiry on the Exner Comprehensive System. *Journal of Personality Assessment, 55,* 647–656.

Roberts, B. W., & DelVecchio, W. F. (2000). The rank-order consistency of personality traits from childhood to old age: A quantitative review of longitudinal studies. *Psychological Bulletin, 126,* 3–25.

Roberts, B. W., Kuncel, N. R., Shiner, R., Caspi, A., & Goldberg, L. R. (2007). The power of personality: The comparative validity of personality traits, socioeconomic status, and cognitive ability for predicting important life outcomes. *Perspectives on Psychological Science, 2,* 313–345.

Roberts, B. W., Luo, J., Briley, D. A., Chow, P. I., Su, R., & Hill, P. L. (2017). A systematic review of personality trait change through intervention. *Psychological Bulletin, 143*(2), 117–141.

Roberts, G. E. (2005). *Roberts Apperception Test-2.* Los Angeles, CA: Western Psychological Services.

Roche, M. J., Pincus, A. L., Rebar, A. L., Conroy, D. E., & Ram, N. (2014). Enriching psychological assessment using a person-specific analysis of interpersonal processes in daily life. *Assessment, 21,* 515–528.

Rorschach, H. (1942). *Psychodiagnostics: A diagnostic test based on perception.* Bern, Switzerland: Verlag Hans Huber.

Ross, J. M., Girard, J. M., Wright, A. G. C., Beeney, J. E., Scott, L. N., Hallquist, M. N., Lazarus, S. A., Stepp, S. D., & Pilkonis, P. A. (2017). Momentary patterns of covariation between specific affects and interpersonal behavior: Linking relationship science and personality assessment. *Psychological Assessment, 29,* 123–134.

Sadler, P., Ethier, N., Gunn, G. R., Duong, D., & Woody, E. (2009). Are we on the same wavelength? Interpersonal complementarity as shared cyclical patterns during interactions. *Journal of Personality and Social Psychology, 97,* 1005–1020.

Sadler, P., Ethier, N., & Woody, E. (2011). Interpersonal complementarity. In L. M. Horowitz & S. Strack (Eds.), *Handbook of interpersonal psychology: Theory, research, assessment, and therapeutic interventions* (pp. 123–142). Hoboken, NJ: Wiley.

Sadler, P., Woody, E., McDonald, K., Lizdek, I., & Little, J. (2015). A lot can happen in a few minutes: Examining dynamic patterns within an interaction to illuminate the interpersonal nature of personality disorders. *Journal of Personality Disorders, 29,* 526–546.

Samuel, D. (2013). Assessing the five-factor model of personality disorder. In T. A. Widiger & P. T. Costa (Eds.), *Personality disorders and the five-factor model* (pp. 221–232). Washington, DC: American Psychological Association.

Schafer, R. (1954). *Psychoanalytic Interpretation in Rorschach Testing: Theory and application.* Oxford, England: Grune & Stratton.

Schroeder, D. G., Hahn, E. D., Finn, S. E., & Swann, W. B., Jr. (1993, June). *Personality feedback has more impact when mildly discrepant from self views.* Paper presented at the fifth annual convention of the American Psychological Society, Chicago, IL.

Searls, D. (2017). *The inkblots: Hermann Rorschach, his iconic test, and the power of seeing.* New York: Crown Publishers.

Sellbom, M. (2019). The MMPI-2-Restructured Form (MMPI-2-RF): Assessment of personality and psychopathology in the twenty-first century. *Annual Review of Clinical Psychology,* (in press).

Shapiro, D. (1965). *Neurotic styles.* Oxford, England: Basic Books.

Siefert, C. J., Stein, M. B., Slavin-Mulford, J., Sinclair, S. J., Haggerty, G., & Blais, M. A. (2016). Estimating the effects of Thematic Apperception Test card content on SCORS—G ratings: Replication with a nonclinical sample. *Journal of Personality Assessment, 98,* 598–607.

Silverstein, M. L. (2013). *Personality assessment in depth: A casebook.* New York, NY: Routledge.

Silverton, L. (1993). *Adolescent Apperception Cards*. Los Angeles, CA: Western Psychological Services.

Simms, L. J., Williams, T. F., & Simms, E. N. (2017). Assessment of the five factor model. In T. A. Widiger (Ed.), *The Oxford handbook of the five factor model* (pp. 353–380). New York: Oxford University Press.

Skodol, A. E. (2012). Personality disorders in DSM-5. *Annual Review of Clinical Psychology, 8*, 317–344.

Smith, J. D., & Finn, S. E. (2014). Therapeutic presentation of multimethod assessment results: An empirically supported framework and case example. In C. J. Hopwood & R. F. Bornstein (Eds.), *Multimethod clinical assessment of personality and psychopathology* (pp. 403–425). New York: Guilford Press.

Spangler, W. D. (1992). Validity of questionnaire and TAT measures of need for achievement: Two meta-analyses. *Psychological Bulletin, 112*, 140–154.

Stein, M. B., & Slavin-Mulford, J. (2018). *The Social Cognition and Object Relations Scale-Global Rating Method (SCORS-G): A comprehensive guide for clinicians and researchers*. New York, NY: Guilford Press.

Stein, M. B., Slavin-Mulford, J., Siefert, C. J., Sinclair, S. J., Renna, M., Malone, J., . . . Blais, M. A. (2014). SCORS-G stimulus characteristics of select Thematic Apperception Test Cards. *Journal of Personality Assessment, 96*, 339–349.

Stein, M. B., Slavin-Mulford, J., Sinclair, S. J., Chung, W.-J., Roche, M., Denckla, C., & Blais, M. A. (2018). Extending the use of the SCORS—G composite ratings in assessing level of personality organization. *Journal of Personality Assessment, 100*, 166–175.

Strack, S. (2005). An integrationist perspective on personality assessment. *Journal of Personality Assessment, 84*, 105–107.

Strack, S., & Lorr, M. (1994). *Differentiating normal and abnormal personality*. New York, NY: Springer Publishing Company.

Stricker, G., & Trierweiler, S. J. (1995). The local clinical scientist. A bridge between science and practice. *The American psychologist, 50*(12), 995–1002.

Su, W. S., Viglione, D. J., Green, E. E., Tam, W. C. C., Su, J. A., & Chang, Y. T. (2015). Cultural and linguistic adaptability of the Rorschach Performance Assessment System as a measure of psychotic characteristics and severity of mental disturbance in Taiwan. *Psychological Assessment, 27*, 1273–1285.

Sullivan, H. S. (1953). *The interpersonal theory of psychiatry*. New York, NY: Norton.

Swann, W. B., Jr. (1997). The trouble with change: Self-verification and allegiance to the self. *Psychological Science, 8*, 177–180.

Tackett, J. L., Lilienfeld, S. O., Patrick, C. J., Johnson, S. L., Krueger, R. F., Miller, J. D., . . . Shrout, P. E. (2017). It's time to broaden the replicability conversation: Thoughts for and from clinical psychological science. *Perspectives on Psychological Science, 12*, 742–756.

Teglasi, H. (2010). *Essentials of TAT and other storytelling assessments* (2nd ed.). Hoboken, NJ: John Wiley & Sons.

Tellegen, A. (1985). Structures of mood and personality and their relevance to assessing anxiety, with an emphasis on self-report. In A. H. Tuna & J. D. Maser (Eds.), *Anxiety and the anxiety disorders* (pp. 681–706). Hillsdale, NJ: Lawrence Erlbaum Associates, Inc.

Tellegen, A., Ben-Porath, Y. S., McNulty, J. L., Arbisi, P. A., Graham, J. R., & Kaemmer, B. (2003). *MMPI-2 Restructured Clinical (RC) Scales: Development, validation, and interpretation.* Minneapolis, MN: University of Minnesota Press.

Tharinger, D. J., Finn, S. E., Hersh, B., Wilkinson, A., Christopher, G., & Tran, A. (2008). Assessment feedback with parents and children: A collaborative approach. *Professional Psychology: Research and Practice, 39,* 600–609.

Thomas, K. M., Hopwood, C. J., Woody, E., Ethier, N., & Sadler, P. (2014). Interpersonal processes in psychotherapy: A reanalysis of the Gloria Films. *Journal of Counseling Psychology, 61,* 1–14.

Thurston, N. S., & Cradock O'Leary, J. (2009). *Thurston Cradock Test of Shame (TCTS).* Los Angeles, CA: Western Psychological Services.

Tracey, T. J., Bludworth, J., & Glidden-Tracey, C. E. (2012). Are there parallel processes in psychotherapy supervision? An empirical examination. *Psychotherapy, 49,* 330–443.

Trobst, K. K., & Wiggins, J. S. (2003). Constructive alternativism in personality assessment. Madeline G. from multiple perspectives. In J. S. Wiggins (Ed.), *Paradigms of personality assessment* (pp. 296–324). New York: Guilford Press.

Tyrer, P., Crawford, M., & Mulder, R. (2011). Reclassifying personality disorders. *The Lancet, 9780*(377), 1814–1815.

Van Denburg, T. F., Schmidt, J. A., & Kiesler, D. J. (1992). Interpersonal assessment in counseling and psychotherapy. *Journal of Counseling & Development, 71,* 84–90.

Van der Kolk, B. (2014). *The body keeps the score: Brain, mind, and body in the healing of trauma.* New York: Viking.

Viglione, D. J., Blume-Marcovici, A. C., Miller, H. L., Giromini, L., & Meyer, G. J. (2012). An initial inter-rater reliability study for the Rorschach Performance Assessment System. *Journal of Personality Assessment, 94,* 607–612.

Viglione, D. J., Meyer, G. J., Jordan, R. J., Converse, G. L., Evans, J., MacDermott, D., & Moore, R. C. (2015). Developing an alternative Rorschach administration method to optimize the number of responses and enhance clinical inferences. *Clinical Psychology and Psychotherapy, 22,* 546–558.

Viglione, D. J., Towns, B., & Lindshield, D. (2012). Understanding and using the Rorschach Inkblot Test to assess post-traumatic conditions. *Psychological Injury and Law, 5,* 135–144.

Ward, R. M. (2008). Assessee and assessor experiences of significant events in psychological assessment feedback. *Journal of Personality Assessment, 90,* 307–322.

Watson, D., & Tellegen, A. (1985). Toward a consensual structure of mood. *Psychological Bulletin, 98,* 219.

Weiner, I. B., & Greene, R. L. (2017). *Handbook of personality assessment* (2nd ed.). Hoboken, NJ: John Wiley & Sons.

Weiss, J. (1993). *How psychotherapy works.* New York: Guilford Press.

Welsh, G. S. (1956). Factor dimensions A and R. In *Basic readings on the MMPI in psychology and medicine* (pp. 264–281). Minneapolis, MN: University of Minnesota Press.

Westen, D. (1998). The scientific legacy of Sigmund Freud: Toward a psychodynamically informed psychological science. *Psychological Bulletin, 124,* 333–371. doi:10.1037/0033-2909.124.3.333

Westenberg, P. M., Hauser, S. T., & Cohn, L. D. (2004). Sentence completion measurement of psychosocial maturity. In M. J. Hilsenroth & D. L. Segal (Eds.), *Comprehensive handbook of psychological assessment, Vol. 2: Personality assessment* (pp. 595–616). Hoboken, NJ: John Wiley & Sons.

Widiger, T. A. (Ed.). (2017). *The Oxford handbook of the five-factor model.* New York: Oxford University Press.

Widiger, T. A., & Frances, A. J. (1994). Toward a dimensional model for the personality disorders. In P. T. Costa, Jr. & T. A. Widiger (Eds.), *Personality disorders and the five-factor model of personality* (pp. 19–39). Washington, DC: American Psychological Association.

Widiger, T. A., & Trull, T. J. (1997). Assessment of the five-factor model of personality. *Journal of Personality Assessment, 68,* 228–250.

Widiger, T. A., & Trull, T. J. (2007). Plate tectonics in the classification of personality disorder: Shifting to a dimensional model. *American Psychologist, 62,* 71–83.

Wiggins, J. S. (1966). Substantive dimensions of self-report in the MMPI item pool. *Psychological Monographs: General and Applied, 80,* 1–42.

Wiggins, J. S. (1973a). Despair and optimism in Minneapolis. *Psyccritiques, 18,* 605–606.

Wiggins, J. S. (1973b). *Personality and prediction: Principles of personality assessment.* Malabar, FL: Krieger.

Wiggins, J. S. (1979). A psychological taxonomy of trait-descriptive terms: The interpersonal domain. *Journal of Personality and Social Psychology, 37,* 395–412.

Wiggins, J. S. (1995). *Interpersonal Adjective Scales: Professional manual.* Odessa, FL: Psychological Assessment Resources.

Wiggins, J. S. (2003). *Paradigms of personality assessment.* New York, NY: Guilford Press.

Winnicott, D. (1971). *Playing and reality.* New York: Basic Books.

Winter, D. G., John, O. P., Stewart, A. J., Klohnen, E. C., & Duncan, L. E. (1998). Traits and motives: Toward an integration of two traditions in personality research. *Psychological Review, 105,* 230–250.

Wood, J. M., Garb, H. N., Nezworski, M. T., Lilienfeld, S. O., & Duke, M. C. (2015). A second look at the validity of widely used Rorschach indices: Comment on Mihura, Meyer, Dumitrascu, and Bombel (2013). *Psychological Bulletin, 141,* 236–249.

Wood, J. M., Lilienfeld, S. O., Garb, H. N., & Nezworski, M. T. (2000). "The Rorschach test in clinical diagnosis": A critical review, with a backward look at Garfield (1947). *Journal of Clinical Psychology, 56,* 395–430.

Wood, J. M., Nezworski, M. T., Lilienfeld, S. O., & Garb, H. N. (2003). *What's wrong with the Rorschach?: Science confronts the controversial inkblot test.* San Francisco, CA: Jossey-Bass.

Zimmermann, J., & Wright, A. G. (2017). Beyond description in interpersonal construct validation: Methodological advances in the circumplex structural summary approach. *Assessment, 24,* 3–23.

Index

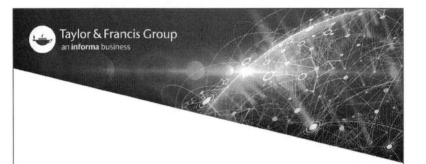